MW01056252

How to Draw Everything

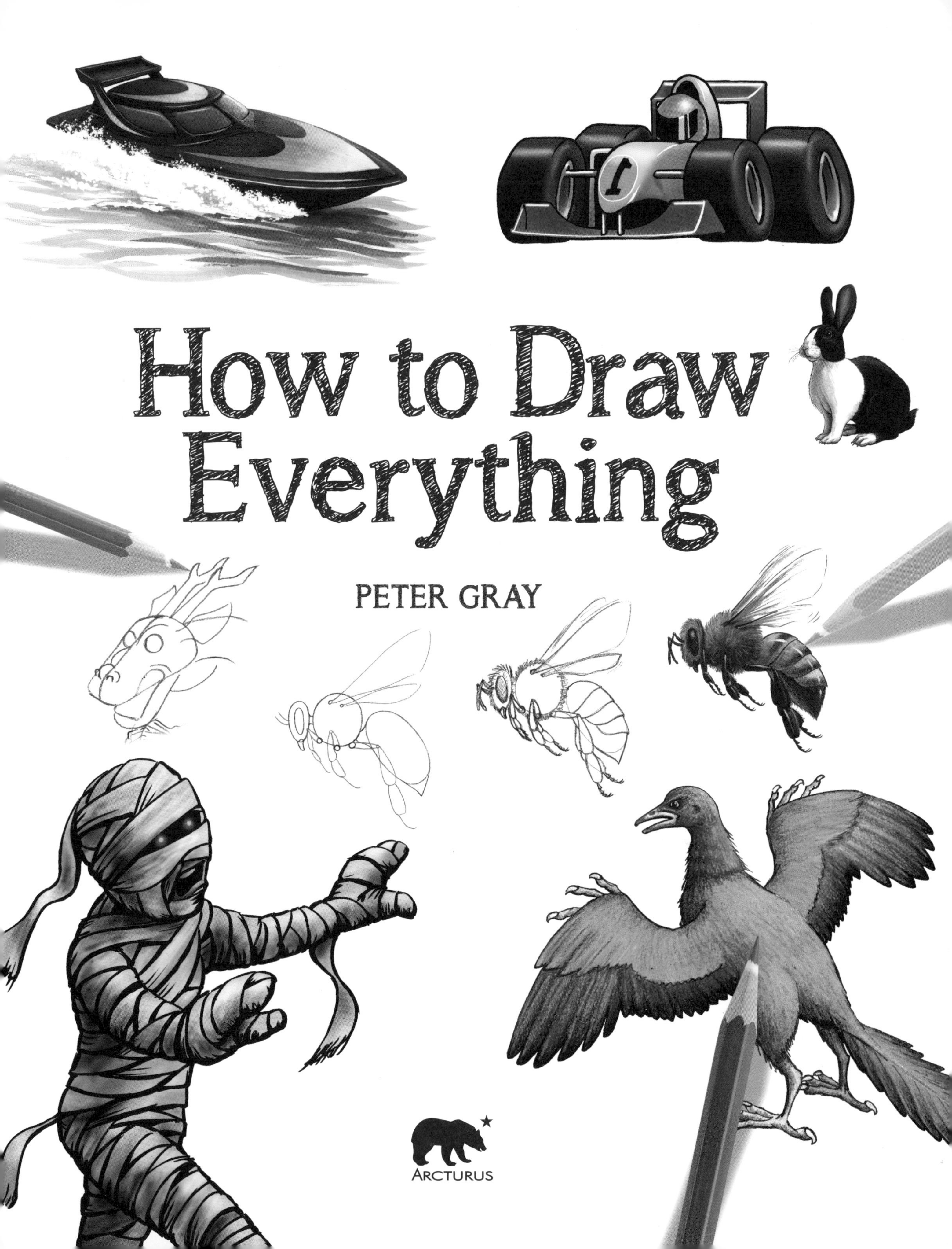

How to Draw Everything

PETER GRAY

ARCTURUS

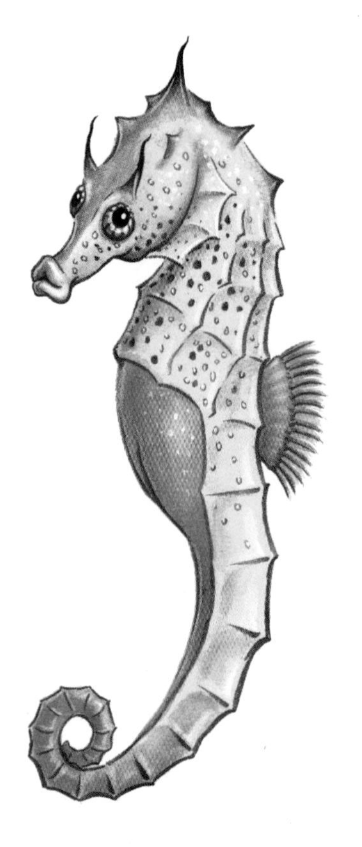

ARCTURUS

This edition published in 2016 by Arcturus Publishing Limited
26/27 Bickels Yard, 151–153 Bermondsey Street,
London SE1 3HA

Designed by Ian Winton
Text and illustrations by Peter Gray

ISBN: 978-1-78599-263-6
CH004936US
Supplier 29, Date 0916, Print run 4846

Printed in China

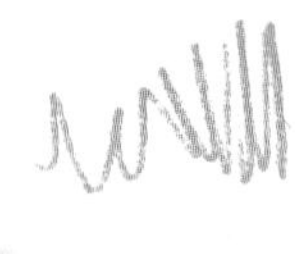

CONTENTS

DRAW IT ALL!

Always wanted to know how to draw? This book is the perfect starting point, since it's packed full of ideas, inspiration, and simple step-by-step guides. You'll discover all types of characters and varying levels of difficulty, with tips and tricks to help your drawings really stand out.

CHAPTERS INCLUDE

ANIMALS

Critters come in all shapes and sizes, and chapters focusing on pets, underwater creatures, and wild animals mean that you can learn to draw a huge variety of the animal kingdom.

PEOPLE

Drawing people can be a challenge, but we'll show you how. Try portraits, full figures, action poses, and discover tips on hands and feet.

MONSTERS AND FANTASY

Drawing characters from your imagination is great fun. These fantasy creatures in step-by-step form will help you master all your favorites.

SPEED MACHINES

If technical drawing is your thing, then try the race cars, speedboats, and space rockets in this chapter.

DINOSAURS

As well as trying terrifying T. rex, why not draw Triceratops, Velociraptor, and Iguanodon, and bring these reptiles back to life.

SCENES

Once you've drawn your characters, learn how to put them together in a scene. Try a jungle, back yard, or underwater masterpiece.

STYLES

REALISTIC STYLE

There are two styles of art in this book. The dinosaur below has been drawn and colored in a realistic style with pencils and watercolor paints. Paying attention to detail and looking for references to copy helps with realistic drawings.

CARTOON STYLE

This dinosaur is pretty different! It has been drawn and colored in a cartoon style. The features are exaggerated, and there is a thick black outline. Cartoon drawings allow you to experiment with shapes and colors as much as you want.

FOLLOW THE LINES

Build up your picture step-by-step by looking at the color of each stroke. Red strokes show you the lines you need to draw, and black strokes show what you have already drawn. All the lines will be red in the first step. After that, only the new lines will be in red.

YOU WILL NEED

Every artist needs essential drawing tools including pencils, pens, a ruler, paints, and paper. As you become more experienced, you can add materials, such as ink pens, gouache paints, or pastel crayons. They will help you to develop your own favorite style.

PENCILS

Pencils come with different weights of lead. Hard lead pencils (H to 9H) are useful for drawing precise, fine lines. Soft lead pencils (B to 9B) work well for shading and softer lines.

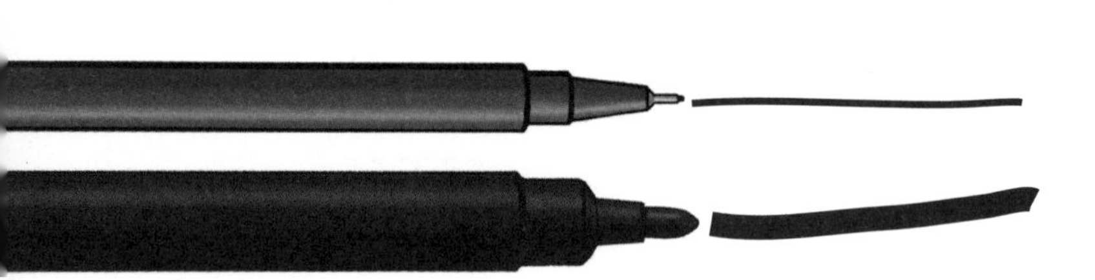

MARKERS

Before coloring, it's a good idea to go over your pencil outline. A marker is perfect for this. You can use a thick or thin one, depending on the effect you want to create.

PAPER

You can use different types of paper for different jobs. When practicing shapes and lines, a rough sketch paper is practical. For final colored-up drawings, a smooth plain paper works well.

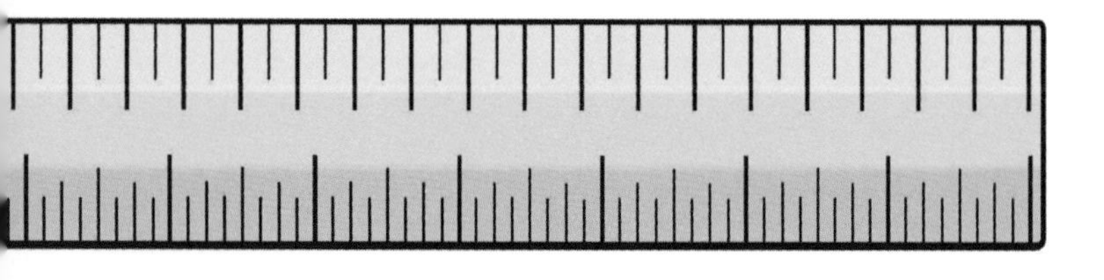

RULER

For technical drawings, a ruler really helps. It will allow you to make your lines straight and angles accurate.

ERASER

From time to time, you'll make mistakes or need to erase guidelines. That's where an eraser comes in handy. Don't worry if you make mistakes—everybody does!

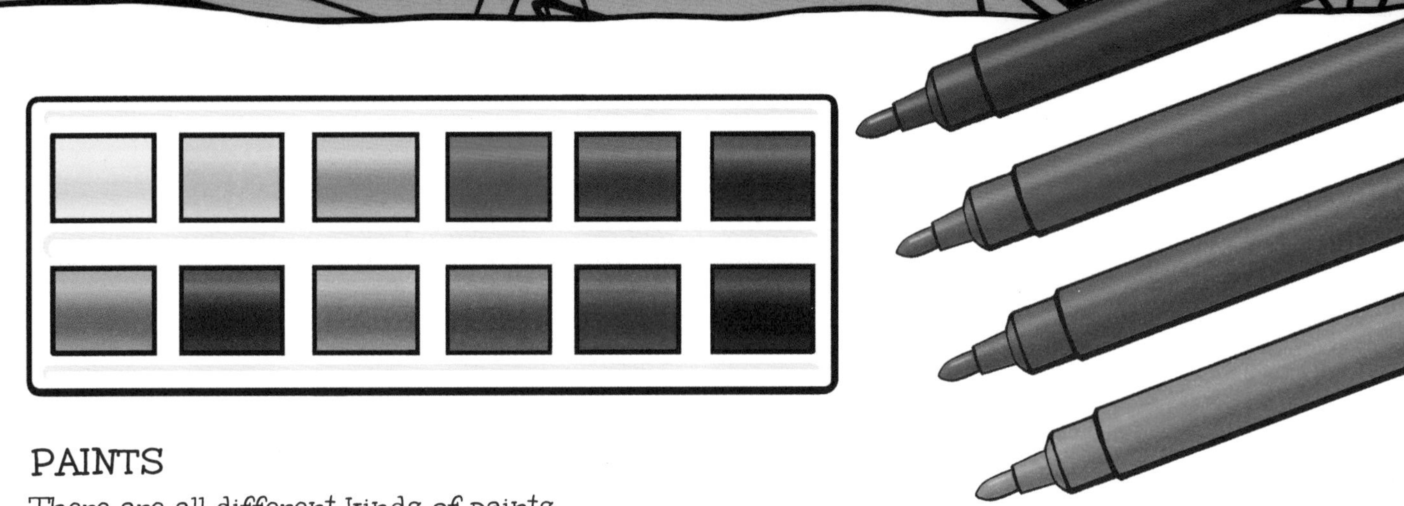

PAINTS

There are all different kinds of paints you can experiment with, but poster paints and watercolors are an excellent starting point. You could also try gouache, which will give you more solid tones.

FELT-TIP PENS

Felt-tips are perfect for coloring drawings that need bold, bright colors. They work especially well for cartoons.

ART IN ACTION

Take a look at the examples below to see how to get the best out of using different pens, brushes, and paints.

This friendly dolphin was colored in watercolor paints to give a smooth effect. Colors can be blended together to create different shades with watercolors.

Felt-tip pens were used to color this cartoon shark, making it look dramatic. The outline was done with a black marker, and the body was highlighted with white chalk.

SHAPES AND LINES

All the drawings in this book start with simple shapes and lines. They give you a basic structure to build on. Then you can work on developing the details.

SIMPLE SHAPES

Here are some examples of the shapes you'll use. It's a good idea to practice drawing them until you feel comfortable. For some of the shapes, such as the squares, rectangles, and triangles, use a ruler to get straight lines.

square

circle

oval

rectangle

different-shaped triangles

curved lines

BUILD IT UP

Once you've mastered drawing shapes, the next step is to build them up into a real picture. This fighter jet is made from different-shaped triangles and straight lines that have been smoothed and softened in places.

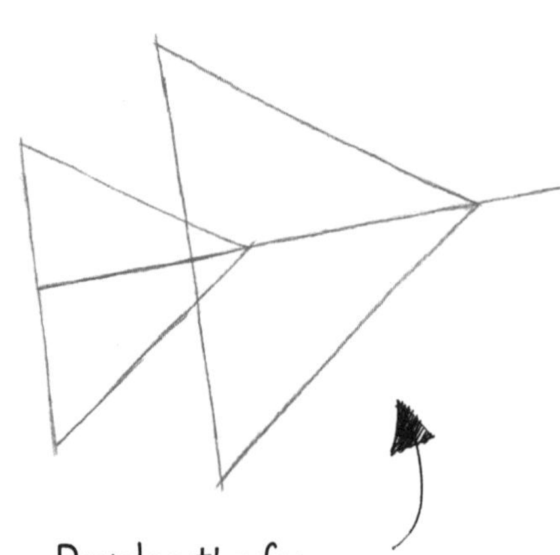

Develop the form through shapes and lines.

Then soften the edges to make the jet real. You'll need your eraser at this stage.

LINES

THICK LINES

You can create different effects depending on the thickness of your line. This tiger looks dramatic because it has a thick bold outline and fur made with jagged short strokes.

SMUDGED LINES

Smudging your lines makes this werewolf seem wild, since it gives the fur a sense of movement. Try soft pencil or charcoal, then smudge the line with your finger. You could also use an old brush and ink to get a scratchy effect.

FINE LINES

A fine line gives a more delicate appearance. It's perfect for creating the wispy fur on this almost cuddly yeti. Notice how the outline is not solid but made up of lots of tiny strokes drawn very close together.

COLOR MAGIC

When you color in your drawings, you instantly bring them to life. As well as working with colors that go well together, think about those that contrast. Using color is also a great way to create a particular mood or feel.

If you're going for realistic hair, then it's a good idea to avoid a single block of color. Brown, yellow, and white have all been blended together here.

Did you know that you can make brown by blending green and red together? Try this with watercolor paints.

To give this elf a truly woodland feel, we decided to color her outfit in many different shades of green.

To add some "pizzazz" to the picture, try including a touch of lime green. You can make this by blending a strong green with bright yellow.

COLOR WHEEL

A color wheel can help you decide how to mix and match color. The primary colors are red, yellow, and blue. You can make up all the other colors by mixing them.

Colors that sit next to each other, such as blue and green, and red and orange, go well together and create almost no contrast.

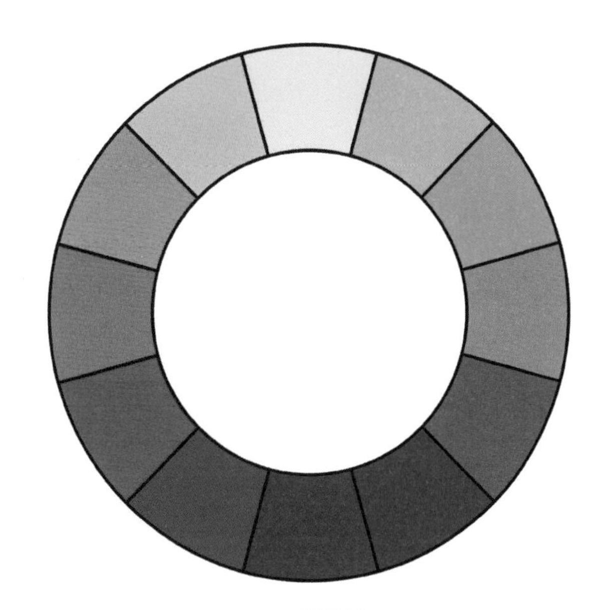

Colors that sit opposite each other, such as red and green, and purple and yellow, provide lots of contrast. They are called complementary colors.

Warm colors are much richer. They include yellow, orange, and red.

Cool colors can create a sense of calm. These include blue and green.

CUDDLY AND CUTE

Changing the color of a picture or adding features can make a huge difference. This green baby dragon looks friendly and sweet.

HOT AND BOTHERED

Turn him bright red, and he becomes more mischievous. Give him a puff of fire, and you know you better not make him angry!

SHADING AND HIGHLIGHTS

Adding darker areas of color to a picture is called shading. Highlights are patches of white. Artists use these techniques to give their pictures bulk and depth, so that they seem three-dimensional and real. Find out how on the Triceratops example below.

1

Once you have outlined your drawing, plot out where the shading needs to go. Darker areas around the neck, underneath the body, and on the legs give this dinosaur its bulk.

A wobbly outline helps to create a bony backbone.

2

Now build up the shading. We have used a watercolor paint because we are working in a realistic style. Make sure that the shading is in a darker color than the main body color.

Notice how the brushstrokes curve and round out the body.

Wrinkly lines give the skin texture.

3

Now cover the whole picture with the main body color, in this case a light brown. Notice how by going over the whole body, including the shaded areas, the colors feel blended together.

4

The final step is to add highlights. Here, we have used white chalk on top of the watercolor. Add most of the highlights around the neck plate, spiny back, and thigh joints to make them stand out.

PERSPECTIVE

In real life, objects look smaller the farther away they are. You can create this feel in your pictures by drawing them in perspective. Using this technique will also help make the objects look solid. Follow the steps below to find out how.

VANISHING POINTS

When creating perspective, you need at least one vanishing point. This is the point where parallel lines would meet in the distance if you kept on looking at them.

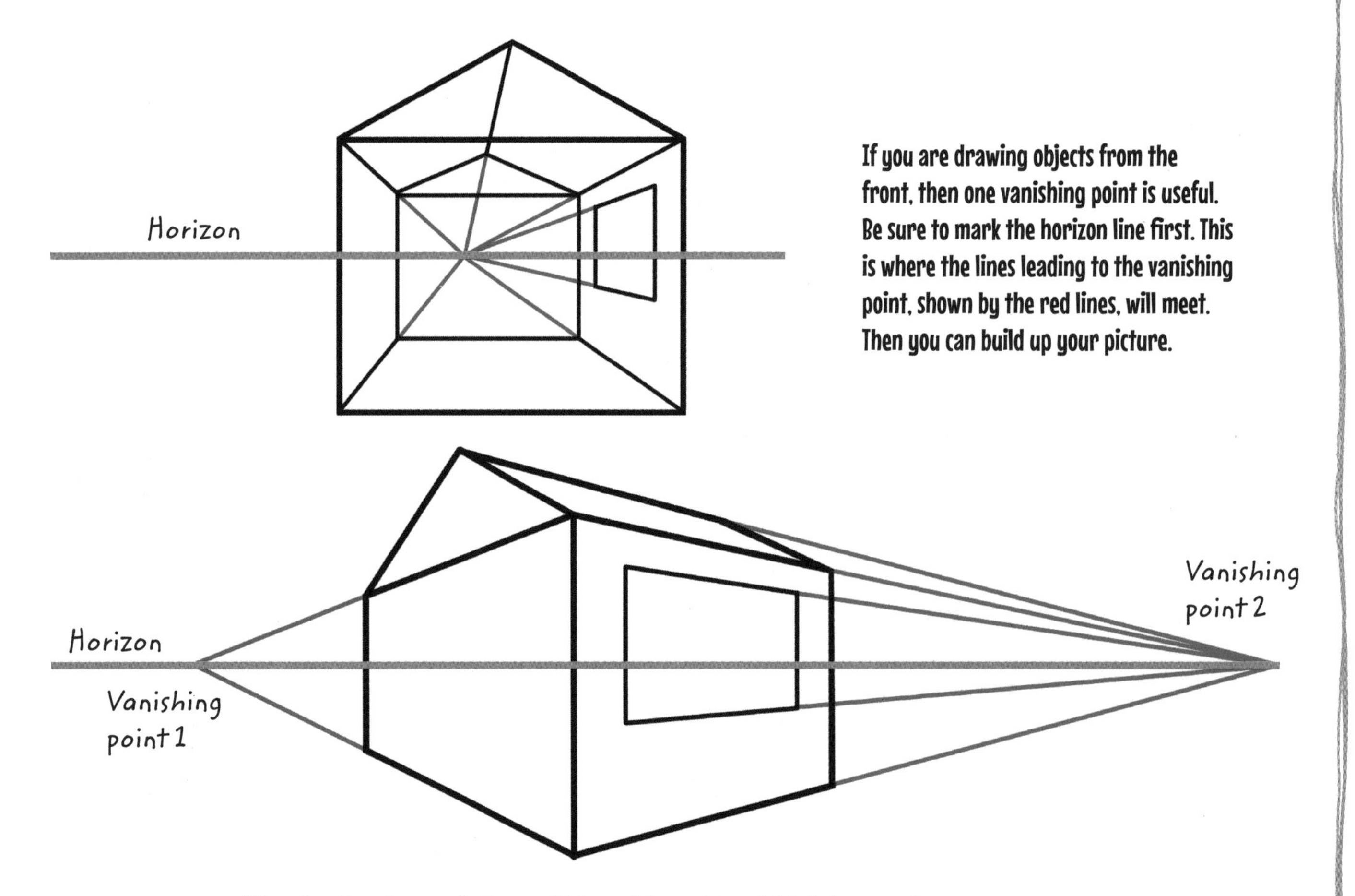

If you are drawing objects from the front, then one vanishing point is useful. Be sure to mark the horizon line first. This is where the lines leading to the vanishing point, shown by the red lines, will meet. Then you can build up your picture.

When drawing at an angle, two vanishing points can be useful to help you get your picture right. Both of the vanishing points should be positioned on the horizon line.

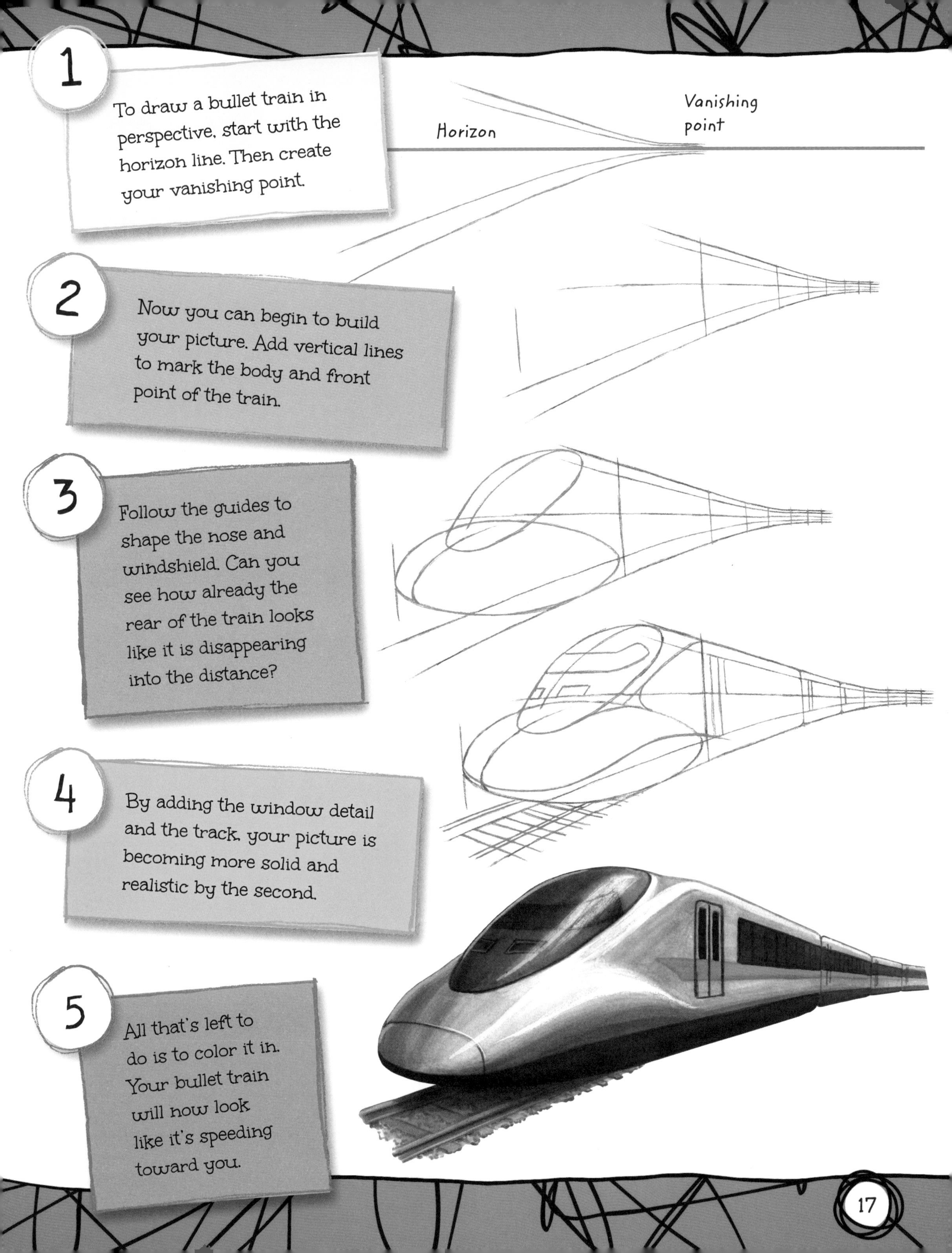
1
To draw a bullet train in perspective, start with the horizon line. Then create your vanishing point.
Horizon
Vanishing point
2
Now you can begin to build your picture. Add vertical lines to mark the body and front point of the train.
3
Follow the guides to shape the nose and windshield. Can you see how already the rear of the train looks like it is disappearing into the distance?
4
By adding the window detail and the track, your picture is becoming more solid and realistic by the second.
5
All that's left to do is to color it in. Your bullet train will now look like it's speeding toward you.

CHAPTER 1

PETS

GOLDEN RETRIEVER

Golden retriever dogs are well-loved pets in many homes. They are gentle, loyal, and very intelligent. They also love playing in water! Their thick golden coat has two different types of fur-a soft under layer that helps to keep the dog warm, and a shaggier outer layer that is water-resistant to keep the dog dry.

1

Dogs come in all shapes and sizes, but the first steps for drawing them are fairly similar—it's just the proportions that change. The golden retriever has a fairly large, long body with a relatively small head. Draw the body and head as simple shapes, an oval and a circle, with a space in between.

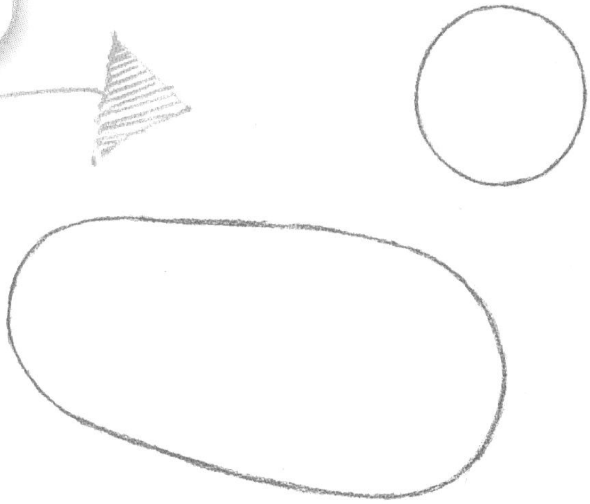

2

Connect the head to the body with curving lines that show the neck leaning forward. Draw the upper part of the rear leg as a broad shape that also forms the dog's rump. Now mark the front edges of the legs, being careful to make them the right length.

3

Finish the leg guidelines, and add paw shapes. The tail is broad, curving to a point. Draw a roughly triangular muzzle, and mark a center line that curves over the top of the head. This will help you to position the eyes on either side of the line and the ears on the sides of the head.

4

Add more detail to the face, and draw some individual toes on each paw. Now start to work on the coat. Show the shagginess of the coat with simple outlines and curving marks around the neck to suggest the direction of growth.

5

With all the guidelines in place, you can now refine the drawing with a sharp pencil. Work on the face, aiming for a friendly expression. Add some more detail to the coat, mainly on the underside of the animal, behind the legs, and around the neck and chest.

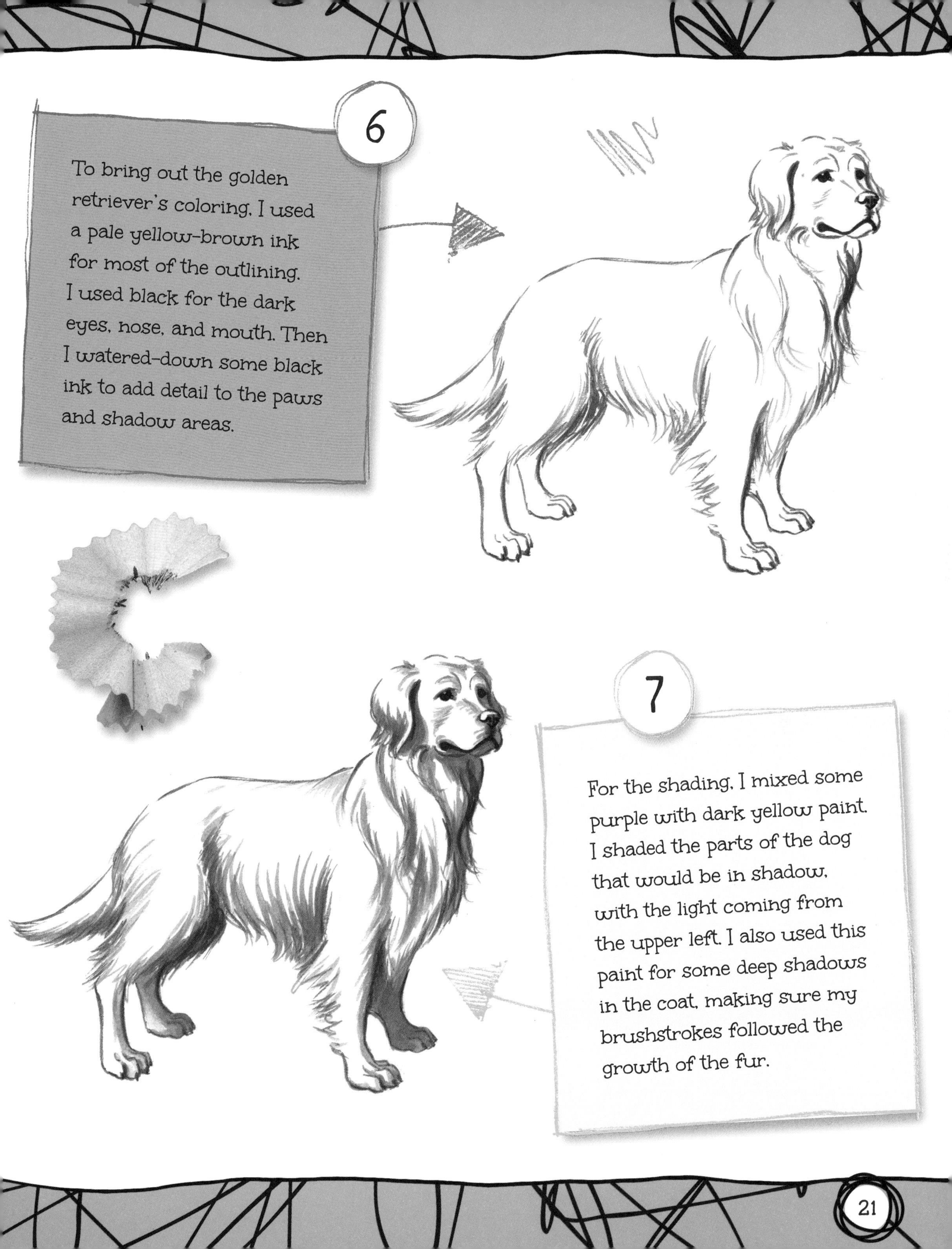

6

To bring out the golden retriever's coloring, I used a pale yellow-brown ink for most of the outlining. I used black for the dark eyes, nose, and mouth. Then I watered-down some black ink to add detail to the paws and shadow areas.

7

For the shading, I mixed some purple with dark yellow paint. I shaded the parts of the dog that would be in shadow, with the light coming from the upper left. I also used this paint for some deep shadows in the coat, making sure my brushstrokes followed the growth of the fur.

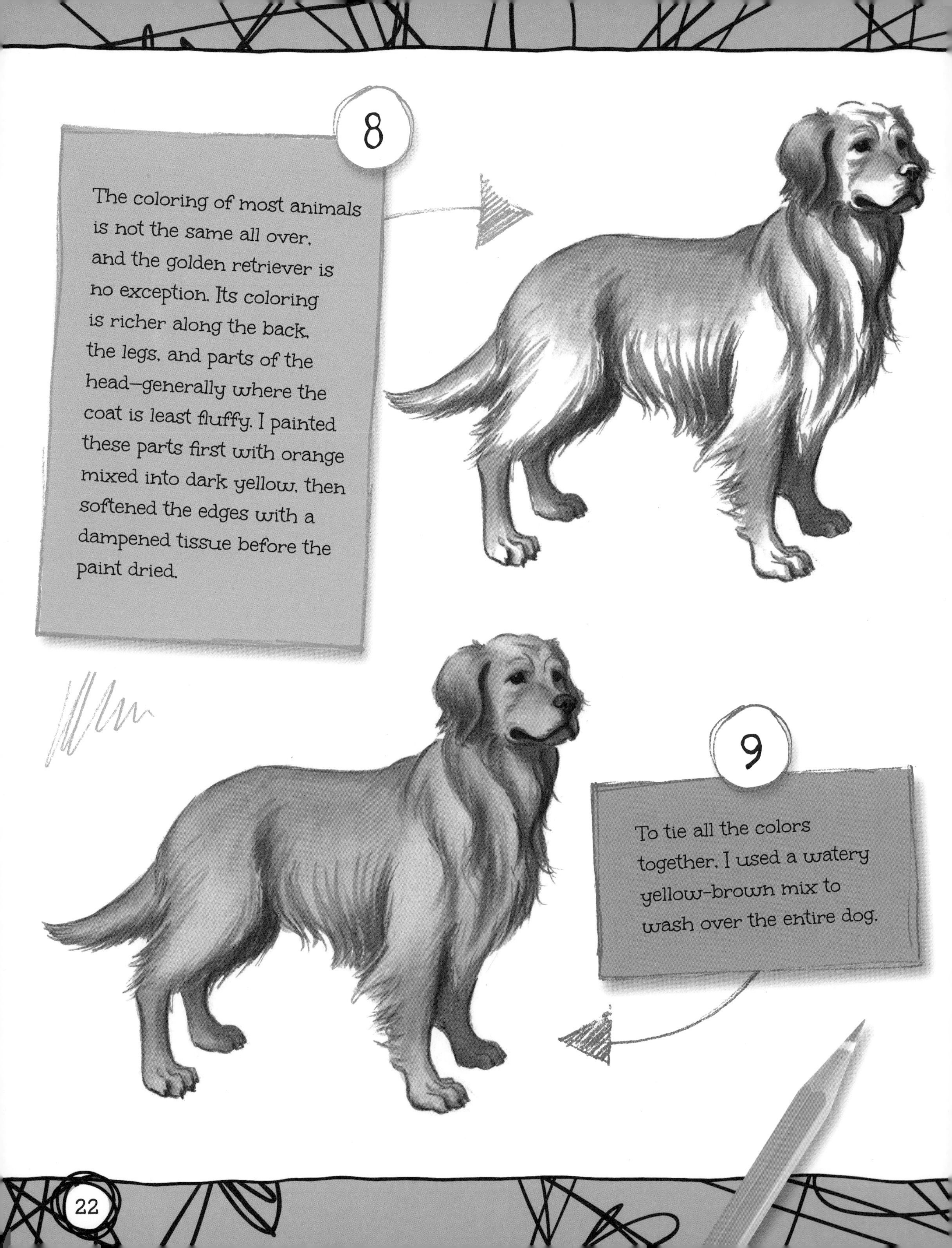

8

The coloring of most animals is not the same all over, and the golden retriever is no exception. Its coloring is richer along the back, the legs, and parts of the head—generally where the coat is least fluffy. I painted these parts first with orange mixed into dark yellow, then softened the edges with a dampened tissue before the paint dried.

9

To tie all the colors together, I used a watery yellow-brown mix to wash over the entire dog.

10

For the finishing touches, I added a few more spots of purple shade under the neck, inside the legs, and on the paws. Then I used diluted white ink to paint on some highlights to make the fur shiny and to bring out the features of the face and paws.

CAT

Cats have strong, flexible bodies. They walk lightly on their toes and are very agile and quick-footed. Like wild cats, such as lions and tigers, many pet cats are hunters. They often catch their prey after dark, helped by their excellent night vision.

1

The view I have chosen shows the cat looking over its shoulder, so the circle that forms the head is placed almost centrally above the larger oval shape of the body. Make sure you leave a gap between the two shapes.

2

Connect the two shapes with a long, arching neck line on the outer edge. For the front leg, continue the neck line down, curving inward. At the rear end, form the shape of the upper leg and rump, then draw the leg shapes in between. The front legs should be wider than the rear.

3

Add the ears and the basic lines of the face—suddenly your drawing looks like a cat. Some feet shapes and a low-slung tail complete the basic outline.

4

Now put in some shaping and markings to the head and toes on the paws. Draw lines around the cat's body to guide you for the fur markings.

Did you know?

CAT TONGUES

Pet cats spend many hours each day grooming-licking their coats to keep them clean. Their tongues are a little bit like mini hairbrushes! The surface of the tongue is covered with tiny, backward-facing spines, which clean and untangle the fur as the cat licks.

5

As you add detail to the drawing, pay attention to the shapes of the shoulders and hips. Make the outlines furry as you go. Draw character into the face and head, then put some striped markings across the body.

6

For the inking stage, I used a fine brush and black ink to create a furry texture with many fine strokes. I did not erase the pencil drawing because I wanted to follow the guidelines for the stripes at the next (painting) stage.

7

After painting the stripes in dark brown, I erased the pencil work. Then I added some orangey color to the legs and feet. Once dry, I painted on some shadow in purple gray, then I washed blue gray over the whole body. I used the same blue gray to paint textural marks to give a rough, shaggy look. Then with watered-down white ink, I brought out more of the shaggy texture as well as the highlights in the eyes, ear hairs, and whiskers.

KITTEN

You could probably do a good job of drawing this cute kitten just by copying the final picture. But if you learn to construct it one step at a time, this will help you when you are drawing more complicated poses and viewpoints.

1

Take a hard pencil and use light lines to draw an oval for the head. To help you make your picture symmetrical, put a vertical and a horizontal line through the center of it—it's good to get used to drawing lines like this freehand rather than using a ruler. For the eyes, draw two ovals with pointed ends. The ears and long fur around the face can be drawn as rough triangle shapes.

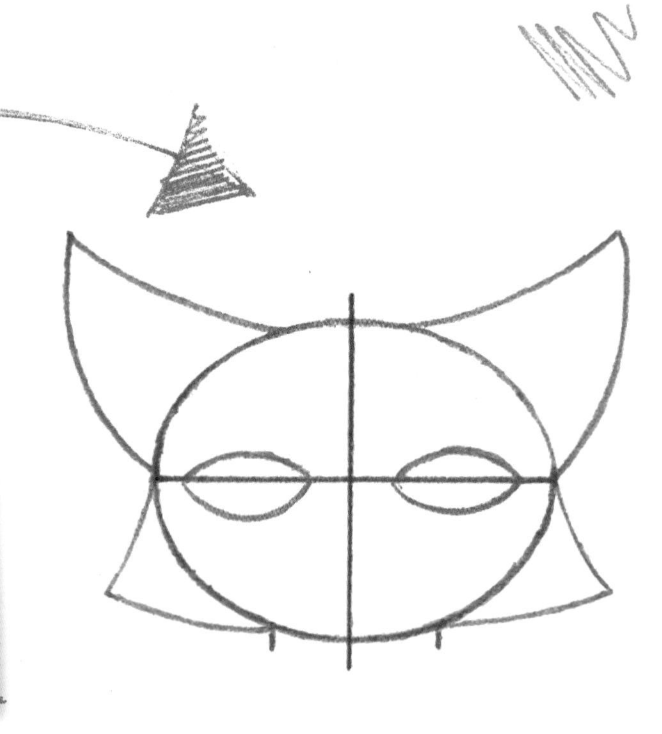

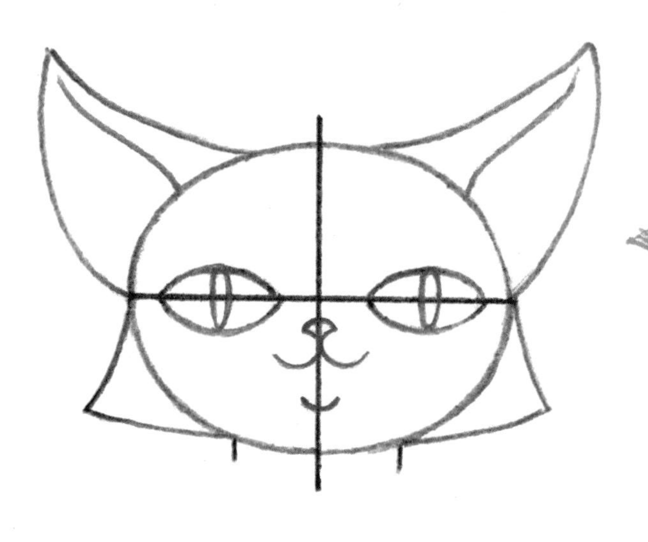

2

Adding a few more simple lines will complete the facial features.

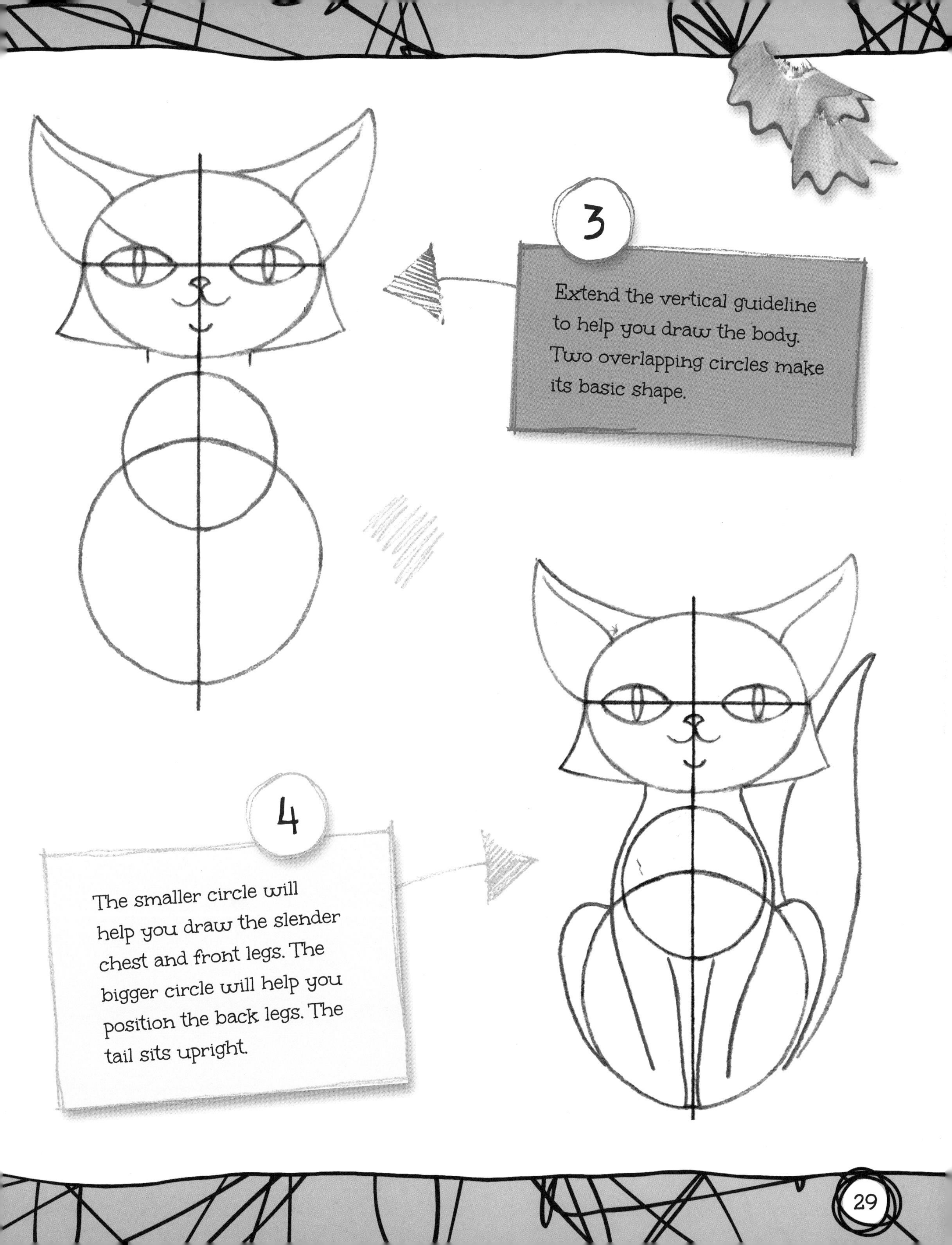
3
Extend the vertical guideline to help you draw the body. Two overlapping circles make its basic shape.
4
The smaller circle will help you draw the slender chest and front legs. The bigger circle will help you position the back legs. The tail sits upright.

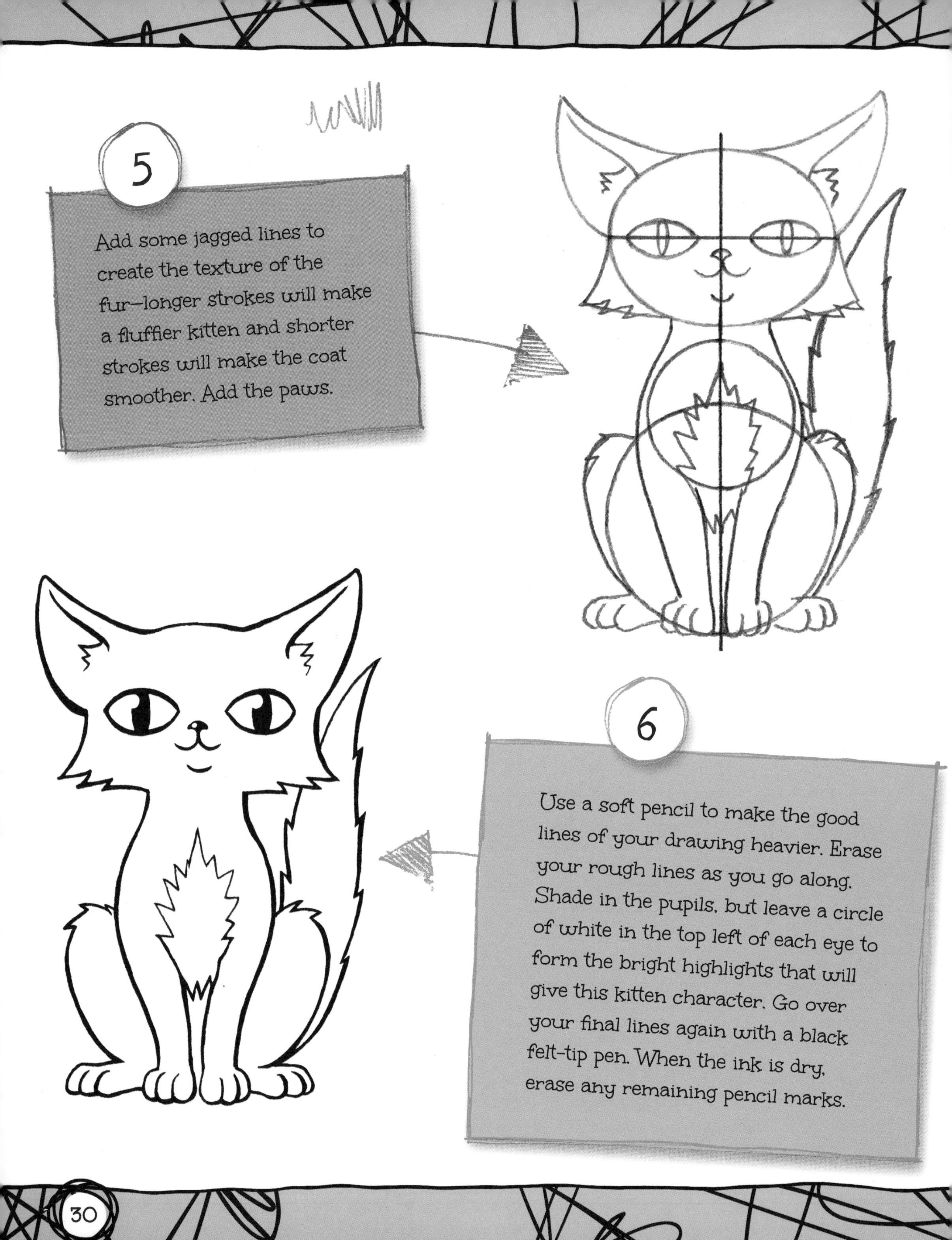
5
Add some jagged lines to create the texture of the fur—longer strokes will make a fluffier kitten and shorter strokes will make the coat smoother. Add the paws.
6
Use a soft pencil to make the good lines of your drawing heavier. Erase your rough lines as you go along. Shade in the pupils, but leave a circle of white in the top left of each eye to form the bright highlights that will give this kitten character. Go over your final lines again with a black felt-tip pen. When the ink is dry, erase any remaining pencil marks.

7

This is what your finished drawing should look like. I've colored mine on a computer—but you might want to color your kitten with pencils, paints, or felt-tip pens instead. I've experimented with an unrealistic color to give the kitten some personality—this is fine when drawing in a cartoon style.

RABBIT

The rabbit's most noticeable features are its long ears. It also has large, powerful back legs that it uses to hop–and to run very fast when necessary. Pet rabbits are often kept in hutches, but some are trained to live freely in people's homes as "house rabbits."

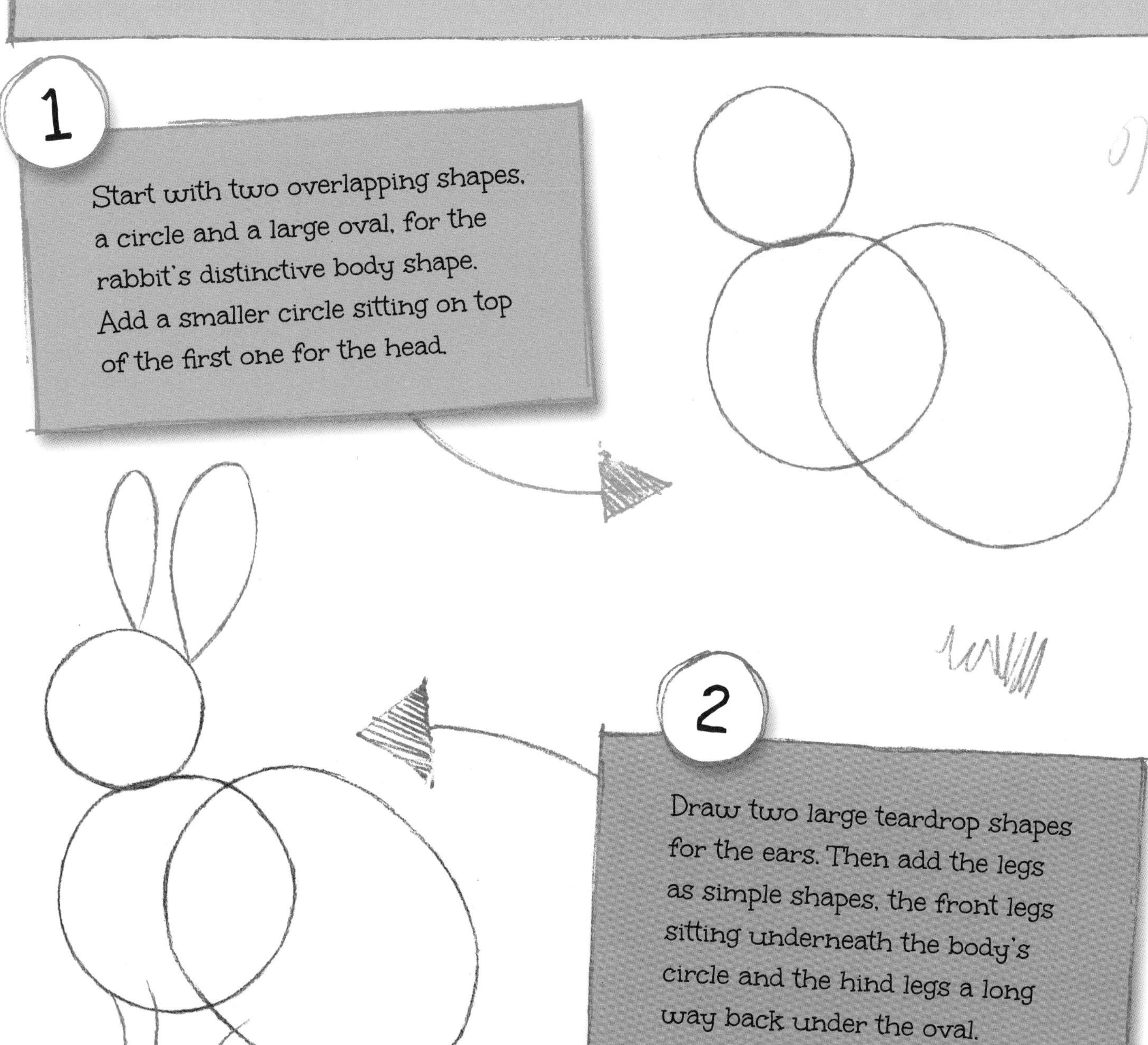

1

Start with two overlapping shapes, a circle and a large oval, for the rabbit's distinctive body shape. Add a smaller circle sitting on top of the first one for the head.

2

Draw two large teardrop shapes for the ears. Then add the legs as simple shapes, the front legs sitting underneath the body's circle and the hind legs a long way back under the oval.

3

Draw two oval shapes in front of the head for the muzzle with a nose in between. Connect the ears to the head. Mark in the eye. Shape the back end, adding a little tail.

4

Work on the outline details around the head and eye. Draw some individual toes on the feet.

Did you know?

THUMPING AND HOPPING

In the wild, rabbits are food for other animals, such as foxes and birds of prey. They warn other rabbits of danger by thumping their powerful hind legs on the ground. If necessary, they hop away in zigzags to try to confuse and outwit their attacker.

5

Now work over the whole drawing to make the rabbit look as soft and friendly as you can. I chose to give mine bold black and white markings, so I drew the outlines of the black patches to guide me at the inking stage.

6

Although this rabbit has patches of solid black, I did not want to use ink for all of these areas because this would make the picture flat and lifeless. I reserved the black ink for the very darkest parts and some delicate outlines around the rest of the animal.

7

For the delicate shading, I used a brown-blue mix, which is less dull than plain gray. I built up the shade in two or three layers, using light marks. For the black, I used a mix of very dark blue and dark red. I built up the black with several layers, blending it into the black ink patches. Some spots of pink and yellow brown added detail to the feet, ears, and nose. For a few highlights on the fur, I used diluted white ink.

THOROUGHBRED HORSE

A thoroughbred is a breed of horse used for racing, jumping, and other equestrian sports. Thoroughbreds are usually agile, quick, and lively.

1

Begin by drawing a large oval with a flat top. This is the main part of the horse's chest and belly. Add a small circle for the head, and a long curve off the animal's rear end for its rump. Leave enough space on the paper for the legs and tail.

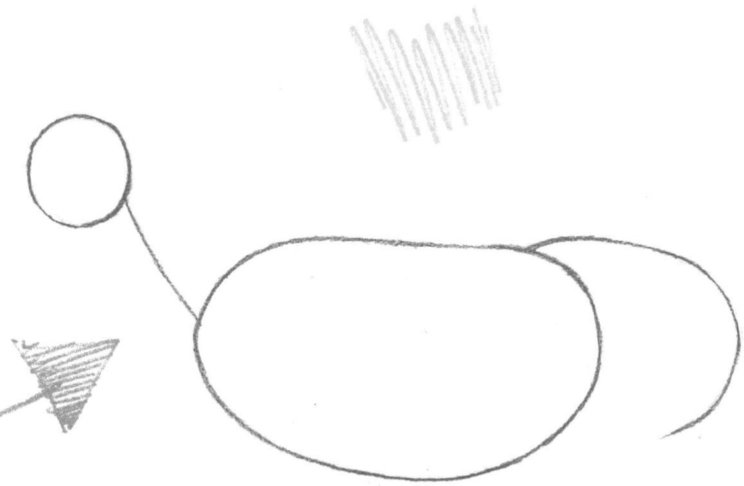

2

Draw the cone shape of the muzzle, then add a line for the back of the neck, arching over the head. Sketch in the long, thin curves of the legs, which become narrower toward the feet.

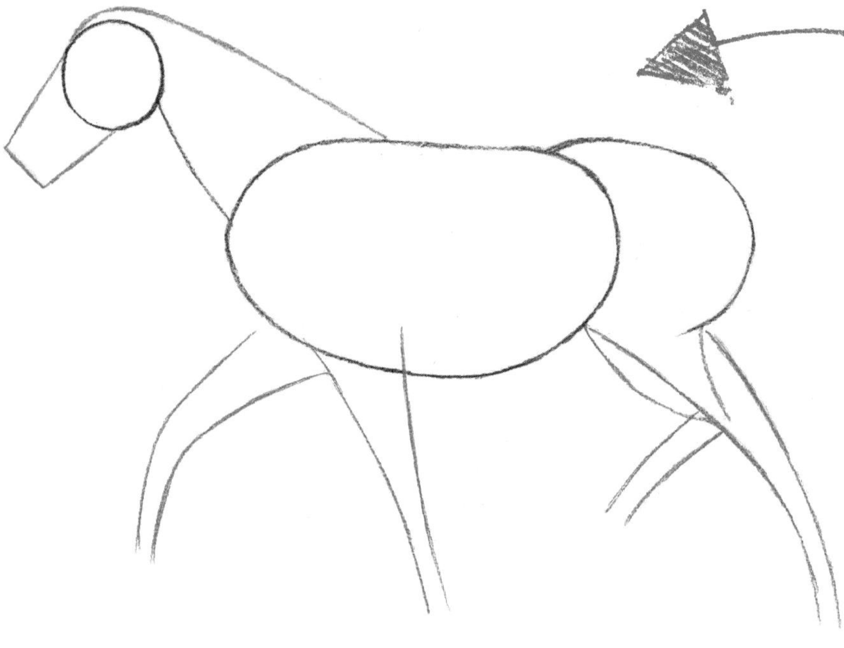

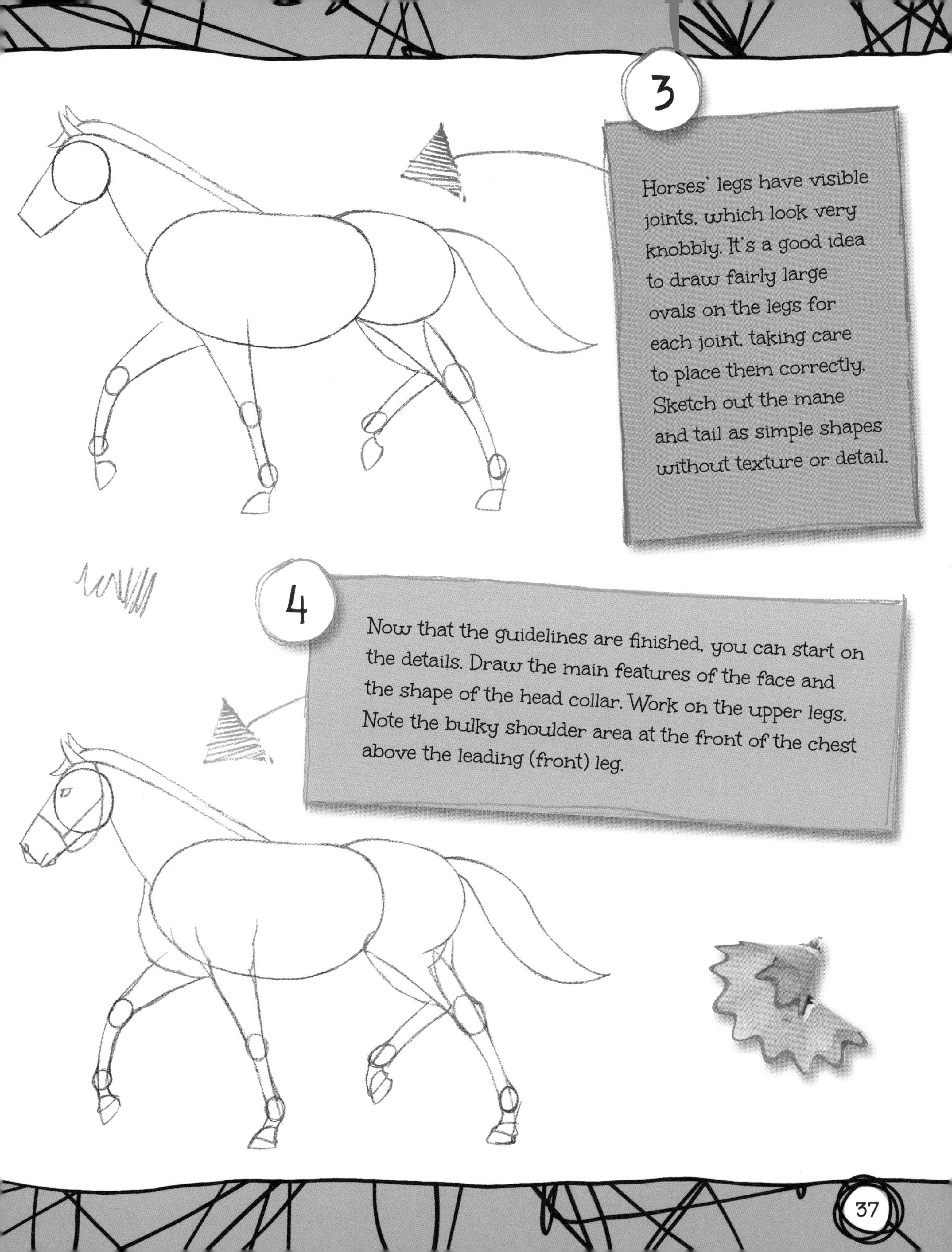

3

Horses' legs have visible joints, which look very knobbly. It's a good idea to draw fairly large ovals on the legs for each joint, taking care to place them correctly. Sketch out the mane and tail as simple shapes without texture or detail.

4

Now that the guidelines are finished, you can start on the details. Draw the main features of the face and the shape of the head collar. Work on the upper legs. Note the bulky shoulder area at the front of the chest above the leading (front) leg.

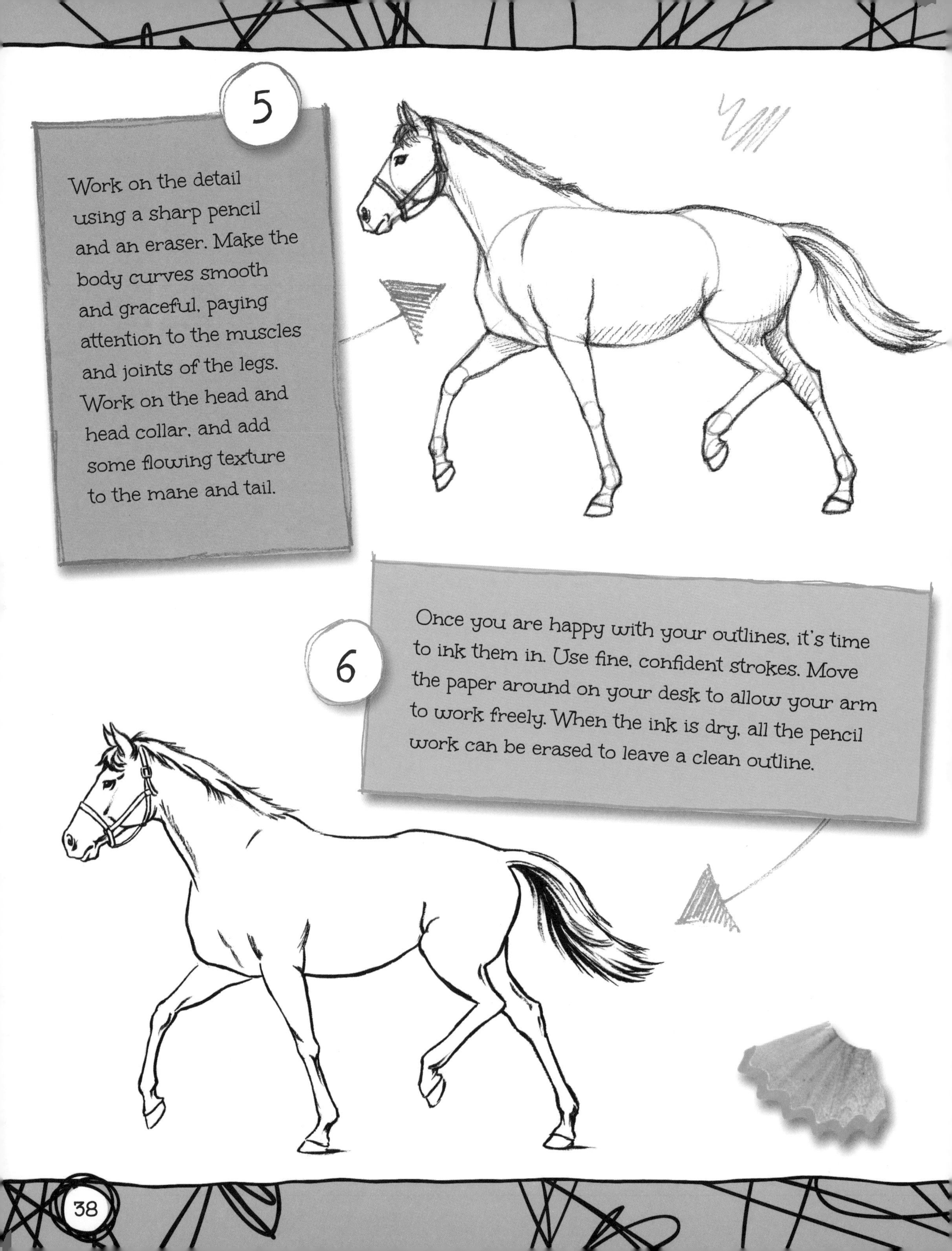

5

Work on the detail using a sharp pencil and an eraser. Make the body curves smooth and graceful, paying attention to the muscles and joints of the legs. Work on the head and head collar, and add some flowing texture to the mane and tail.

6

Once you are happy with your outlines, it's time to ink them in. Use fine, confident strokes. Move the paper around on your desk to allow your arm to work freely. When the ink is dry, all the pencil work can be erased to leave a clean outline.

7

You can break the coloring process down into stages. For this horse, I decided to start with the dark markings. I mixed dark brown and blue to make black. Where the markings blend into the upper leg, I used a dampened brush to soften the hard edge of the paint marks. I also added some shading to the ankles and hooves.

Did you know?

FAMOUS HORSES

Thoroughbreds are ridden by people in a wide variety of sporting events. Many are trained to be racers–either on flat courses with no jumps or in races with fences and ditches. The most successful of these horses have become racing legends, with names such as Peppers Pride, Colin, and Personal Ensign.

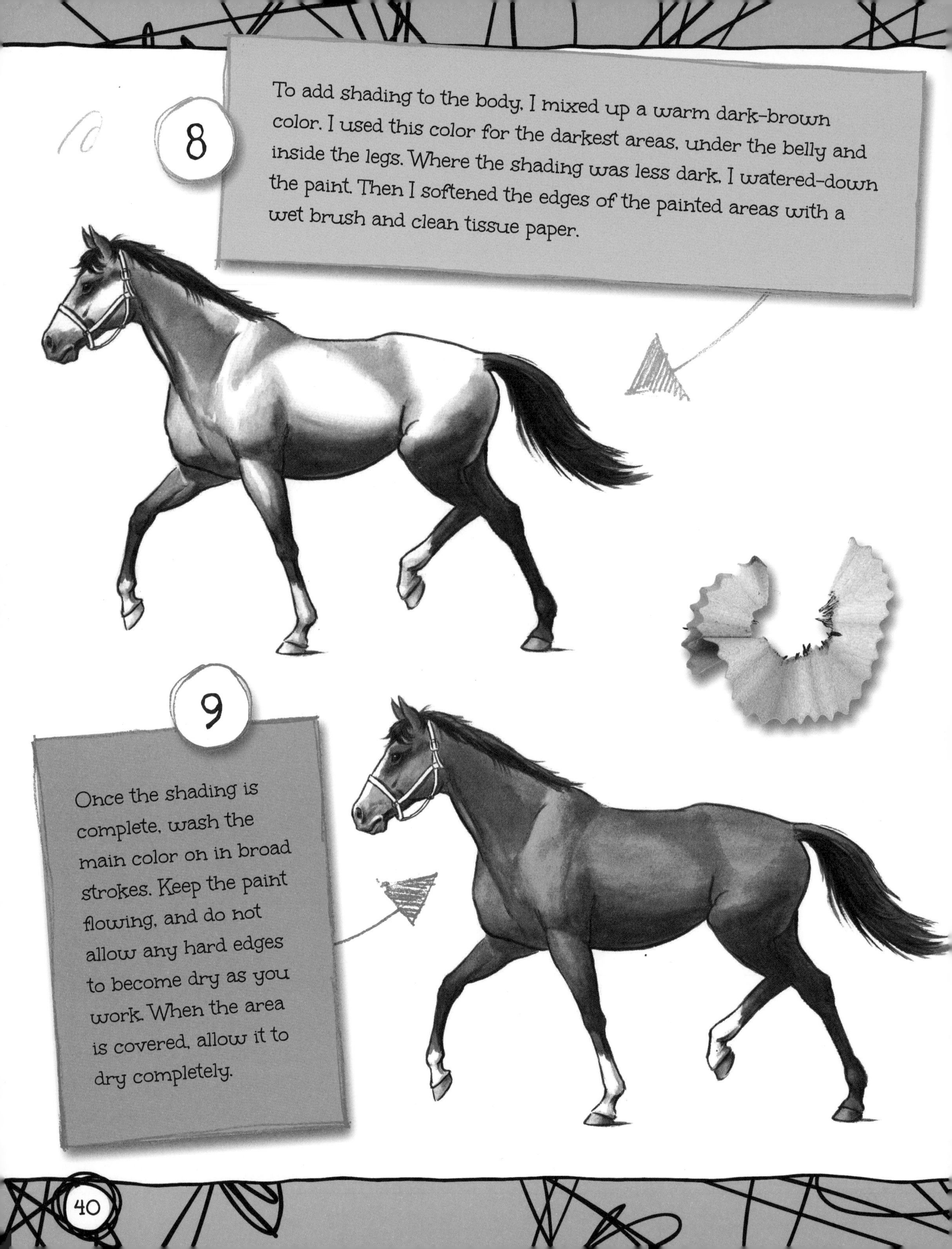

8

To add shading to the body, I mixed up a warm dark-brown color. I used this color for the darkest areas, under the belly and inside the legs. Where the shading was less dark, I watered-down the paint. Then I softened the edges of the painted areas with a wet brush and clean tissue paper.

9

Once the shading is complete, wash the main color on in broad strokes. Keep the paint flowing, and do not allow any hard edges to become dry as you work. When the area is covered, allow it to dry completely.

10

Once the paint is dry, you can add other small areas of color and strengthen the shading. Then work on the sheen, to make the horse look glossy. I wet the areas of highlight with a brush, then dabbed off the moistened paint with a clean tissue. You might prefer to create highlights with watered-down white ink or chalk. Add a few spots of white ink to bring out the highlights on the head.

FOAL

A foal is a baby horse, up to one year old. Foals have very long legs and small, slim bodies. Their manes and tails are short. After its first birthday, a foal is known as a yearling.

1

Although a foal is much leaner than a fully-grown horse, you start with a similar oval for the chest and belly. Add a circle for the head and a long curve off the animal's rear end for its rump.

2

Draw in the muzzle and the neck, arching over the head. Sketch in the legs, which are very long and thin on a foal.

3

Draw the head as a roughly rectangular box at this stage. The knees are very knobbly, and the tail and mane are short. To place the legs firmly on the ground, draw a neat shape on the floor to guide you.

4

Now draw in the main features of the face and the ears. Work on the upper legs, bringing out the curves of the foal's muscles. Add some detail to the hooves.

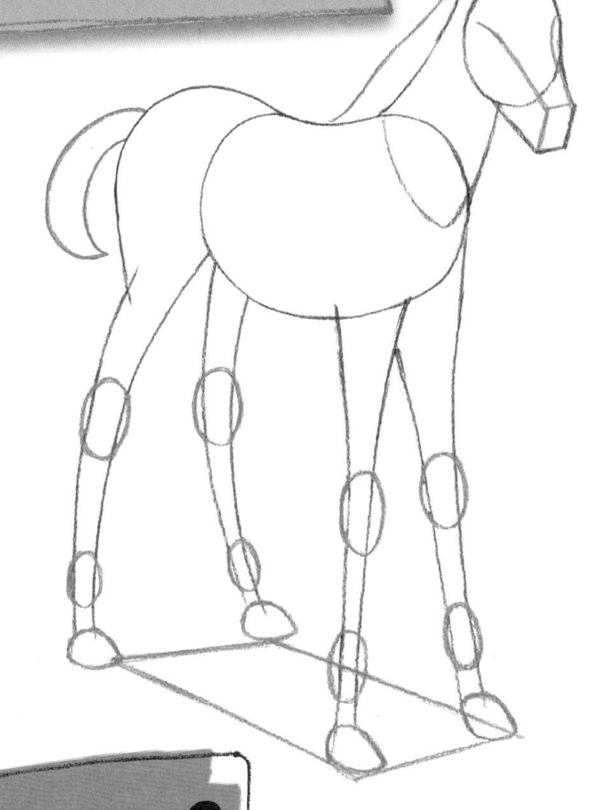

Did you know?

LONG LEGS

When a foal is born, its legs are almost as long as they will be when it has grown into an adult horse. Unlike human babies, foals use their legs almost right away. A foal will be standing within an hour of birth. By one day old, it will be trotting and galloping next to its mother.

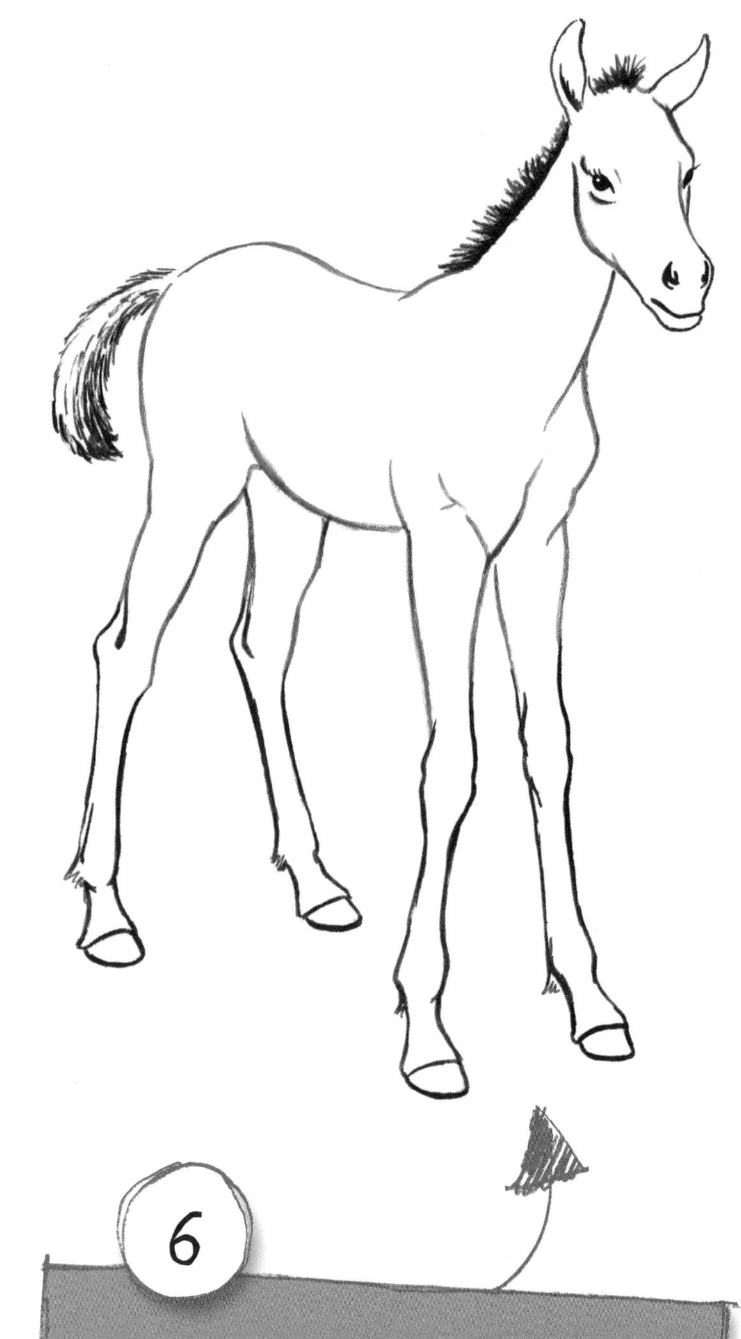

5

Continue working on the detail of the head, mane, and short tail. Make the body curves smooth, and pay attention to the joints on the foal's long legs.

6

To give a softer feel for this young animal, I decided on colored ink for part of the outline. I used a yellow-brown color for the body and upper legs, and black ink for the darker parts.

7

Although the nose is as dark as the legs and tail, it is more gray in color. A young horse is not as sleek and shiny as an adult. To give a sense of the fluffier coat, I painted some short, soft strokes on the foal's body.

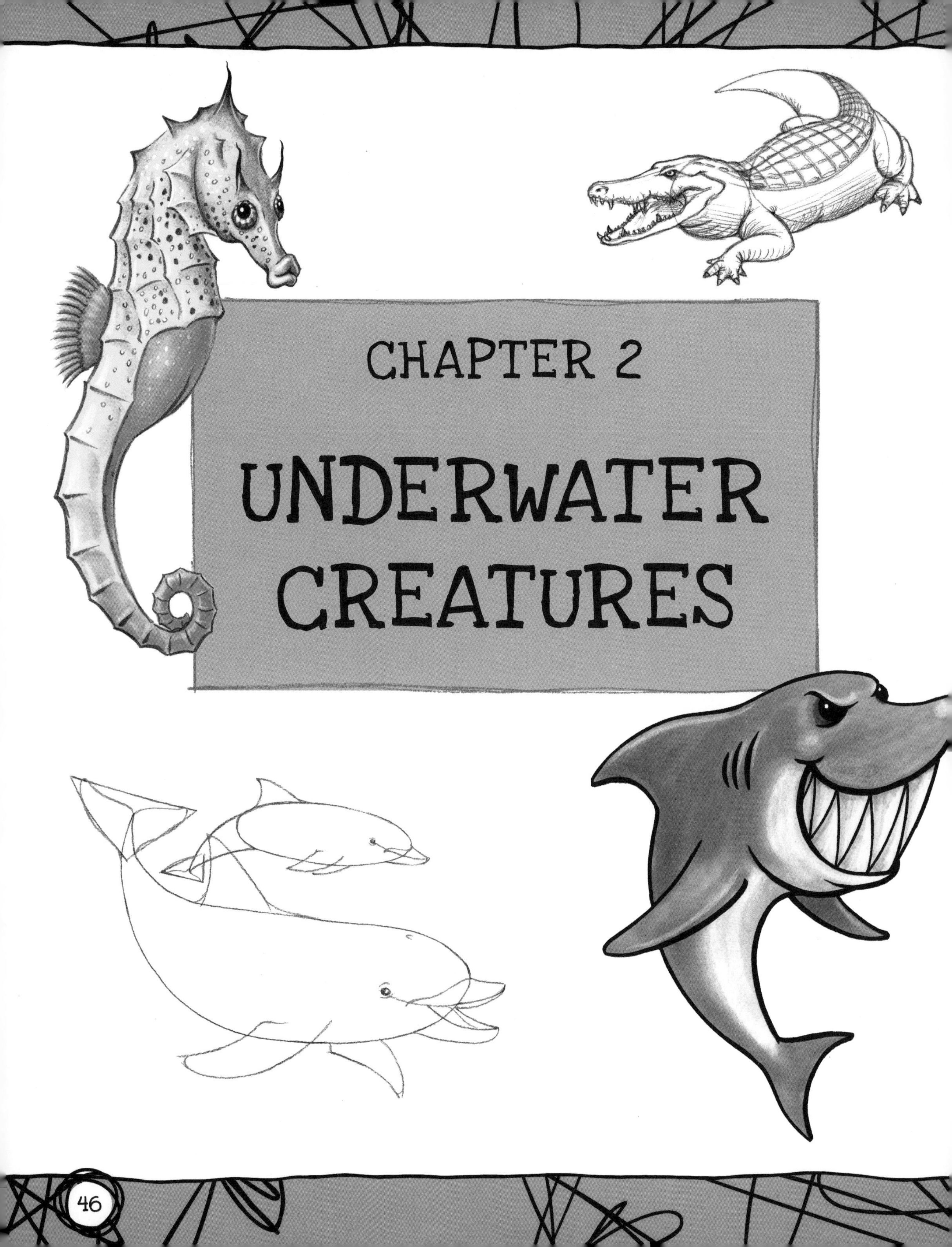

CHAPTER 2

UNDERWATER CREATURES

CROCODILE

The biggest and heaviest of all living reptiles, the crocodile is a fearsome hunter in water and on land. It has powerful jaws and sharp teeth for grabbing prey. The scales on the underside of the crocodile are small and smooth. On its back, it has large, ridged scales that act as protective armor.

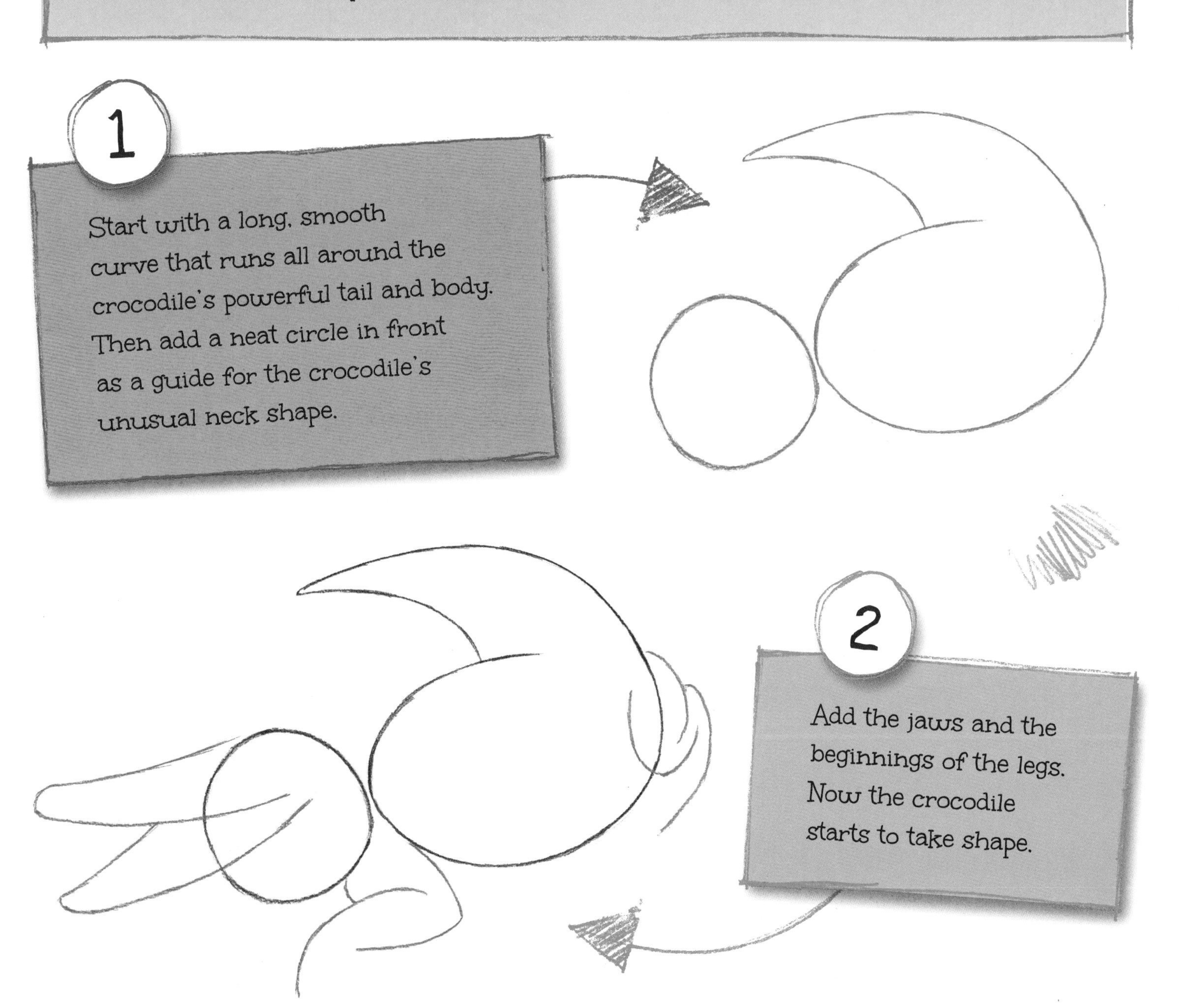

1

Start with a long, smooth curve that runs all around the crocodile's powerful tail and body. Then add a neat circle in front as a guide for the crocodile's unusual neck shape.

2

Add the jaws and the beginnings of the legs. Now the crocodile starts to take shape.

3

Connect the head, neck, and body with a few lines, and add eyebrow ridges. Sketch in the feet—five toes on the front feet, four on the back. Start to map out the ridges on the back, drawing the outer edges and center line.

4

Now flesh out the details—the lines of the mouth and teeth, the claws and webbed toes. Fill in the guidelines for the back ridges. They should be evenly spaced on the body but should get smaller along the tail.

5

This is where the fun starts! Now that the guidelines are all in place, you can work up the details with your pencil, refining and reshaping the drawing wherever necessary. You can erase the guidelines as you go.

6

For this example, I did most of the inking with a brush. I also used a fine felt-tip pen for the delicate details of the teeth. For the shadow and texture of the crocodile's underside, I used crisscross shading to follow the curve of the rounded body.

7

The first stage of painting is the shading. Decide on a direction for the light to come from—here it is upper right. Mix up a neutral gray color. Try to avoid using black paint—it's much better to mix up a gray from other colors, for example, purple with a little brown and blue.

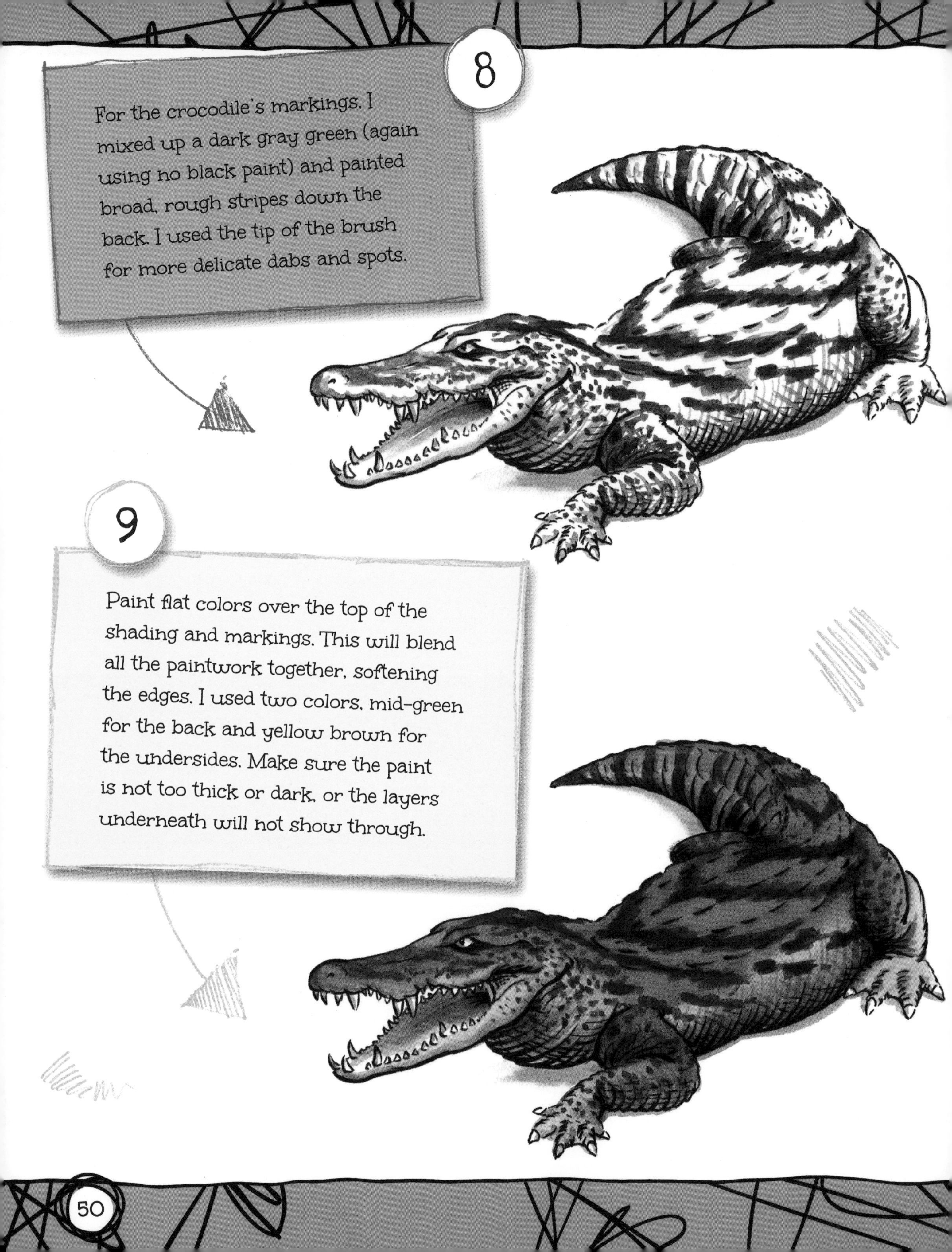

8

For the crocodile's markings, I mixed up a dark gray green (again using no black paint) and painted broad, rough stripes down the back. I used the tip of the brush for more delicate dabs and spots.

9

Paint flat colors over the top of the shading and markings. This will blend all the paintwork together, softening the edges. I used two colors, mid-green for the back and yellow brown for the undersides. Make sure the paint is not too thick or dark, or the layers underneath will not show through.

10

Now it's time to add tiny spots of color for highlights, on the eyes and claws, for example. Look hard at your picture to see if any areas need brightening. For highlights, you will need some white paint or ink, or you could use a sharpened piece of chalk. The highlights bring out the shine on a subject and show up its texture.

CARTOON CROC

You wouldn't want a real-life croc snapping at your feet, but this cartoon version is a lot more friendly! Compare this style of drawing to the realistic crocodile on the previous pages.

1

Draw two ovals for the body and tail. With cartoon animals, it's a good idea to make the head fairly big, so add a large triangular shape for this.

2

Next, plot out the head with eyes and nostrils and a line for the snout. Add curves for the back and tail. Start to form the legs.

3

Have fun working on the face to make it appealing. Add toes to the legs, then draw rounded squares on the back and lines on the tail to make the bumpy skin.

4

Before coloring in, go over the outlines with a black felt-tip pen. When it's dry, erase your pencil lines.

CARTOON CORNER

Try different expressions for your croc. Study yourself in the mirror making these faces first to help.

1

For an angry face, scrunch up the eyes and make the nostrils wide. Close most of the mouth, but leave some teeth on show.

2

For a happy face, make the mouth wide and smiling with lots of teeth on show. The eyes should be wide open.

3

Use props to help. As well as drawing your croc licking his lips, add a knife, fork, and napkin to make him look really hungry!

SHARK

This cartoon shark looks scary and funny at the same time! When you're an expert at drawing him this way, try varying the length of his tail and the size of his teeth.

1

Start with an extra-large circle for the head. Then draw two curved lines that meet at a point for the body and tail.

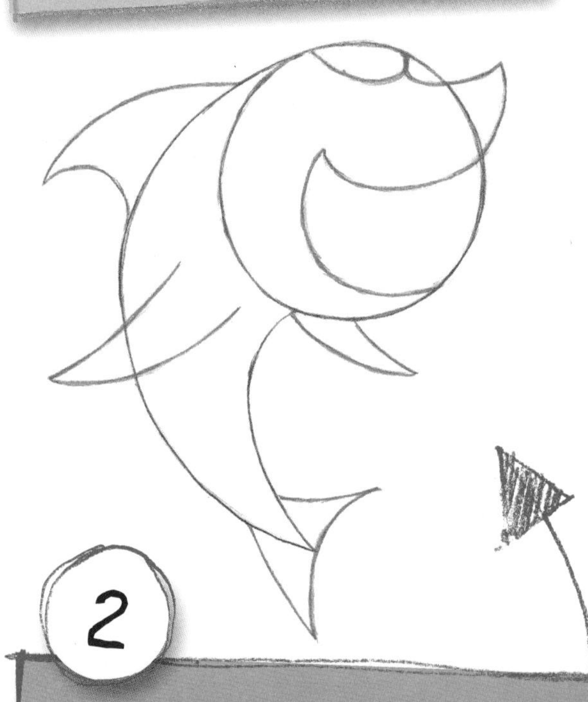

2

You can add movement by drawing more pointed curves for the fins and tail. Copy the picture carefully, especially the head and mouth.

3

Now draw the pointed teeth and scary eyes. Add three gill lines, and round off the tips of the fins and tail. This will make the teeth look even sharper!

4

Erase the circle around the head, and color your shark in two shades of blue. Give it some pale yellow and white teeth.

CARTOON CORNER

Here are some tips for drawing other crazy cartoon fish.

As with the shark, start this goldfish with a circle and a pointed curve. Give it large wonky eyes and a lopsided mouth to make it look really silly. Add fine lines for the tail, fin, and flippers.

To draw this tropical fish, use two overlapping triangles. Experiment with different angles and sizes. Try different colors, too, and add wavy lines or stripes instead of spots.

DOLPHIN

Dolphins live in the world's warmer seas and oceans, usually in groups known as "pods." These are bottlenose dolphins-they are called that because their long snouts look rather like bottles! They can vary in color from light bluish gray to almost black.

1

I decided to draw a pair of dolphins swimming together. You can, of course, choose to draw only one. The body shape of the main dolphin is two curves meeting at a broadly rounded head. The other dolphin is a long oval with a separate tail.

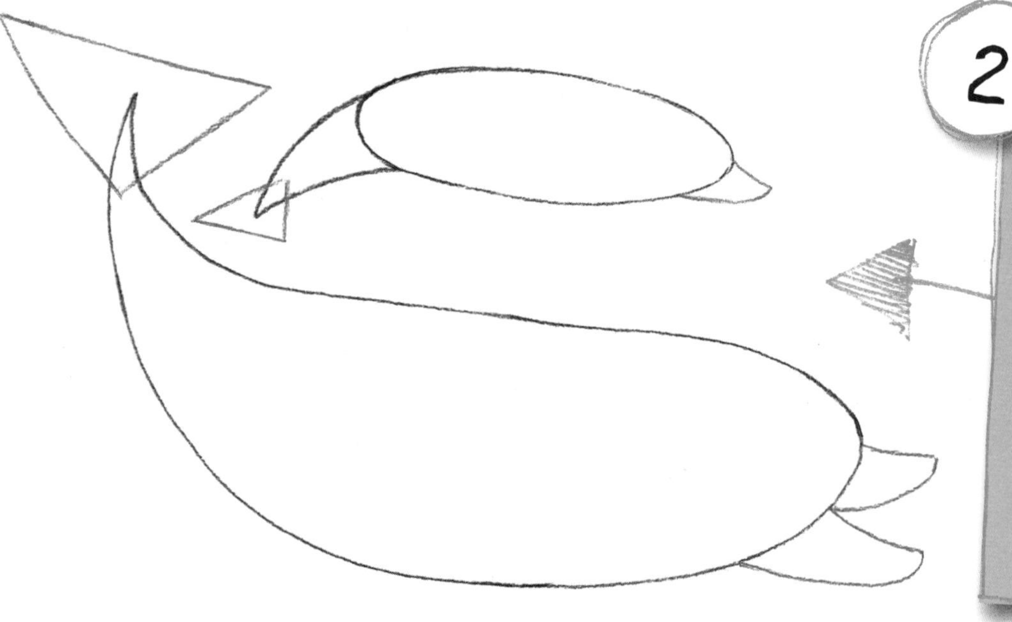

2

Add the shapes of the snouts, one closed and the other open. The tail fins start as simple triangles. Make sure these triangles fit symmetrically on to the body.

3

Draw the back fins and flippers. Note that the back fins sit to the rear of the bodies. Add mouth openings that extend into the head—these will help you to position the eyes.

4

Shape the tail fins neatly within the triangles. Then work on the other fins, rounding off the corners and blending them smoothly into the bodies. Complete the snout shapes with curved lines where the upper jaw joins the head.

5

Make sure your drawings are sleek and streamlined, then erase any confusing guidelines. Because the shapes of these animals are quite simple, you need to be careful with every outline.

6

For the inking stage, try to ink each part of your drawing with continuous, unbroken lines. Use a fine but well-loaded brush, so that the ink doesn't run out halfway along a graceful curve. Make the outline slightly broader on the shaded undersides and finer along the upper surfaces.

7

Even simple coloring like that of the dolphin requires several stages to be really effective. Work on the shading first. For this picture, I used a blue-gray color. Before each section dried, I softened the edges with a wet brush to blend the dark parts into the light, to suggest smoothly rounded bodies.

Did you know?

DOLPHIN SENSES

Dolphins are highly intelligent creatures. When they are hunting, they make clicking sounds and then listen for the echo of the sound as it bounces back. The time it takes for the sound to return tells the dolphin how far away its prey is. This is called echolocation. Dolphins also "talk" to each other with a wide range of whistles and other sounds.

8

Now add the plain gray coloring. For this, I mixed some golden brown into the gray. Mix up plenty of paint, so that you don't run out halfway through the painting. I painted this layer in swift, broad strokes and softened the bottom edges to blend into the pale undersides.

9

To bring some roundness to the shapes of the dolphins and to show where the light falls, I lightened the upper surfaces. I used a soft, damp brush to moisten the paint and lift it off the surface, cleaning the brush frequently.

10

For the final touches, I diluted white ink with water to pick out the delicate highlights on the upper parts, and to neaten up the mouth and eye areas. Then I mixed some blue into the white ink to paint some fine strips of color on the dolphins' undersides.

SEAHORSE

These strange little creatures look like miniature horses-that's where their name comes from. However, they are in fact bony fish. They swim upright in some of the world's warm seas and oceans by fluttering the small fins on their backs. To rest, they attach themselves to corals or seagrasses with their long spiral tails.

1

Start the seahorse's long head and body with two slightly squashed ovals. The head should be fairly flat on top and more rounded underneath. The body dips in at the back, in a bean shape.

2

Connect the two ovals with an arching line for the outside of the neck. The tail begins as a long curve that runs from the back and ends in a loose spiral. Add in the triangular nose part.

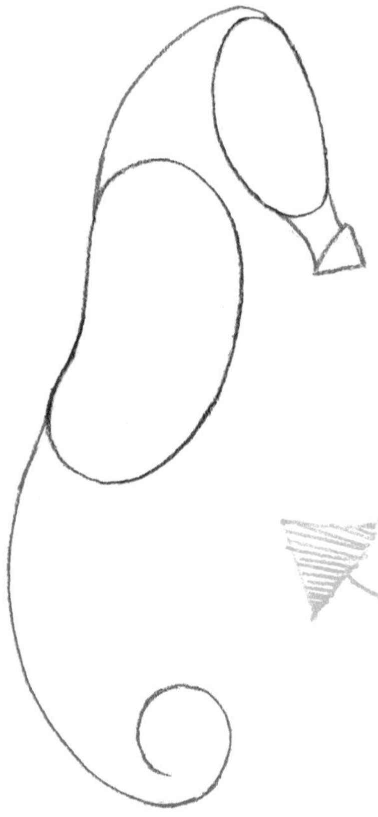

3

Draw the inside line of the tail, which forms a tight spiral at the end. Add facial features and fins around the jawline and in the middle of the back.

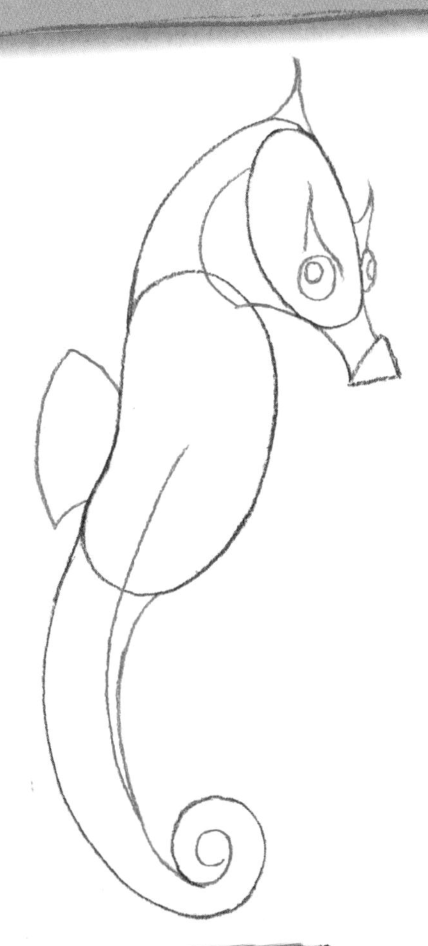

4

Mark some guidelines for the ridges on the seahorse's body. Be sure to make them regular in size on the body and smaller as you work down the tail.

Did you know?

SEAHORSE SNACKS

Seahorses use their long snouts to suck in tiny sea creatures for food. They have no teeth and no stomach! This means that seahorses must feed almost constantly in order to process enough food to keep them alive.

5

Now you can refine your drawing, adding detail and texture to the guidelines. Work on the ridges of the body to give them some depth. Then spend some time working on the features of the face and the back fin.

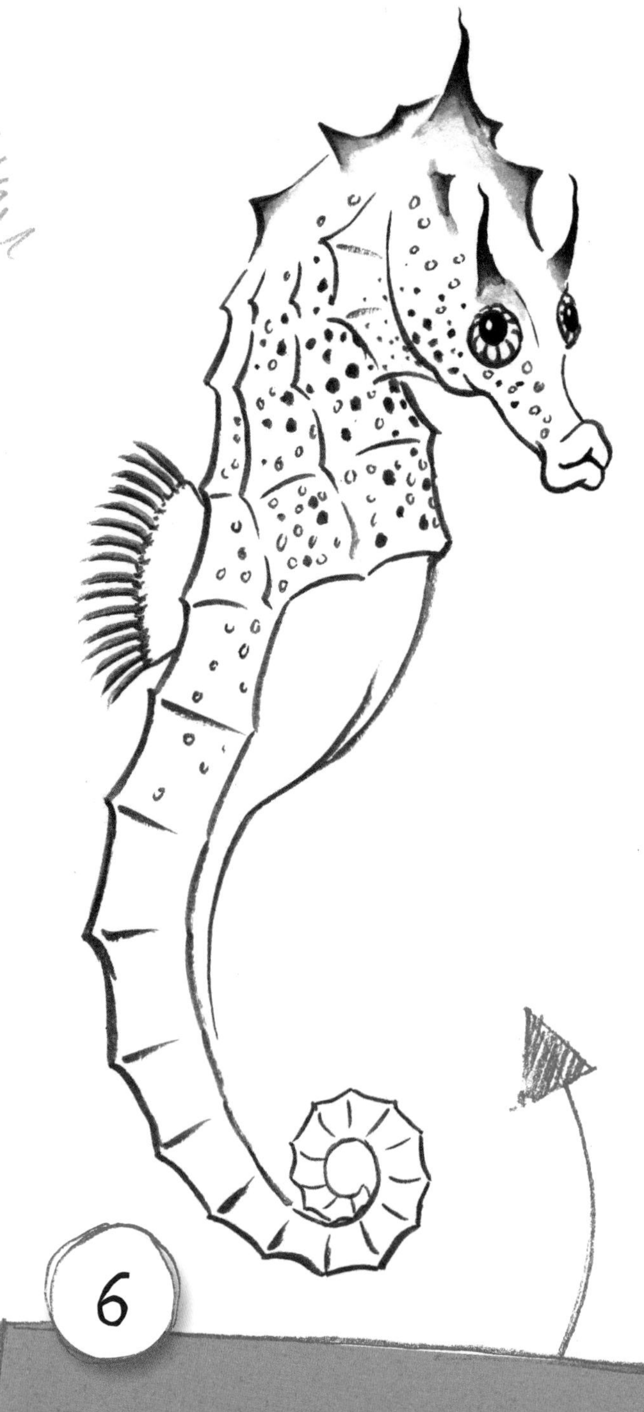

6

For such a delicate and colorful creature, I chose a warm red-brown color for the inking stage. I used black ink for the eyes and the tips of the horns. I also added some small dots and circles around the face and chest.

7

Like many fish, seahorses come in a remarkable range of colors and markings. Some are dull brown and gray, but I chose a more colorful example. I used orange and yellow, blending into a greenish tint around the face. White highlights help to bring out the various ridges and bumps on the seahorse's body.

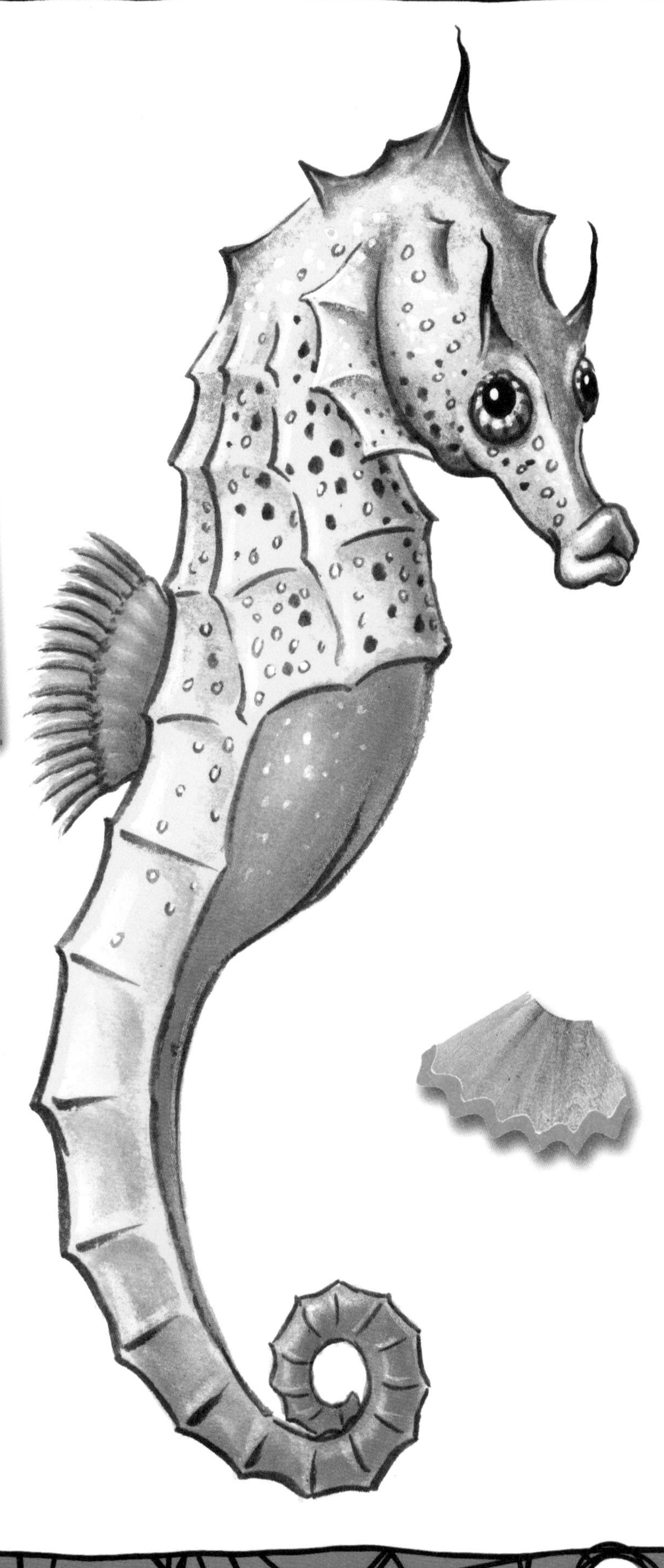

CHAPTER 3

WILD ANIMALS

BUTTERFLY

There are many thousands of different types of butterflies, and they live in nearly all parts of the world. The striking shapes, colors, and patterns of their wings have inspired some beautiful butterfly names, such as "painted ladies," "hairstreaks," "coppers," "metalmarks," and "swallowtails."

1

Butterflies are symmetrical down a center line, so a grid is a helpful guide to start your picture. Use a ruler to draw two squares side by side. The center line is where the squares meet. Then draw more guidelines inside the boxes as shown. The lines do not have to be exact, so long as they are the same on each side.

Working either side of the center line, sketch in the three parts of the butterfly's body (head, thorax, and abdomen). Add the wing shapes with curves that fit inside the grid guidelines.

3

Draw the divisions between the wings, and then add the outlines of the wing markings, branching out smoothly from the thorax. I decided to draw the two antennae at slightly different angles, to break up the symmetry a bit.

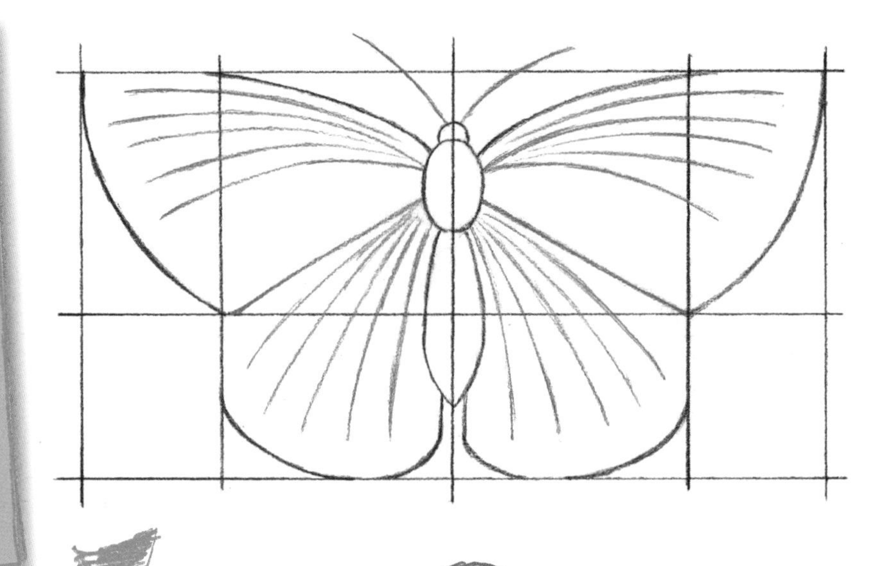

4

Work on the wing markings and the outer shapes of the wings. Then add some detail to the head, and mark the curved divisions along the abdomen.

5

The grid lines will help you to place the finer details and markings of the wings symmetrically. Keep going from one side of your picture to the other, making sure each mark is followed by its mirror image.

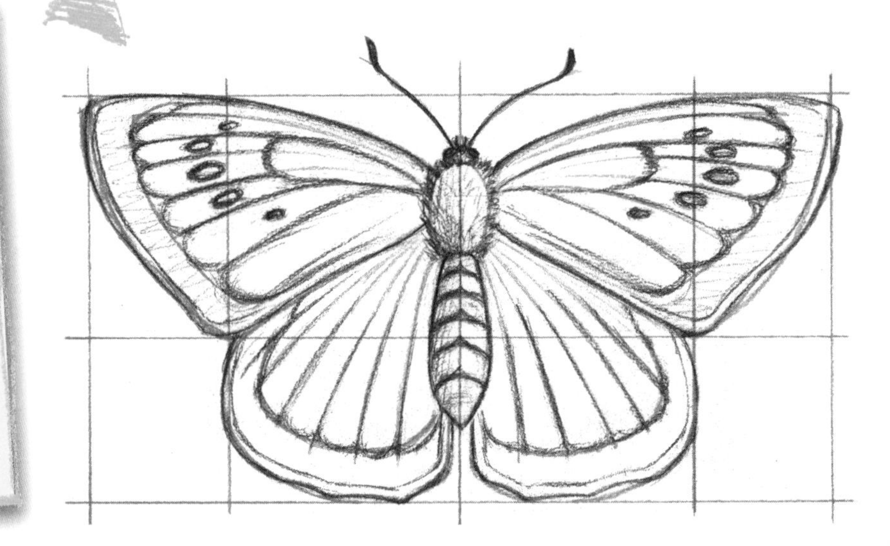

6

For the inking stage, I used a rich blue instead of black, to avoid making the outlines too heavy. I inked in the darker lines of the body and the markings with the tip of a fine brush. Each time the brush started to run dry, I switched to more delicate markings. For the outer edges of the wings, I used tiny strokes of thin brown ink.

7

There is not a lot of shading to be done on a relatively flat subject such as this. But a touch of purple or blue around the body and the inner parts of the wings gives the drawing some solidity and depth.

8

Now apply some color to the main parts of the wings to create a pattern. I used some pale pink with a fairly dry brush to stroke a subtle sheen on the inner parts of the wings. For the bolder outer markings, I avoided black paint, which would be too heavy here. Instead, I mixed up some brown and blue to make a dark shade.

9

For the main color, I mixed up a large batch of pale blue. The important thing here is to wash the color on quickly, so as not to disturb the paint you have already put on the wings. Paint with a fairly broad brush, following the direction of the wing markings.

10

For the final detailed touches, I used some white ink and a very fine brush to lift out the delicate highlights of the wing markings. You can also add fine highlights to the fluffy thorax and the shiny abdomen.

TIGER

The largest of the big cats, the tiger is a strong and ferocious hunter. Its beautiful striped coat makes it difficult to spot in the grasslands and forests that are its home.

1

Although the tiger is a strong and thickset animal, its body shape is in fact fairly slender. Begin with a long oval, and make it bow slightly in the middle. Mark a neat circle at the front end for the basic head shape.

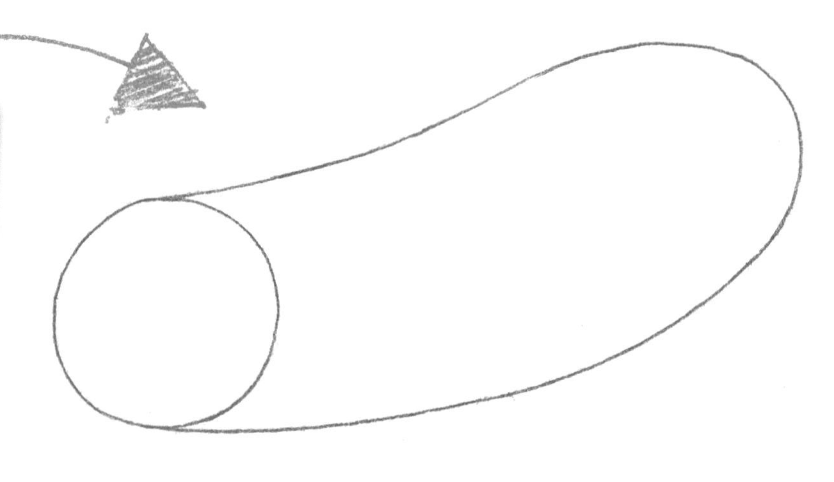

2

Draw curving lines around the head to mark the center of the face and the level of the eyes. Add in the lines of the powerful upper legs.

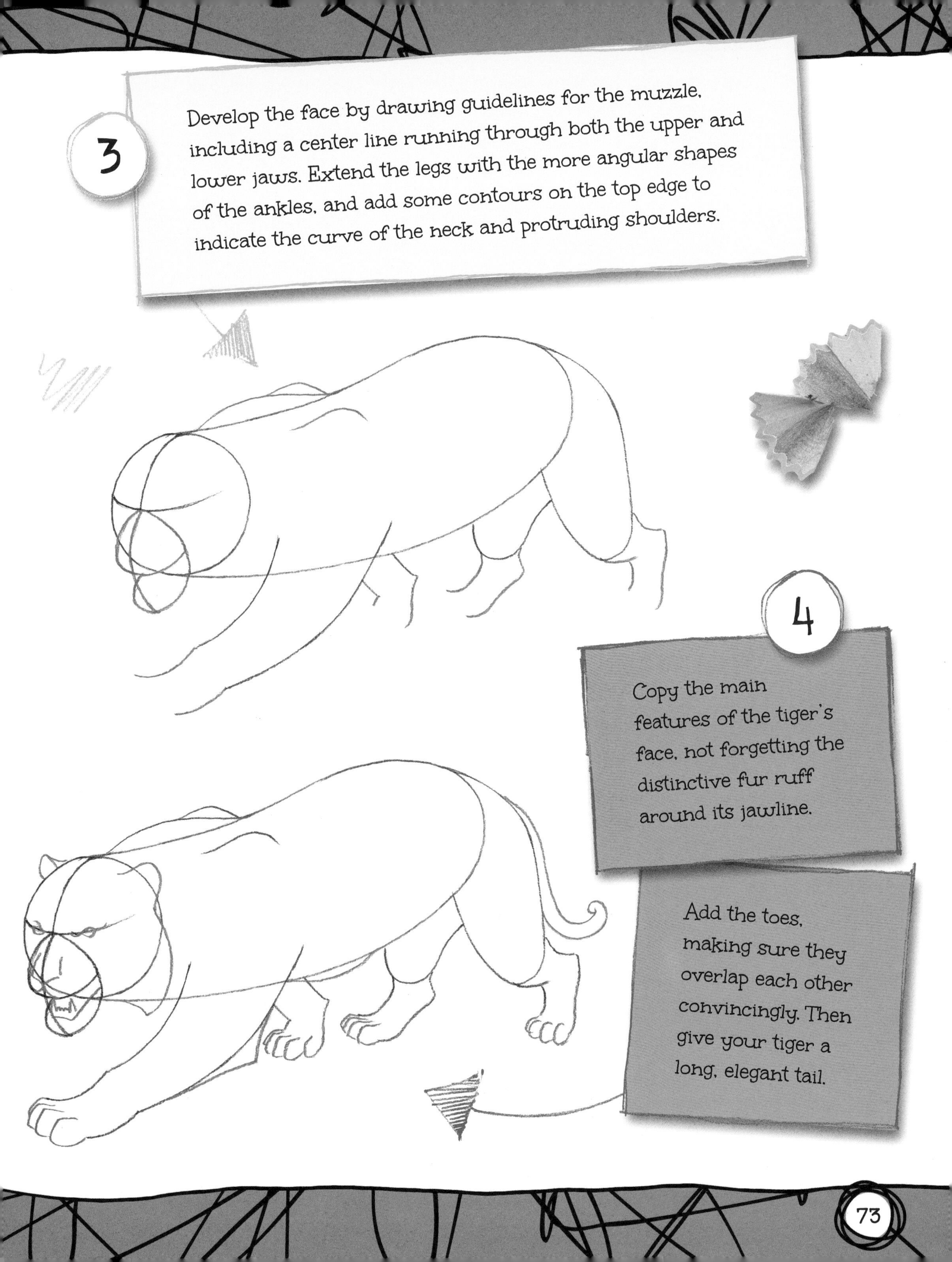

3

Develop the face by drawing guidelines for the muzzle, including a center line running through both the upper and lower jaws. Extend the legs with the more angular shapes of the ankles, and add some contours on the top edge to indicate the curve of the neck and protruding shoulders.

4

Copy the main features of the tiger's face, not forgetting the distinctive fur ruff around its jawline.

Add the toes, making sure they overlap each other convincingly. Then give your tiger a long, elegant tail.

5

With the guidelines all established, you can now enjoy working on the fine detail. Switch to a softer pencil, and make sure it is sharp. Include a center line down the tiger's back and some rough guidelines for the curves and spacings of the stripes.

6

For the inking stage, keep the outlines smooth and simple, allowing the brush to vary the weight of the lines. Use the tip of the brush, lightly loaded, to ink the eyes, mouth, and nose. The black claws can be inked with single strokes.

Don't erase the guidelines yet, as you will need them for the markings.

7

The tiger's markings are black stripes, so I have done them in ink. Work either side of the center guidelines down the tiger's back and head, to make the stripes symmetrical and give them a rough, hairy texture. Don't do too many—leave some space between each stripe.

Did you know?

COOL CATS

Unlike many cats, tigers love water. In the heat of the day, tigers often choose to cool off by taking a dip in lakes or streams. With their powerful bodies and webbed paws, tigers are strong swimmers. They can cover many miles in the water, crossing rivers or chasing prey.

8

With your watercolors, mix up some watery gray using dark blue, red, and maybe a touch of brown. Be sure you have decided the direction of the light—here it is coming from the upper right. Then apply some shading to the parts facing away from the light.

9

Mix some red and brown to make orange, and paint the upper back, face, and shoulders. Once it is dry, use an orangey brown to paint across the entire colored area, which will blend the darker orange with the new color. Remember to leave some white patches on the face, belly, and tail.

10

To finish the painting, add patches of color to the eyes and mouth. Then put in any extra shading or richer color that seems necessary. Use a fine brush and white ink to paint delicate highlights around the teeth, nose, and ears and to add some very fine whiskers.

IGUANA

The iguana is a large lizard that lives in Central America and the Caribbean. Male iguanas can grow to up to six feet (two meters) in length. The iguana uses its sharp eyes to look for food. If attacked, it lashes out with its long, whiplike tail.

1

Draw a long egg shape for the iguana's body, then the outer edge of the tail flowing smoothly on from its back.

The head should be drawn separately, and is roughly triangular in form.

2

Now connect the head and body with curving lines to make the iguana's shape.

Start to work on the legs by carefully marking the outer edges. The tail should get narrower toward the tip.

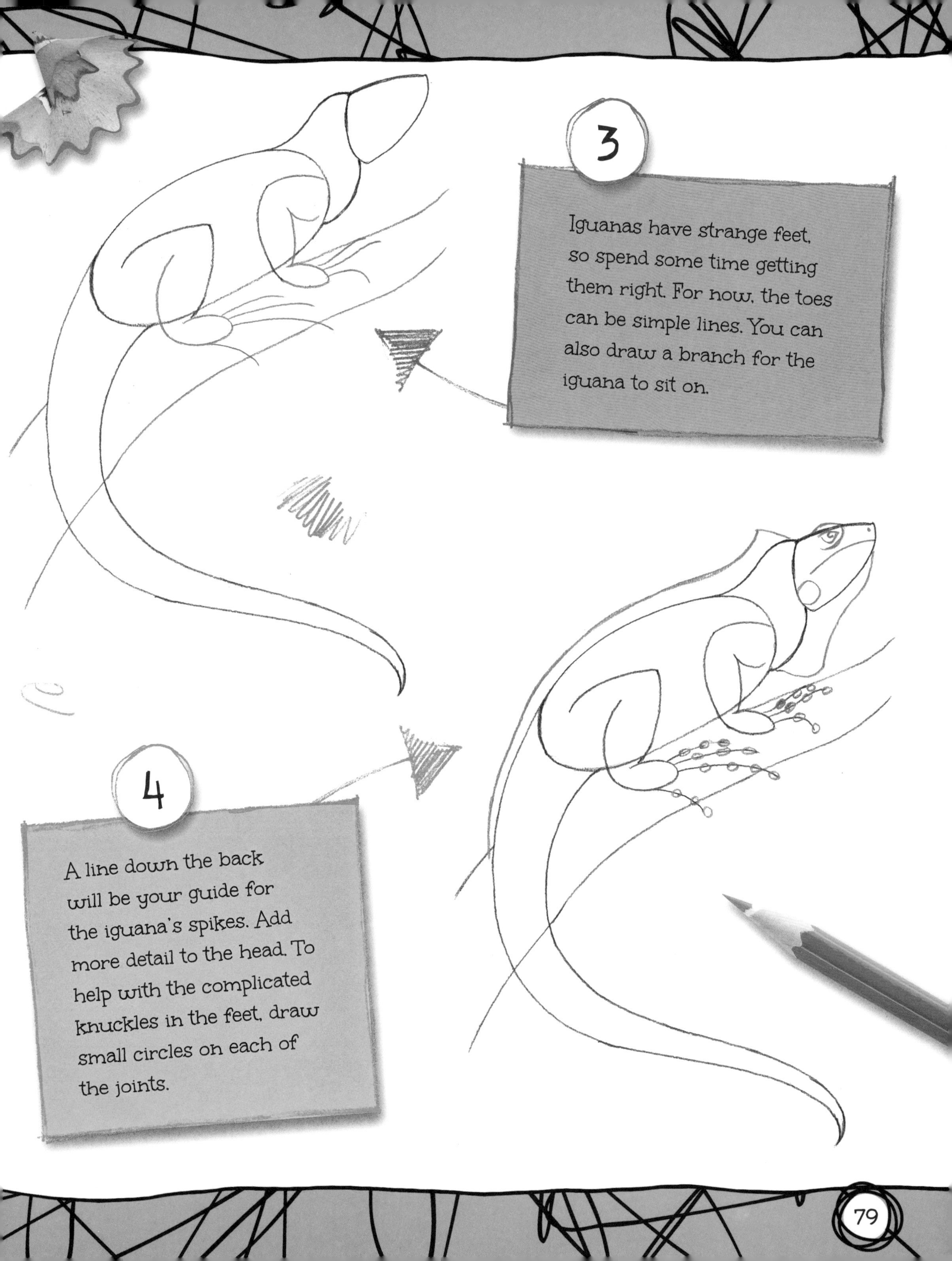

3

Iguanas have strange feet, so spend some time getting them right. For now, the toes can be simple lines. You can also draw a branch for the iguana to sit on.

4

A line down the back will be your guide for the iguana's spikes. Add more detail to the head. To help with the complicated knuckles in the feet, draw small circles on each of the joints.

5

Now you can add the finishing touches to your pencils. Follow the guidelines drawn in step four as you add detail to the feet.

6

Use a thin brush or a fine pen for the delicate lines of the spikes, claws, and fingers. You can ink more heavily in some of the shadow areas and add texture to the branch.

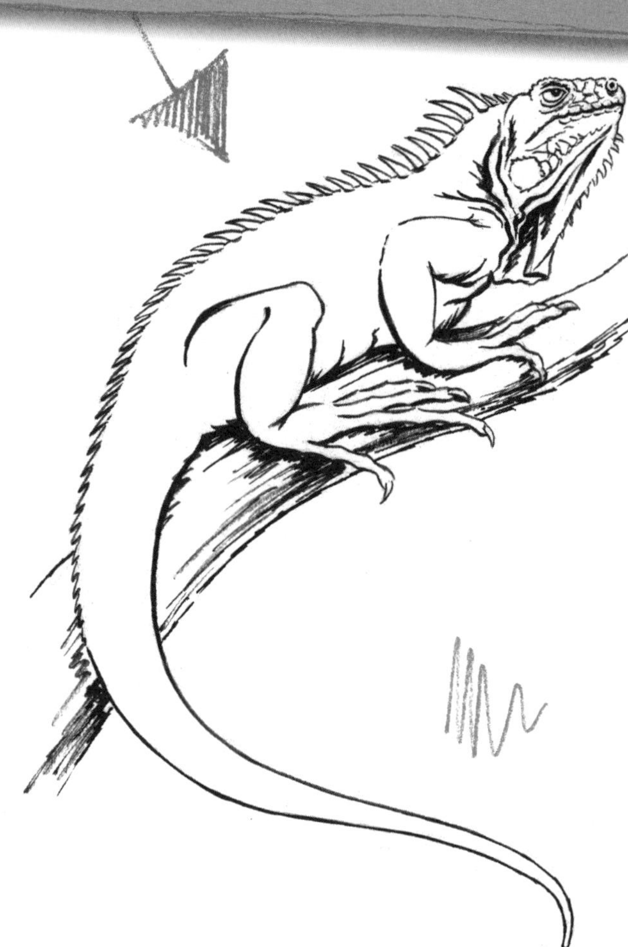

Did you know?

TAIL TRICKS

If an attacker grabs hold of an iguana's tail, the iguana has a clever trick. It allows its tail to drop off and then runs away! In time, a perfect new tail will grow in its place.

7

For creatures of more than one color, try to blend the colors into each other. This effect is tricky with felt-tip pens, but pretty easy with colored pencils. If you are using paint, you should work the two colors together while they are wet.

WILD PONY

Wild ponies are usually fairly broad and sturdy animals, with short legs. Their coats are coarse and thick to keep them warm in winter, and they have long manes and tails. These hardy little ponies have to be able to survive all weathers.

1

This wild pony is a sturdy creature, so make the oval of the body extra deep and rounded. Add a circle for the head and a line to start the back leg.

2

Draw the cone shape of the muzzle, and a line to indicate the neck. The neck is wide and strong. The legs are short and thick.

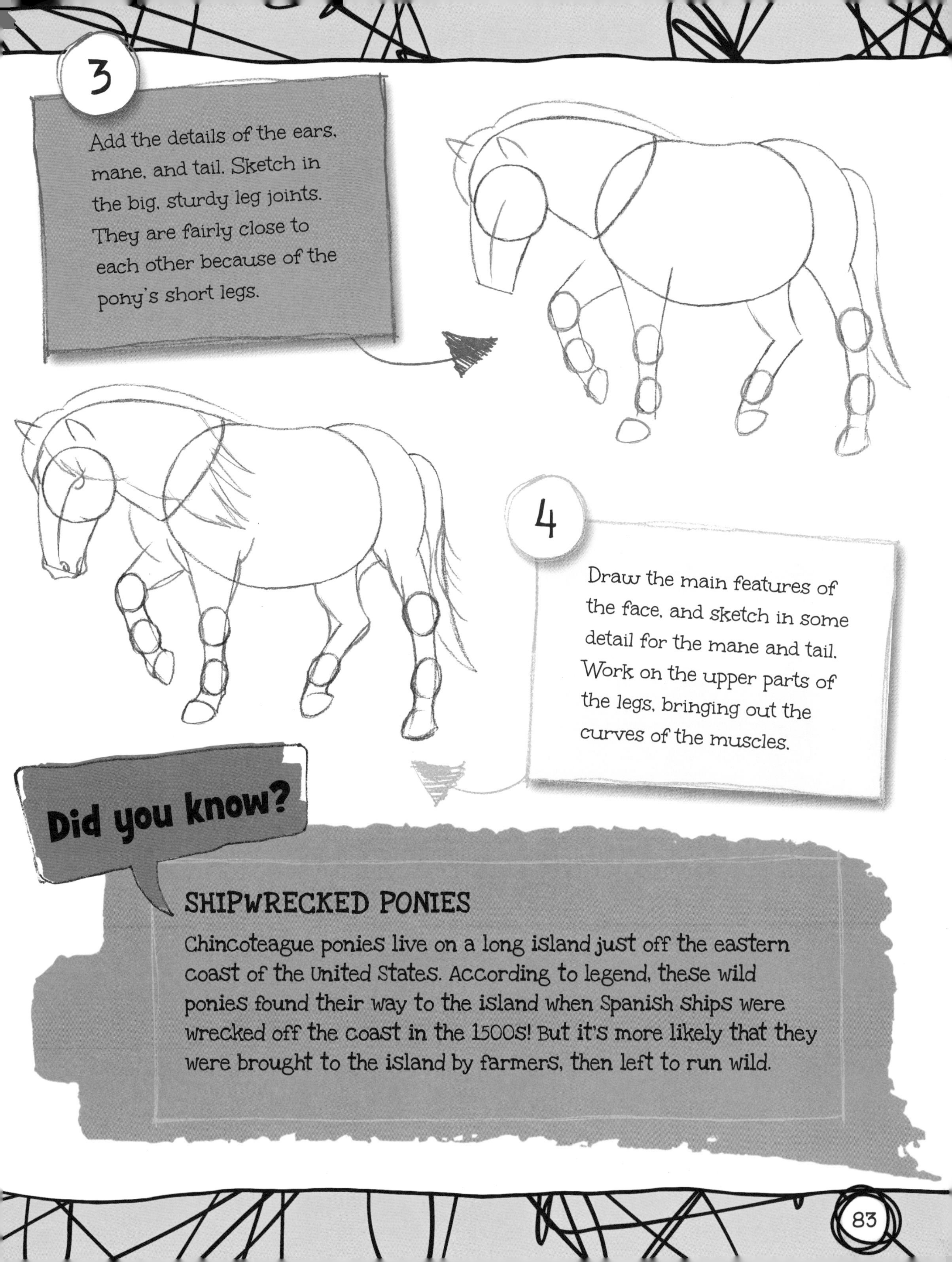

3

Add the details of the ears, mane, and tail. Sketch in the big, sturdy leg joints. They are fairly close to each other because of the pony's short legs.

4

Draw the main features of the face, and sketch in some detail for the mane and tail. Work on the upper parts of the legs, bringing out the curves of the muscles.

Did you know?

SHIPWRECKED PONIES

Chincoteague ponies live on a long island just off the eastern coast of the United States. According to legend, these wild ponies found their way to the island when Spanish ships were wrecked off the coast in the 1500s! But it's more likely that they were brought to the island by farmers, then left to run wild.

5

I wanted to make the mane look windswept, so I drew the general flow of its movement. Don't try to put in every detail—it will look more natural to ink and paint the hair in the next steps. I also added a suggestion of scruffy hair around the hooves and lower legs.

6

I inked the flyaway hair in swift strokes with black ink diluted with water. A small amount of ink on the brush allows the texture of the brush hairs to show. I made the general outlines fairly rough to capture the shaggy appearance of the pony's coat.

7

Once I had colored and shaded the animal, I added lots of fine strokes to capture the texture of the coat. This pony's rough coat has little natural sheen, so I kept the highlights to a minimum on the body. I used white ink for the mane, tail, and shaggy legs.

HONEYBEE

Bees live on the nectar and pollen produced by flowering plants. Honeybees are a particular type of bee that make honey from the nectar they collect, and they store it in a honeycomb. Only female bees make honey.

1

Start with the three main body parts: an upside-down egg shape for the head, a circle for the thorax, and a large oval for the abdomen. Make sure you leave spaces in-between.

2

Connect the body parts, and add the sting at the end of the abdomen. Then draw the large oval eye and the mouth shape. Mark the places where the legs and wings join the thorax with small circles.

Did you know?

DRONES AND WORKERS

Male bees, or drones, don't collect nectar or pollen. It's up to the female worker bees to do all the hard work-collecting nectar, cleaning up, and guarding the hive (the bees' home). Queen honeybees rule the hive and can lay up to 2,000 eggs in one day!

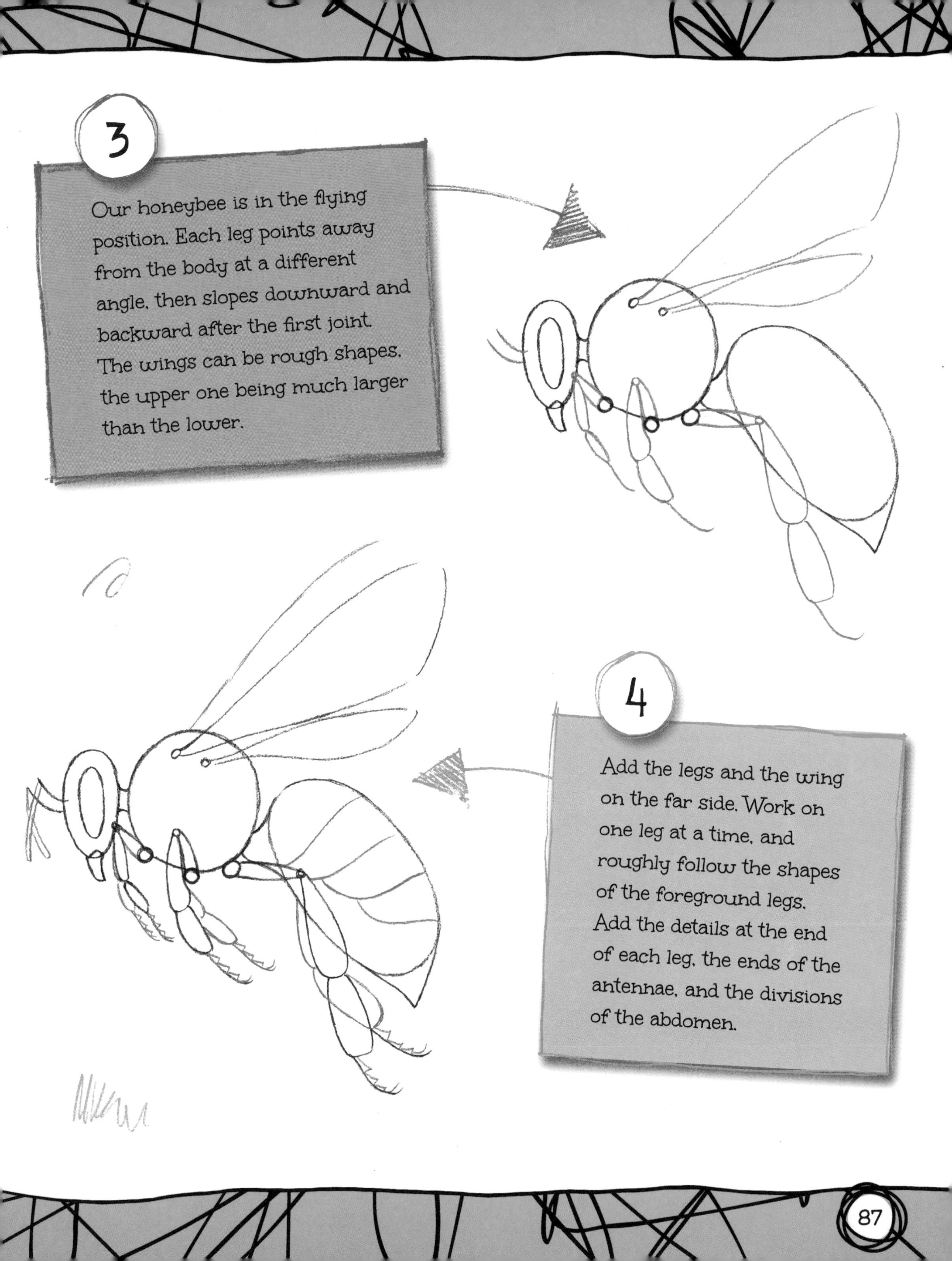

3

Our honeybee is in the flying position. Each leg points away from the body at a different angle, then slopes downward and backward after the first joint. The wings can be rough shapes, the upper one being much larger than the lower.

4

Add the legs and the wing on the far side. Work on one leg at a time, and roughly follow the shapes of the foreground legs. Add the details at the end of each leg, the ends of the antennae, and the divisions of the abdomen.

5

Now work on the details, particularly the characteristic fluffy texture of the thorax, which increases its size on the page. Add more fluffy marks around the head.

6

For the inking stage, use black ink in firm strokes for the hard parts of the abdomen and the legs. Use lots of soft strokes for the furry parts and the fast-moving wings, with fine hatched lines for the eye.

7

To color the bee, I used layers of browns and yellows for the thorax and head to build up a textured feel. The blurry wings needed only a few swift strokes. The abdomen took somewhat longer, since I blended black stripes into the yellow. For the highlights, I used tiny soft strokes for the fluffy parts, with bold, shiny marks for the smooth abdomen.

LION

The lion is king of the animals, with powerful legs for chasing prey. The male lion has a thick mane of hair around his neck. This bushy mane makes the lion look larger, which helps to frighten rivals. The mane also protects the lion's neck during fights.

1

Start with the lion's head by drawing a triangle, pointing downward. Position the triangle to the right of the page. Then draw a long egg shape almost touching it. Leave enough space around the shapes to fit the rest of the lion on your paper. Look at the example to make sure your shapes are the right sizes in relation to each other.

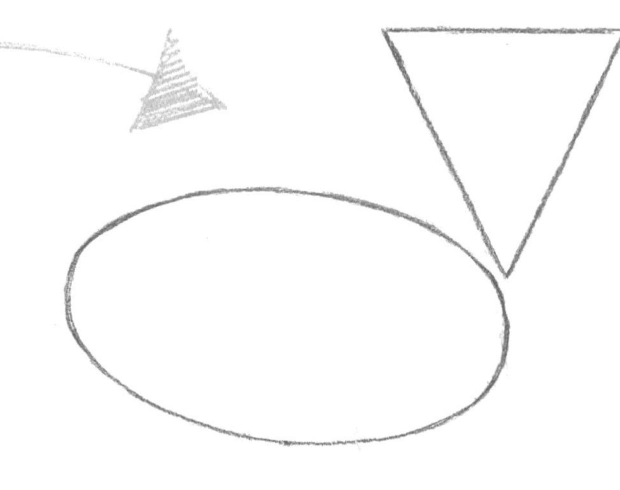

2

Next, you can add the strong upper parts of the lion's legs. Draw four long ovals, being careful to pay attention to the sizes and how they fit onto the body. You can then connect the chest and the hips with curved lines.

3

Complete the basic lion shape with the powerful lower legs and the tail. Draw in a rough outline for the mane. Mark a center line down the lion's head and a line across at the level of the eyes.

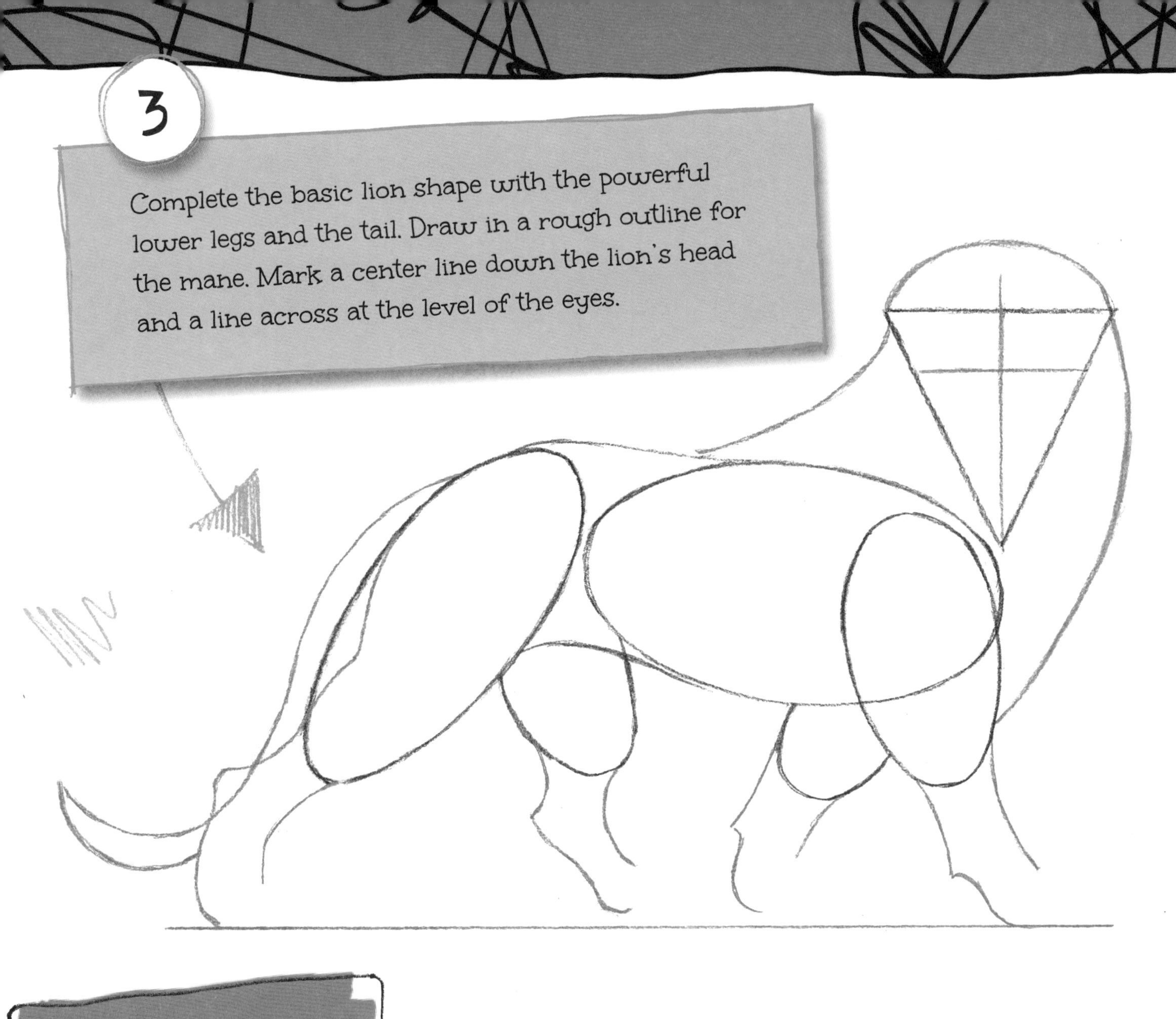

Did you know?

HUNTERS

Many lions live in groups called prides. While the male lions protect the pride's territory, it is the lionesses (female lions) that do most of the hunting for food. They are smaller and more agile than the males, and they often work together to kill their prey.

4

Continue to work on the lion's face. Use the guidelines to make sure the mouth, nose, and eyes are symmetrical. Then draw the ears and add some texture to the outline of the mane. Draw the feet as individual rounded toes.

5

Now that the basic lion shape is complete, you can start to look at the details. At this stage, it's a good idea to work some texture into the mane to guide your ink drawing. You can also plan where the shading will appear on the lion's body.

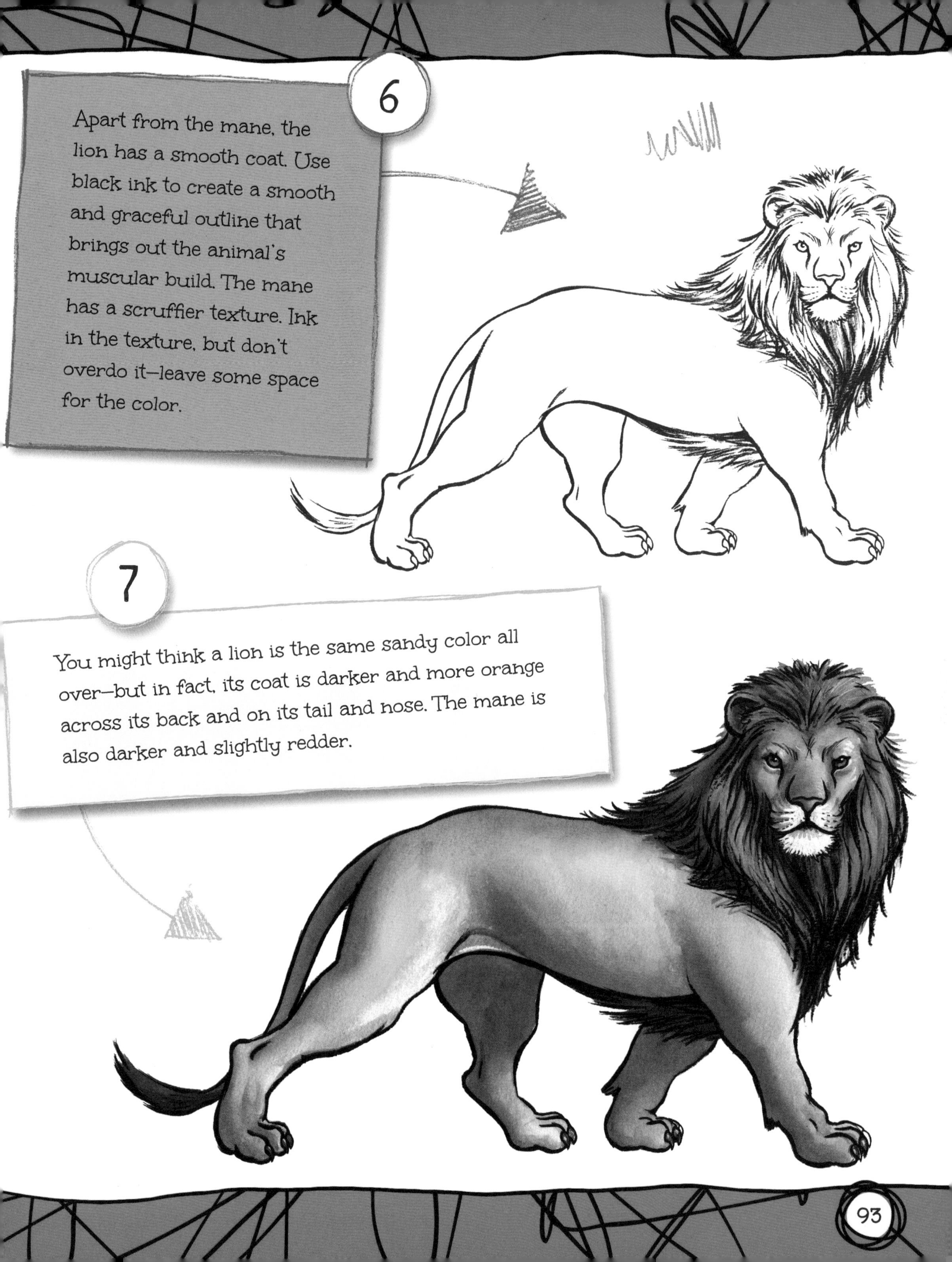

6

Apart from the mane, the lion has a smooth coat. Use black ink to create a smooth and graceful outline that brings out the animal's muscular build. The mane has a scruffier texture. Ink in the texture, but don't overdo it—leave some space for the color.

7

You might think a lion is the same sandy color all over—but in fact, its coat is darker and more orange across its back and on its tail and nose. The mane is also darker and slightly redder.

TOUCAN

For this picture, you're going to work with a set of boxes, or a grid, to draw a toucan from the side. When you draw animals or people side-on, it is called a profile.

Carefully copy the grid above. You can use a ruler to help you make the lines straight and at right angles.

2

Work inside the boxes, drawing curves for the bill, head, and body.

Outside, add circles for the feet and curved, crossing lines to start the tail feathers. Don't forget the eye.

Now shape the body, including the triangular wings. Add a rectangle around the tail feather lines, and draw a branch between the feet.

4

Work on the detail of the eye and bill. Add evenly spaced lines for the feathers. Make the feet grip the branch, then erase the grid.

5

Color the bird black with a white neck and tail patches. Contrast this with a bright red, orange, and yellow bill.

TOP TIPS

A good artist always works hard on the details. This will help make your pictures look more realistic.

Birds' feet are scaly, so draw dark curved lines to bring this out. Study how the feet grip the branch.

Instead of using solid black, blend in deep blue and gray to show light catching the feathers.

OWL

Try your hand at capturing a brown owl swooping down from the sky. This time, you're going to draw the whole outline first, so all the hard work is done up front!

1

Start by drawing a circle with a curved line down the middle for the head. Copy the torpedo-shaped body, then add wings and a squashed semicircle for the tail.

2

Next, concentrate on the owl's face. Use the center line as a guide for placing the beak and large eyes. Owls have feathered legs, so make these thick and rounded.

3

Now work on the wing and tail feathers. Follow the outline carefully, making each feather shape even and about the same size. Then erase the outlines.

4

Brown owls are dull in color to allow them to hide easily, so use shades of brown and cream. Make the wing tips darker to help them stand out.

CARTOON CORNER

Here are some different-shaped birds you can practice drawing.

1

A mighty eagle has large black wings. Make its hooked beak and sharp talons stand out by coloring them bright yellow.

2

Tiny hummingbirds come in lots of colors. Give them long pointed beaks for drinking sweet nectar from flowers.

3

Draw a penguin as if it's wearing a black jacket, and give it a rounded white belly. Notice how its webbed feet are fairly large.

JAGUAR

The jaguar is the largest cat in Central and South America. It is a swift and agile hunter with a very powerful bite. Its name means "one that kills with one leap."

1

Start with a circle for the jaguar's head. The oval of the body has a shallow curve running up the back, with a deeper curve to follow the more rounded tummy.

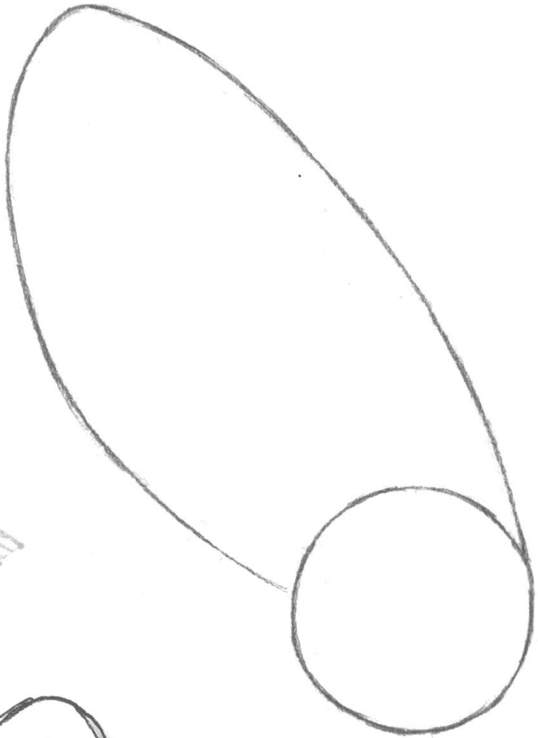

2

Start the rear end by extending the curve of the back around the rump and into the rear thigh. The front leg should be drawn right up into the shoulder and arched over the back. The guidelines should already have a solid, catlike form.

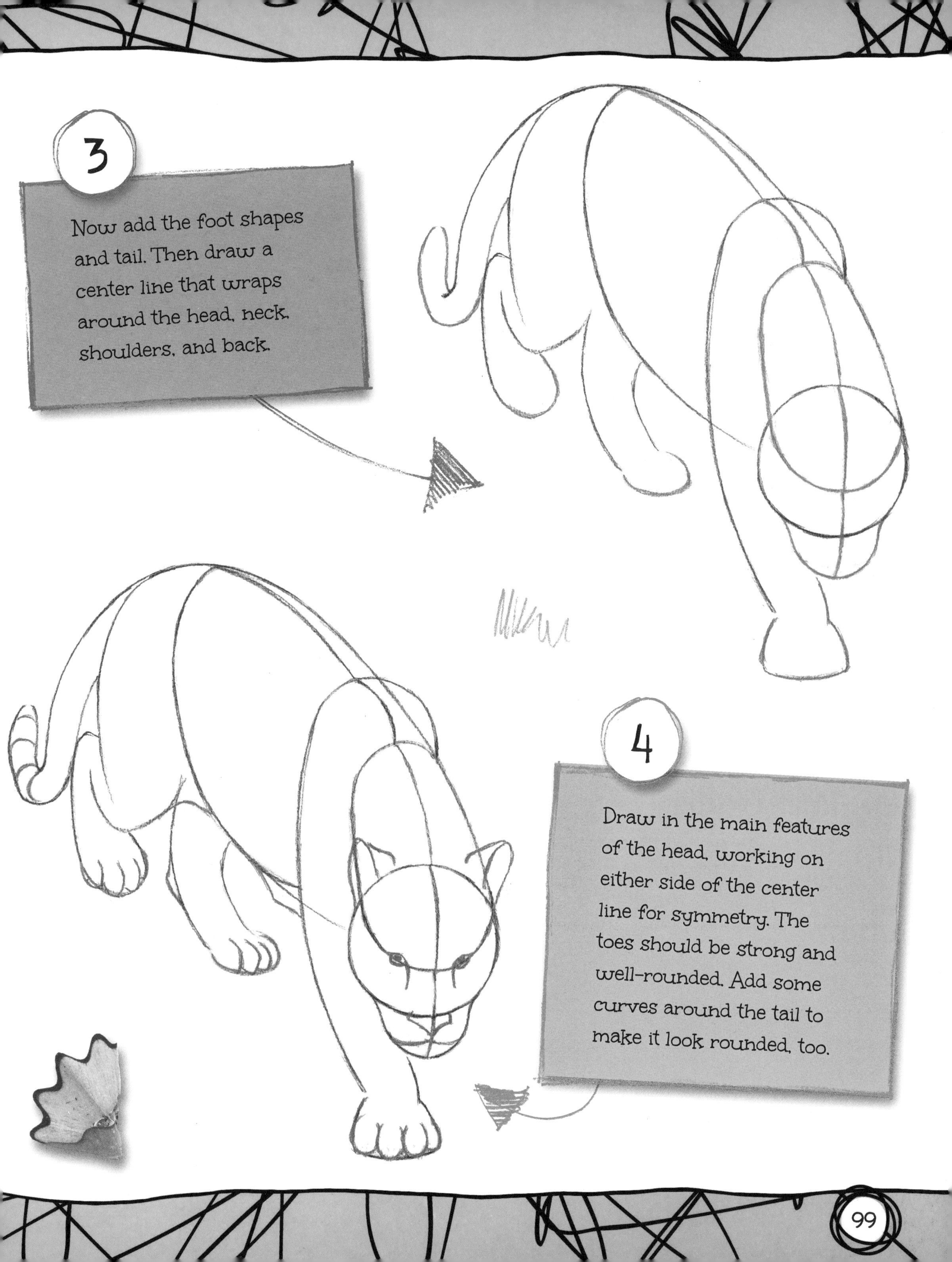
3
Now add the foot shapes and tail. Then draw a center line that wraps around the head, neck, shoulders, and back.
4
Draw in the main features of the head, working on either side of the center line for symmetry. The toes should be strong and well-rounded. Add some curves around the tail to make it look rounded, too.

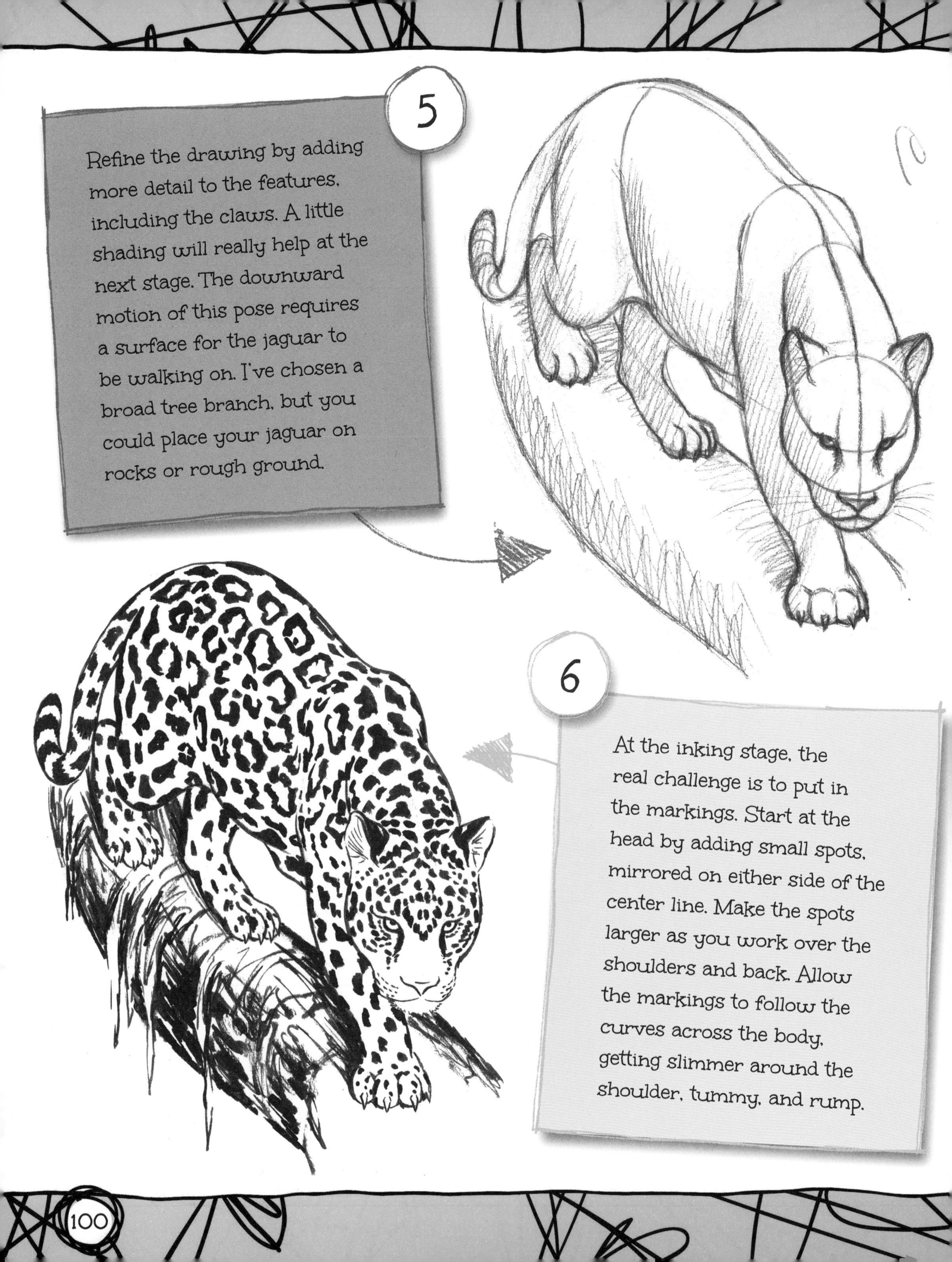

5

Refine the drawing by adding more detail to the features, including the claws. A little shading will really help at the next stage. The downward motion of this pose requires a surface for the jaguar to be walking on. I've chosen a broad tree branch, but you could place your jaguar on rocks or rough ground.

6

At the inking stage, the real challenge is to put in the markings. Start at the head by adding small spots, mirrored on either side of the center line. Make the spots larger as you work over the shoulders and back. Allow the markings to follow the curves across the body, getting slimmer around the shoulder, tummy, and rump.

Did you know?

CLIMBING CATS

The jaguar stalks its prey before attacking with one deadly pounce. Jaguars are good at climbing trees, and they are also excellent swimmers.

7

The jaguar's coloring is very simple—just a little richer across the top of the head, inside the ring marking, and around the rear end. Leave the paws and lower face pale. Then concentrate on making the ground surface look natural. Some highlights may be helpful here.

DRAGONFLY

Dragonflies-with their lacy wings and pencil-thin bodies-are one of the fastest flying insects in the world. Follow the steps to draw a beautiful dragonfly that is about to land.

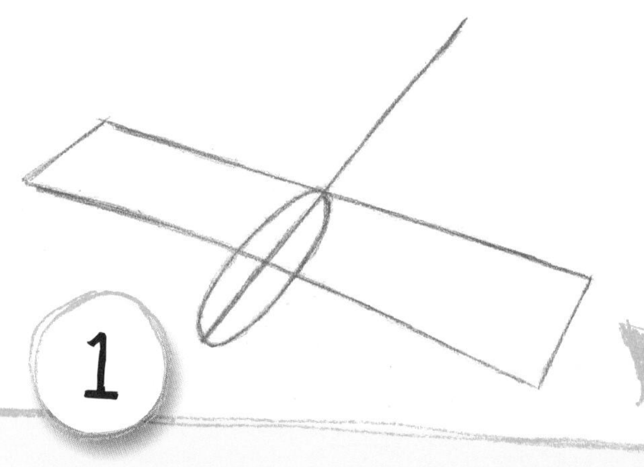

1

For this first step, look closely at the angles. Draw a straight, angled line for the body, then add a rectangle for the wings. An oval forms the upper body and head.

2

Now draw the four long curved wings neatly inside the rectangle. Notice that the back wings are a little shorter and thicker than the front wings.

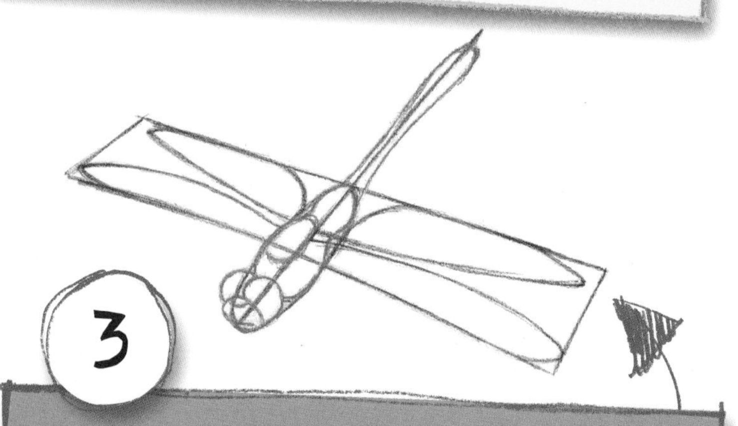

3

Following the guideline, draw the body. Make the upper body thicker than the rest. Copy the head, making sure that you have drawn two huge eyes.

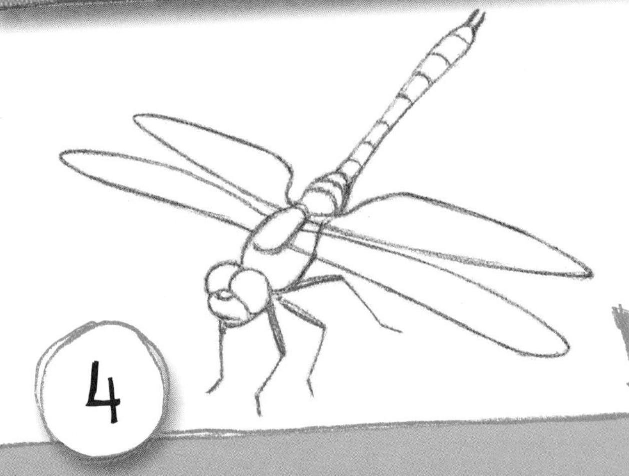

4

Carefully erase the guidelines, and add the thin bent legs and feet. To make the lower body rounded, draw curved lines. Develop the shape of the lower wings.

Go over the outline with a fine black felt-tip pen before you color it in. Leave gaps along the wings to make them look transparent.

5

TOP TIPS

When you get a chance, watch insects outside. Looking at a real dragonfly close-up can help you draw it accurately.

A dragonfly's huge eyes allow it to see in many directions at once. Copy them closely. Notice the fine hairs around the mouth as well.

You could draw the wings in detail. Use lots of linked rectangles to give them a lacelike effect.

ZEBRA

Zebras belong to the same family as horses, and their shape is very similar. Every zebra has a unique pattern of black and white stripes, so try different markings if you draw more than one zebra.

1

A circle, an egg shape, and two triangles form the basis of this zebra's head and body. Be sure to make them the right size in relation to each other.

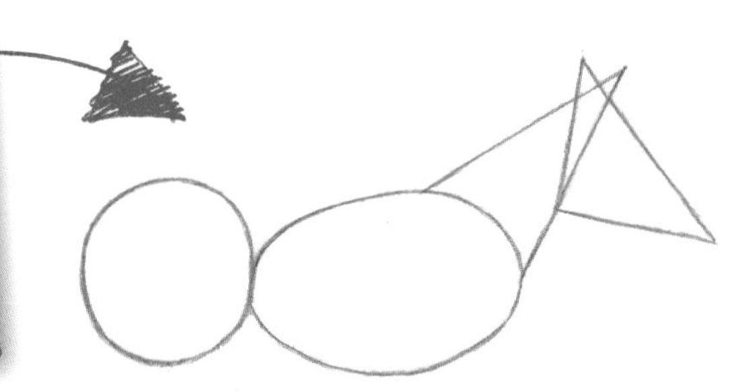

2

Deal with one leg at a time in this step. For the joints of the legs, a series of circles will really help to give the legs convincing shapes at the next stage.

3

Now you need to connect the shapes. Look closely at how each line curves either in or out. Add the detail to the head and ears, too.

4

Now use ink to create the outline of your zebra, erasing your pencil lines when it's done. Add detail to the mane and tail, and lines to create your stripes.

5

It may be tempting to color your zebra's stripes black. Although black will produce a striking graphic effect, if you would like your zebra to look more realistic, then use dark brown.

TOP TIPS

The stripes on a zebra are a very important feature, and it's a good idea to put a little planning into them.

First, pencil in the general direction that the markings will follow and how they curve around the animal's body and legs.

The stripes are broadest on the body and get narrower toward the extremities, except along the mane, where the stripes fan out.

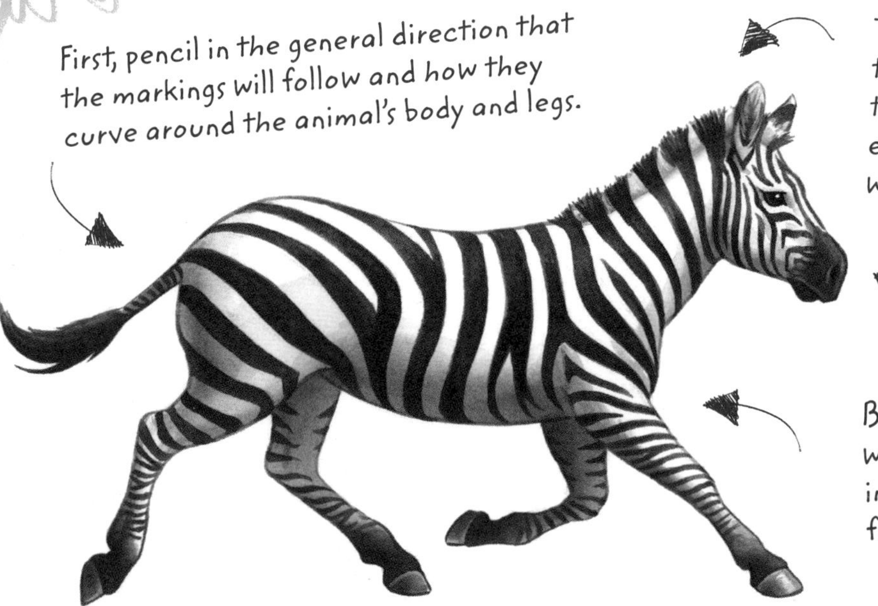

Be clear about those parts where the stripes break into forks, around the foreleg and on the face.

CHAPTER 4

PEOPLE

COMIC BOOK FACE

Faces and their features come in all shapes, and they can be tricky to draw accurately. But by working from a framework for the head, you'll have no problem creating your character.

1

Start by making a basic framework. First, draw a vertical line to help you make your picture symmetrical. Draw a circle over it, and add four lines to form the sides of the face and jaw. Draw a horizontal line halfway down this whole shape. Add a short pencil stroke for the mouth.

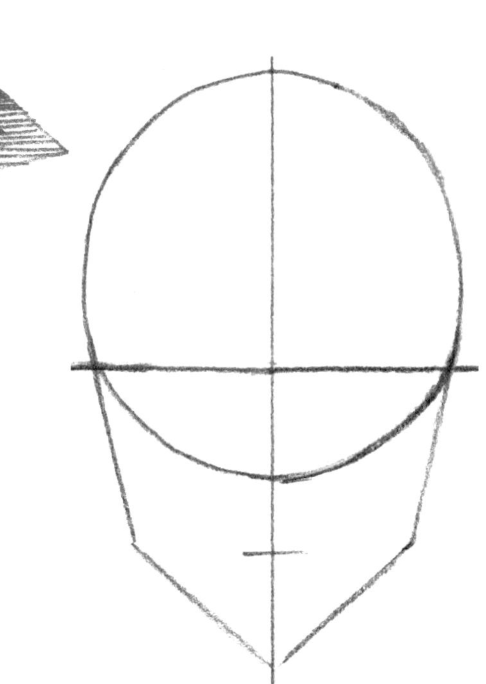

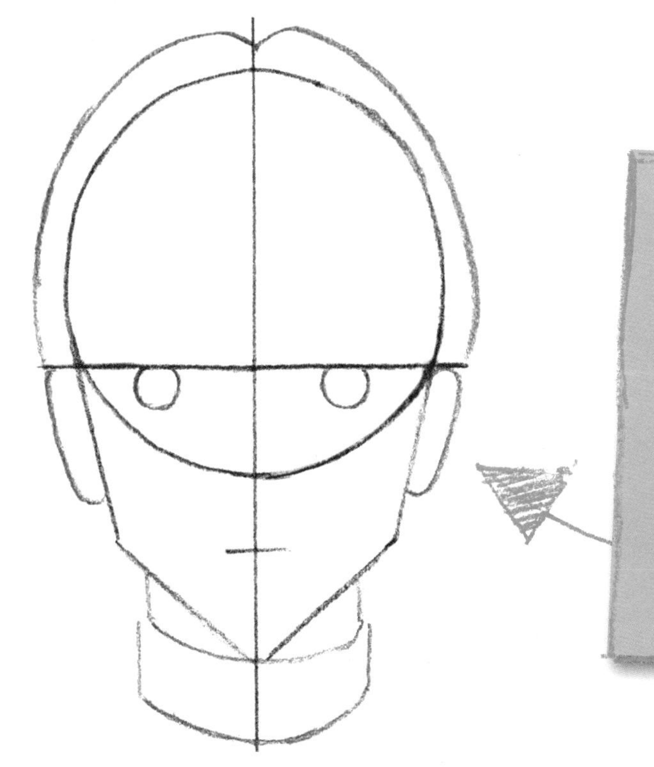

2

Eyes are roughly halfway down the head, and I've made the irises round. The tops should touch the underside of the horizontal line. To draw the ears, start level with the tops of the eyes. The ears should finish level with where the bottom of the nose will be. Draw outline shapes for the hair, neck, and collar, too.

3

Add the pupils, eyelids, and eyebrows, then use two long curved lines to mark the hairline.

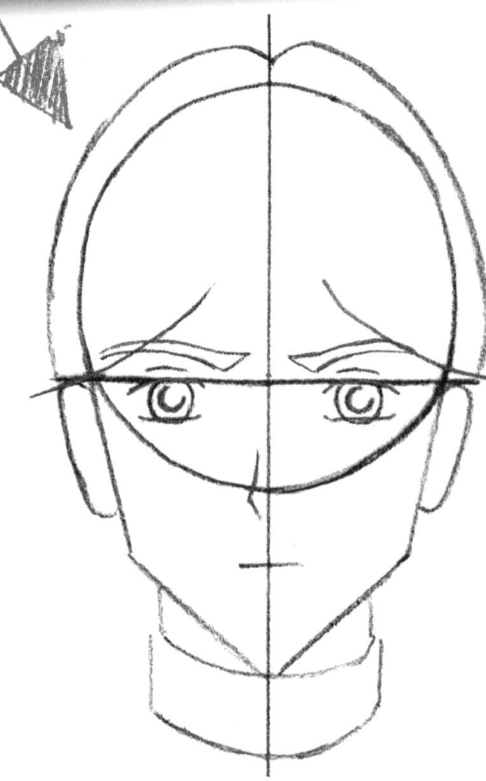

4

The main feature to work on here is the hair. This male has a middle part, so the hair will hang symmetrically.

5

A small circle in the top right of each eye makes the bright highlights that characterize cartoon artwork.

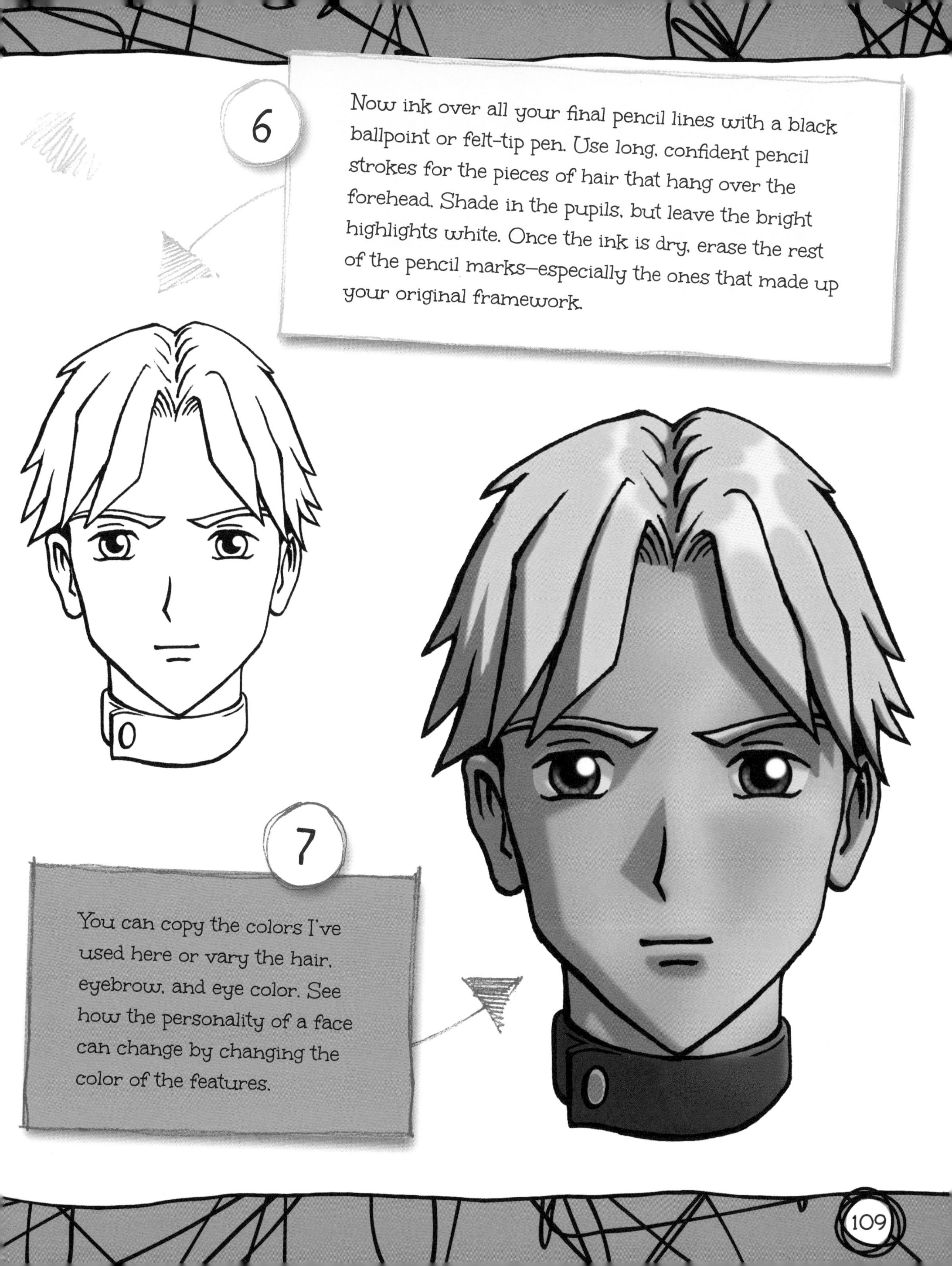

6

Now ink over all your final pencil lines with a black ballpoint or felt-tip pen. Use long, confident pencil strokes for the pieces of hair that hang over the forehead. Shade in the pupils, but leave the bright highlights white. Once the ink is dry, erase the rest of the pencil marks—especially the ones that made up your original framework.

7

You can copy the colors I've used here or vary the hair, eyebrow, and eye color. See how the personality of a face can change by changing the color of the features.

REALISTIC FACE

To draw a realistic face well, you need to pay attention to the details. Once you've mastered this face, how about getting a family member to sit for you while you paint their portrait?

1

Draw an egg shape. Then add guidelines down and across the middle. Mark four equally spaced points on the horizontal line. In the lower half of the face, draw lines for the nose and mouth.

2

Copy the position of the eyes, carefully following the horizontal guide, then draw two lines down to the nose. Add the ears, eyebrows, and mouth shape. Start to form the slender neck.

3

With the guides in place, you can now work on the details. Look in the mirror or at faces in magazines to get a feel for the shapes of different types of features.

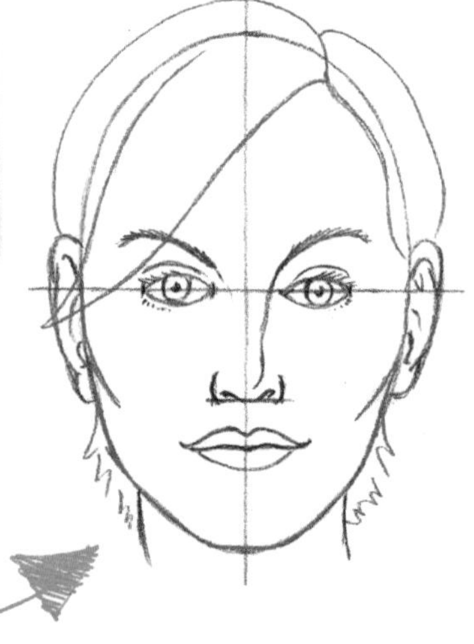

When working on the hair, think about the overall shape. Remember that hair has thickness and stands out from the head. Finally, touch up the face, paying attention to the jawline and cheekbones.

5

When you have erased the guides, work on the skin tones and hair color. Notice how the hair is made up of several different colors. Try not to make the lips too pink.

TOP TIPS

Follow these tips to make your face look even more realistic.

The eye color should be subtle and not too bright. I have used shades of gray here. Make sure that the eyelashes are well defined.

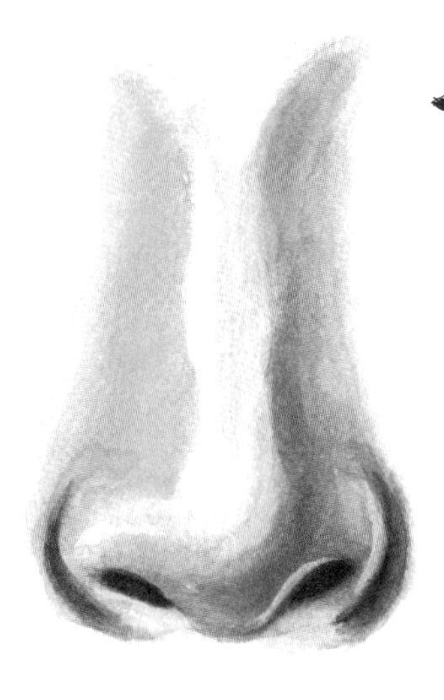

Allow white paper to shine through on areas where light would catch the face, such as on the bridge of the nose, lips, and cheekbones.

MALE FIGURE

When drawing a human figure, you need to get the proportions right-that's the size of their head, bodies, arms, and legs in relation to one another. A grid can help you with this.

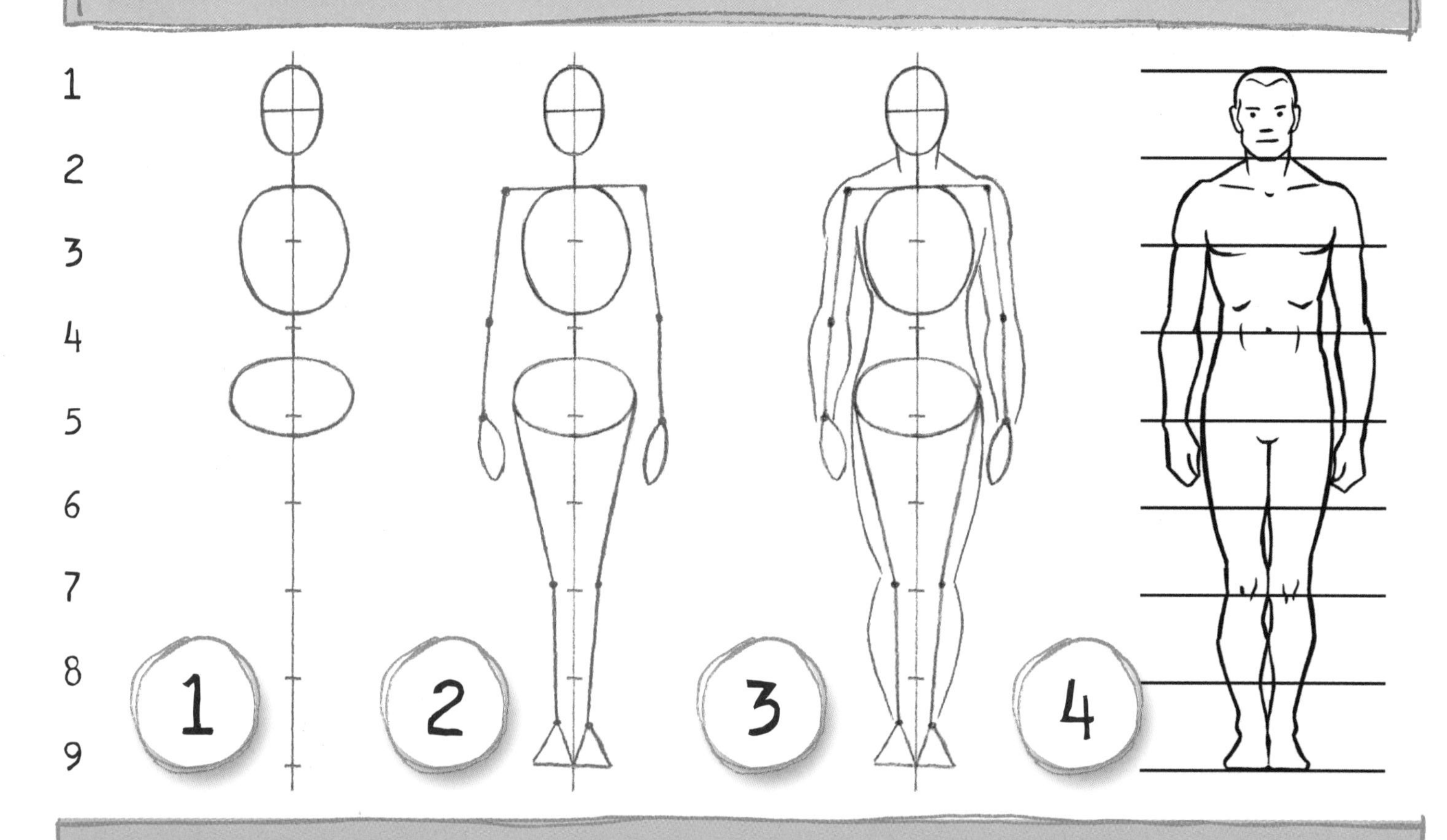

1. Draw a grid with nine marks all the same distance apart. Add an oval for the head between the first two marks, and draw a line across the middle. Draw more ovals, positioning them as shown.

2. Form the shoulders with a straight line, and draw stick arms and legs. Use the grid to get the lengths right. Mark the joints with dots. Then draw simple shapes for the hands and feet.

3. Now flesh out your skeleton with an outline. Notice how the outline nips in around the joints but bulges elsewhere to create a muscular body.

4. Erase your basic shapes, and add definition to the body with curved lines. Then fill in the face. Here, you can clearly see the man's height against the grid.

5

This figure is wearing a T-shirt and jeans, but you can give your person any clothes you like. These simple clothes follow the figure's outline. Try adding bigger, bulkier clothes to change the shape of the body.

TOP TIPS

Draw children so that they have a larger head in relation to their body. This young boy stands about six heads high. A toddler would be about four heads high.

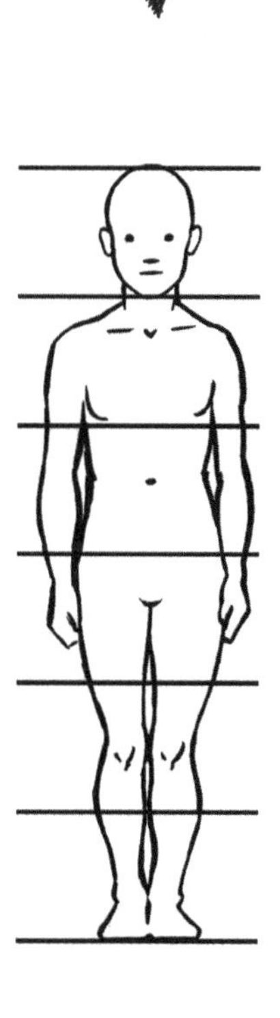

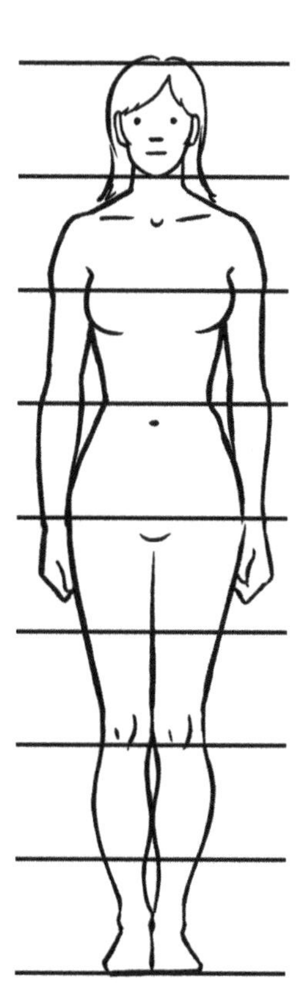

You can use the same basic skeleton for drawing a female as you did for the man. But make the shoulders and chest narrower, and the legs and arms more curvy in shape.

BODY LANGUAGE

Here you're going to use body language and pose to convey a mood. Take a look at this grumpy teacher-you wouldn't want to mess with her!

1

Start with three ovals for the head, chest, and wide hips. Overlapping the shapes will help to make the cartoon figure look old and hunched. Don't forget to include the face guidelines.

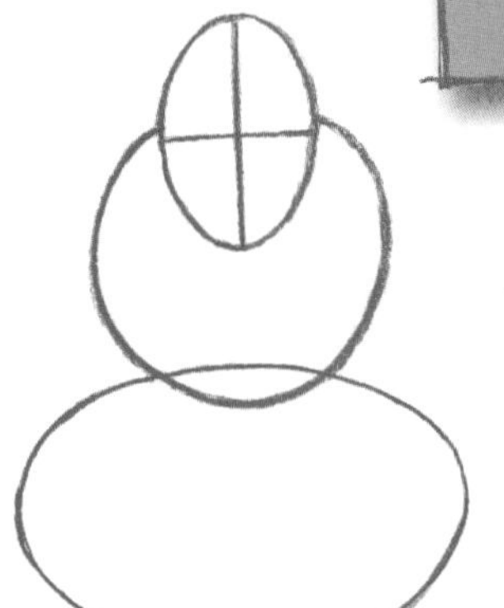

2

Now add the shoulders and arms. Follow the angles carefully, so that the hands can sit on the hips. Draw stick legs, and mark the joints. Make the shoes really pointy.

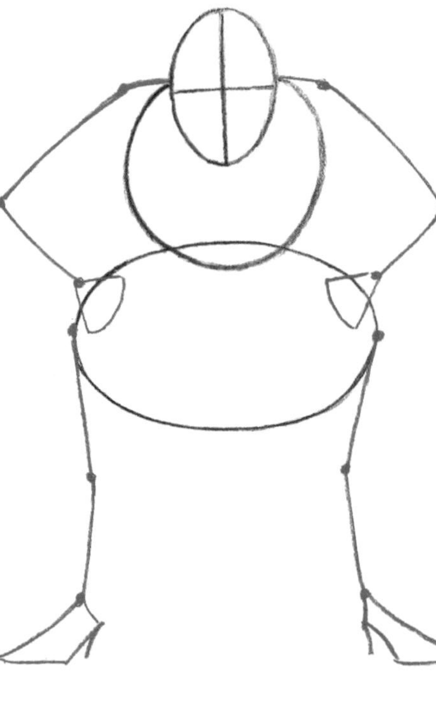

3

Finally, give your teacher her bulging shape. Work on her rounded arms and chest. Add a collar for her shirt and a long wide skirt. Finish off her legs and create a frightful face.

4

When designing costumes and hairstyles, look at pictures to help you. This grumpy teacher has a bun, round glasses, and old-fashioned clothes in drab colors.

CARTOON CORNER

Work on different poses and body language to get a mood across!

1

This figure, with its folded arms, doesn't want to do what you're asking it to.

2

To make a character look shy, give it knocked knees and pigeon toes.

3

With its legs apart and open hands, this character seems really shocked.

EXPRESSIONS

The human face is capable of revealing a very broad range of emotions. Good comic artists are able to show different moods and reactions in their drawings to help with telling a story and building character types.

Here, two characters are making some of the facial expressions that are common to cartoon characters. With the aid of a mirror, you can use your own face as a model for any expression you want to capture in your drawings.

Curious

Injured

Angry

Perturbed

Relieved

Playful

Confrontational

Alarmed

ASTRONAUT

An astronaut wears a heavy spacesuit when in space. It matches the human body shape, but is padded and so becomes more shapeless, making this figure much easier to draw.

1

For the astronaut's body and head, draw a large tilted oval with an overlapping circle on top. A curved line running down the center of the oval will act as a guideline later.

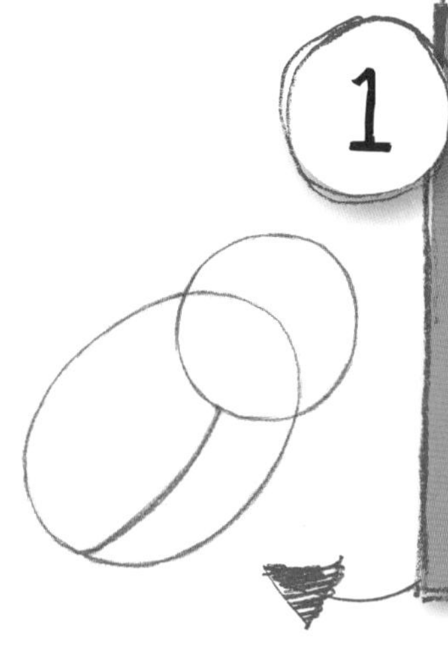

2

Start with sticks for the arms and legs to set out their length and position. Look at where they join the body. For the hands and feet, oval shapes will do for now.

3

Draw around the framework of the arms and legs. A spacesuit is heavily padded, so the limbs look thick and shapeless. Also add detail to create the chest pack, gloves, and helmet.

4

This stage is all about inking in the details. Add some wrinkle marks to the spacesuit, to give it texture and show how the backpack attaches to the suit. Notice the shape of the visor.

5

Try different shades of gray to shade different parts of the suit, but use bright colors for the flags and markings. The visor should show the reflection of what the astronaut is looking at!

TOP TIPS

Shading gives detail to objects that are white, such as this spacesuit.

Be clear about the direction of light when you're shading. Here, the light is coming from the top left corner of the picture, so those parts that face the light are pure white, while those that face the lower right are darker.

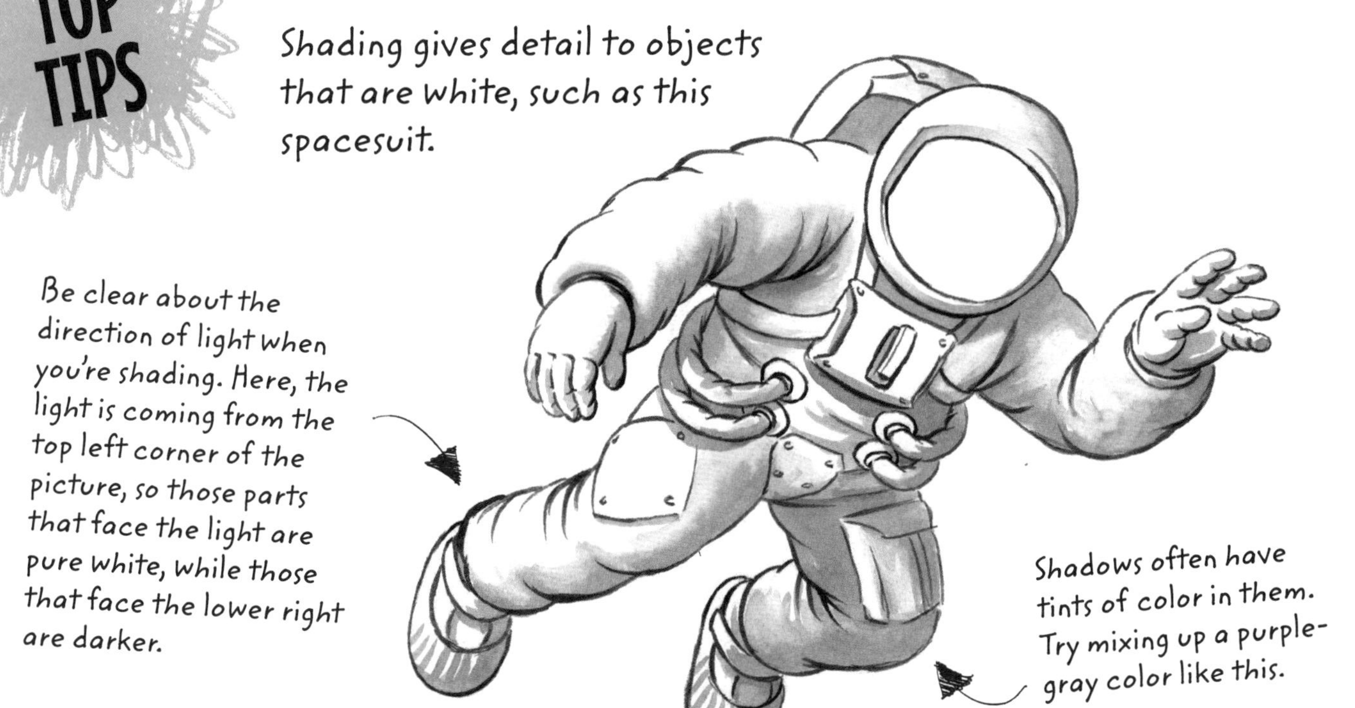

Shadows often have tints of color in them. Try mixing up a purple-gray color like this.

FEMALE CLOTHING

When you draw this graceful fashion model, spend lots of time developing her clothing. Don't forget that clothes can really give a character their personality.

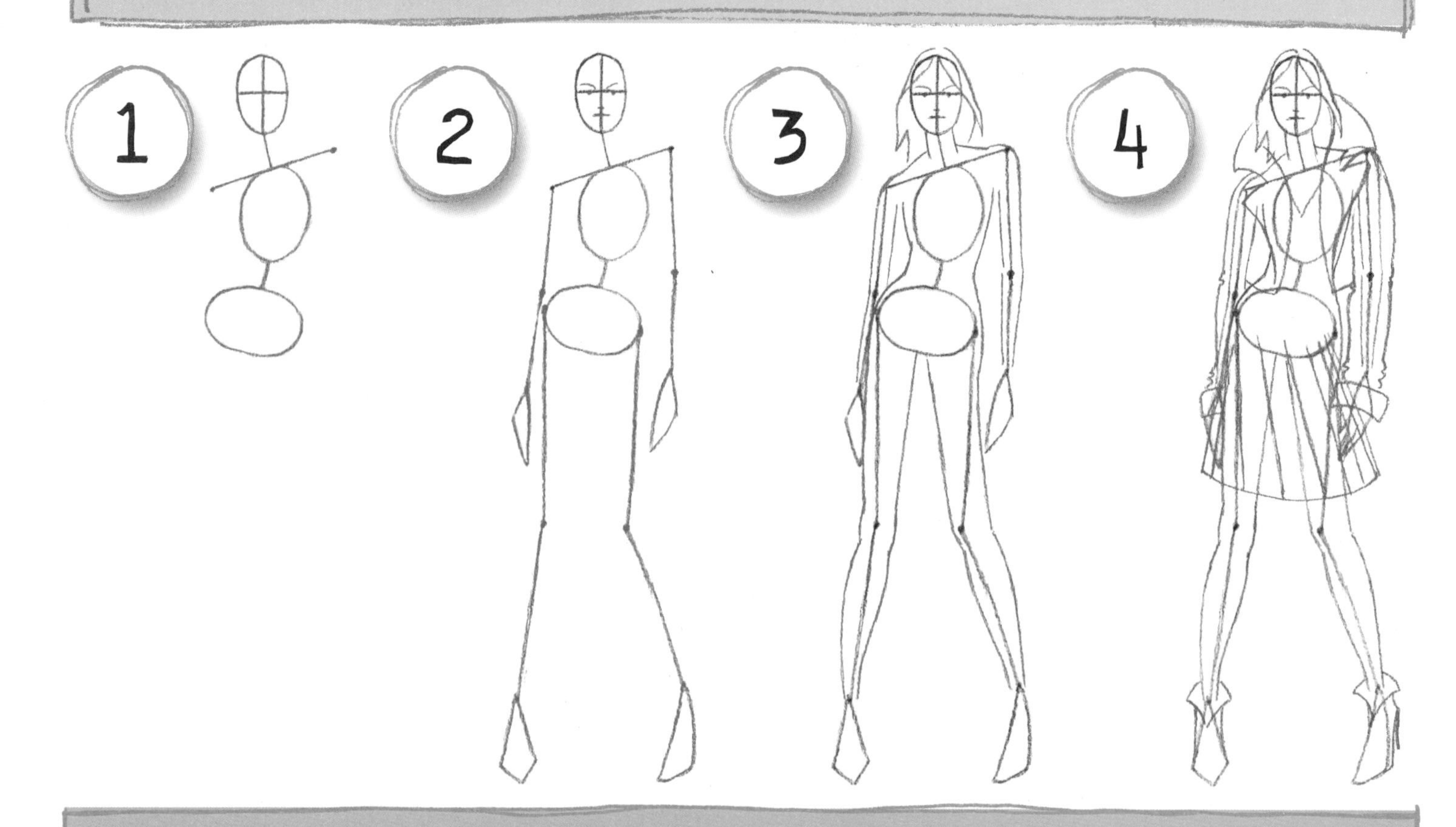

1. Draw three ovals for the head, chest, and body. Add an angled line for the movement of her shoulders, and give her a long neck. Draw the face guides.

2. When you add the stick arms and legs, remember how tall catwalk models are. Shape the hands and feet, then position the facial features.

3. Although much of the model's body will be covered up, it is still worth drawing an outline to make her seem real and to develop her pose. Shape her hair, too.

4. Now add the clothes and boots. Make her thick jacket sit away from her slim arms. Give her dress movement by drawing flowing lines on the skirt.

5

When adding the final touches, work swiftly and use smooth lines. Do the same when you add color—try to cover the paper with as few strokes as possible. This is how real fashion illustrators work!

TOP TIPS

When drawing and coloring clothing, try to capture the texture of the different materials.

Use bold dark lines and bright highlights for the shiny leather. In contrast, make the sheepskin soft and fluffy with a broken outline.

Although these boots are also made of leather, they have a mat look. Blend the colors gently, and add almost no highlights to the top of the boot.

RUNNING GIRL

The tricky thing to achieve in this cartoon drawing is the twist as the girl runs. But if you follow the steps carefully, you'll soon have her sprinting in all directions!

1

Copy the stick drawing, concentrating on the angles of the lines and the different shapes. Notice how large the head is. Also notice how the shoulder line cuts across the chest.

2

There is no need to draw the full body outline, so work on the baggy top instead. Outline the legs, and shape the hair, making sure it flows back. Position the facial features including the open mouth.

3

Develop the face further, paying attention to the jawline. Work on the hands, then finish the sneakers and the clothing. The position of the hood makes it clear that her shoulders are turning away.

4

When you have erased the guides, go over the outline with a dark felt-tip pen and color your figure. To turn the girl into a boy, simply shorten the hair, lose the long eyelashes, and change the color scheme.

CARTOON CORNER

Motion lines create the illusion of speed. Check out these tips for drawing different types of lines.

1

Create a sense of movement in the arms and legs with short curved lines. Draw a ground line to show how the girl's feet are in the air.

2

To give the sense that your character is speeding forward, draw straight lines behind her. Add long curves by the arm to show it lifting up.

3

This time, the girl is racing by in a blur! Draw a smoke trail behind her, angle lines upward, and blend her bottom half into a spiral of color.

BALANCING BALLERINA

Try drawing an elegant ballerina in this graceful pose, then find pictures of other dance positions to copy. You could even show a whole ballet sequence step by step.

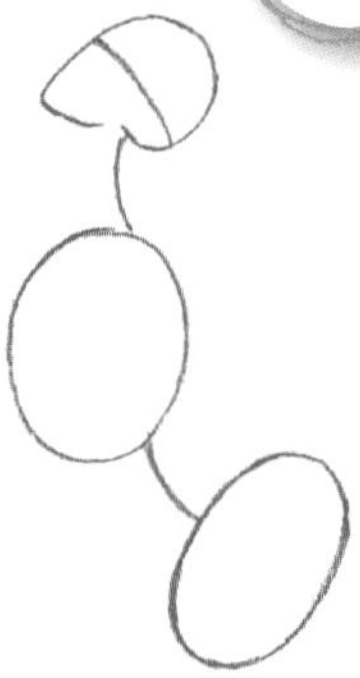

1

Draw three ovals linked by a curved line. Leave plenty of space between the shapes to keep the body looking slender. Make the head small, and include the face guide.

2

Sketch the legs and arms with graceful strokes. These need to be long and stretched out. Sketch the hands and feet, so that they are fully extended, too.

3

Continue working on the legs and arms, fleshing them out with outlines. Keep checking to make sure that your drawing looks balanced and the body well-rounded and realistic.

4

Spend time on the hands and feet, so that they appear delicate. Then draw simple swirls for the ballet dress. Take time with the dancer's expression, so that it looks effortless.

5

When you finish the dress and outline the body, work with a fine brush in dark pink to avoid harsh lines. Notice the tiny shadow that connects her with the floor—this shows you that she is holding a pose rather than leaping.

TOP TIPS

A ballerina needs a graceful hairdo and the right kind of pumps. Here's how to draw and color them.

A neat bun makes the perfect hairstyle. Draw the overall shape first. Then use fine brushes or pencils in shades of brown to create the hair strands.

Work with different shades of pink for the ballet pumps, and give them white highlights. Notice that she's wearing pink tights as well. This creates a delicate and subtle look.

SKATEBOARDING BOY

You can have lots of fun with this cartoon skateboarder. Draw him performing this trick, then experiment with his clothing and the designs on his board.

1

In this picture, you are looking up at the skater boy, so the soles of his feet are on view. Copy the drawing carefully to get the position of the skeleton just right.

2

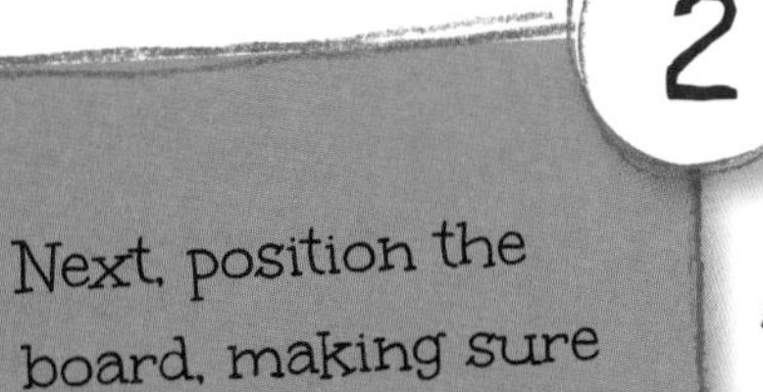

Next, position the board, making sure that the boy's toes are peeping out. Keep the shape of the boy slim, but flare out the end of the arms for the cuffs. Draw the face and outline the hair.

3

Finally, work on the details. Develop the face, add texture to the hair, and shape the fingers. Draw the baggy shorts, and give the skateboard its wheels. Erase the guides.

4

Skateboarders often wear bold colors and like dramatic designs. This boy has a flame design on his board and a T-shirt to match. Instead of the skull motif, you could draw more flames.

CARTOON CORNER

Why not try to create some different sporty characters?

1

Copy the pose for this soccer player carefully, noticing how his arms are outstretched, his back leg is bent, and that he is looking down toward the ball. Choose a color scheme, and add motion lines.

2

The pose of this tennis player is very different. She has her arms raised and is looking up toward the ball to give the idea that she is about to serve. Her flying pigtails add to the effect, but you can give her any hairstyle.

TRIUMPHANT WARRIOR

In this exercise, we're going to draw a dramatically posed action character. The drawing involves a lot of the aspects we've covered so far, such as expression, muscle build, and dynamic pose. Take your time with each step.

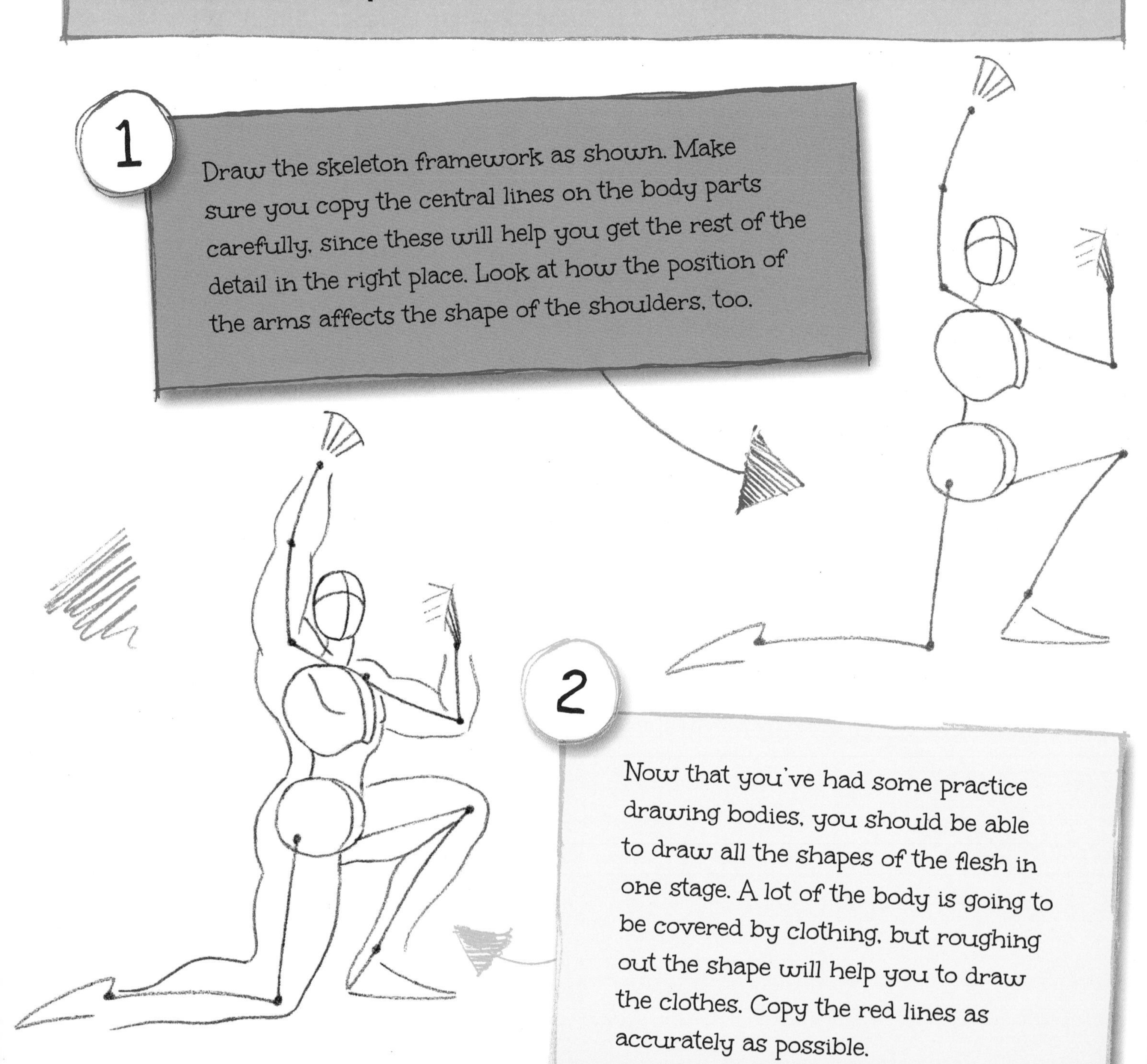

1

Draw the skeleton framework as shown. Make sure you copy the central lines on the body parts carefully, since these will help you get the rest of the detail in the right place. Look at how the position of the arms affects the shape of the shoulders, too.

2

Now that you've had some practice drawing bodies, you should be able to draw all the shapes of the flesh in one stage. A lot of the body is going to be covered by clothing, but roughing out the shape will help you to draw the clothes. Copy the red lines as accurately as possible.

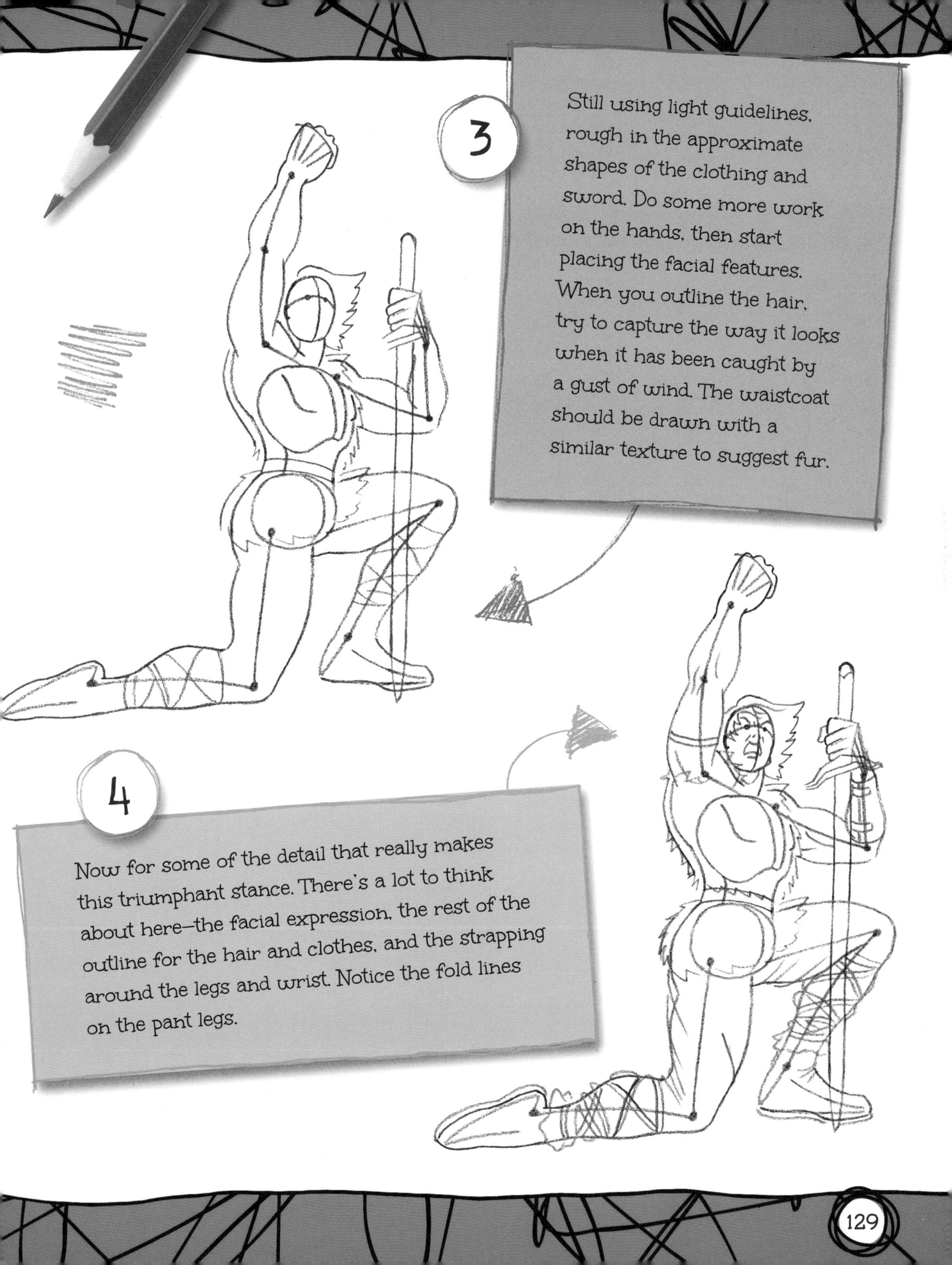

3

Still using light guidelines, rough in the approximate shapes of the clothing and sword. Do some more work on the hands, then start placing the facial features. When you outline the hair, try to capture the way it looks when it has been caught by a gust of wind. The waistcoat should be drawn with a similar texture to suggest fur.

4

Now for some of the detail that really makes this triumphant stance. There's a lot to think about here—the facial expression, the rest of the outline for the hair and clothes, and the strapping around the legs and wrist. Notice the fold lines on the pant legs.

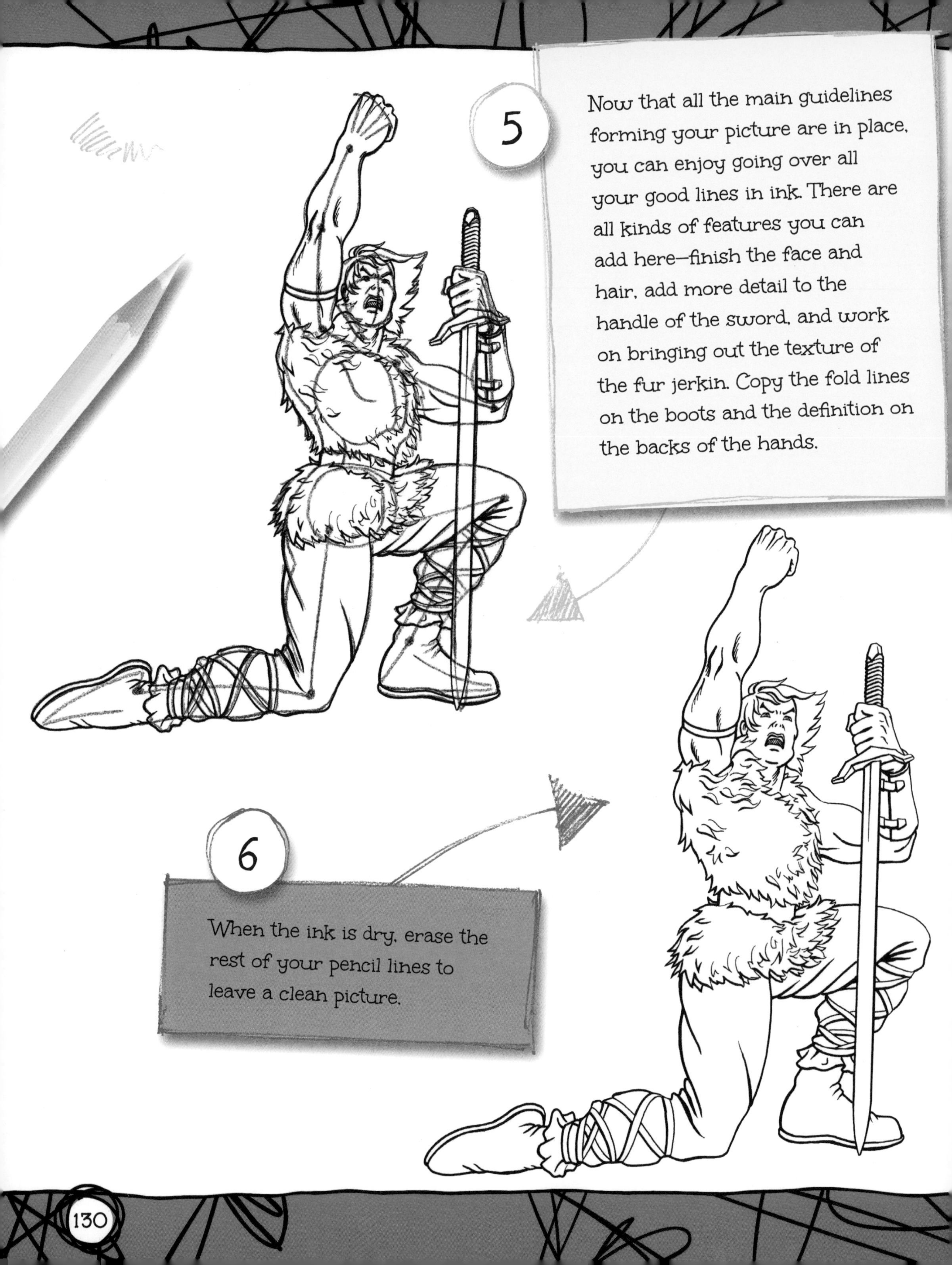

5

Now that all the main guidelines forming your picture are in place, you can enjoy going over all your good lines in ink. There are all kinds of features you can add here—finish the face and hair, add more detail to the handle of the sword, and work on bringing out the texture of the fur jerkin. Copy the fold lines on the boots and the definition on the backs of the hands.

6

When the ink is dry, erase the rest of your pencil lines to leave a clean picture.

7

You can copy this color scheme to complete your drawing, or you could use different colors and patterns. You might want to draw the figure again and add different details of your own. The clothing style could change, or you could put a different expression on the face. You could make the arms slimmer or show them in a different position.

HANDS

If you want to make a human figure look really convincing, then you need to get the hands right. Here, you can learn how to draw hands in different positions.

CLENCHED FIST

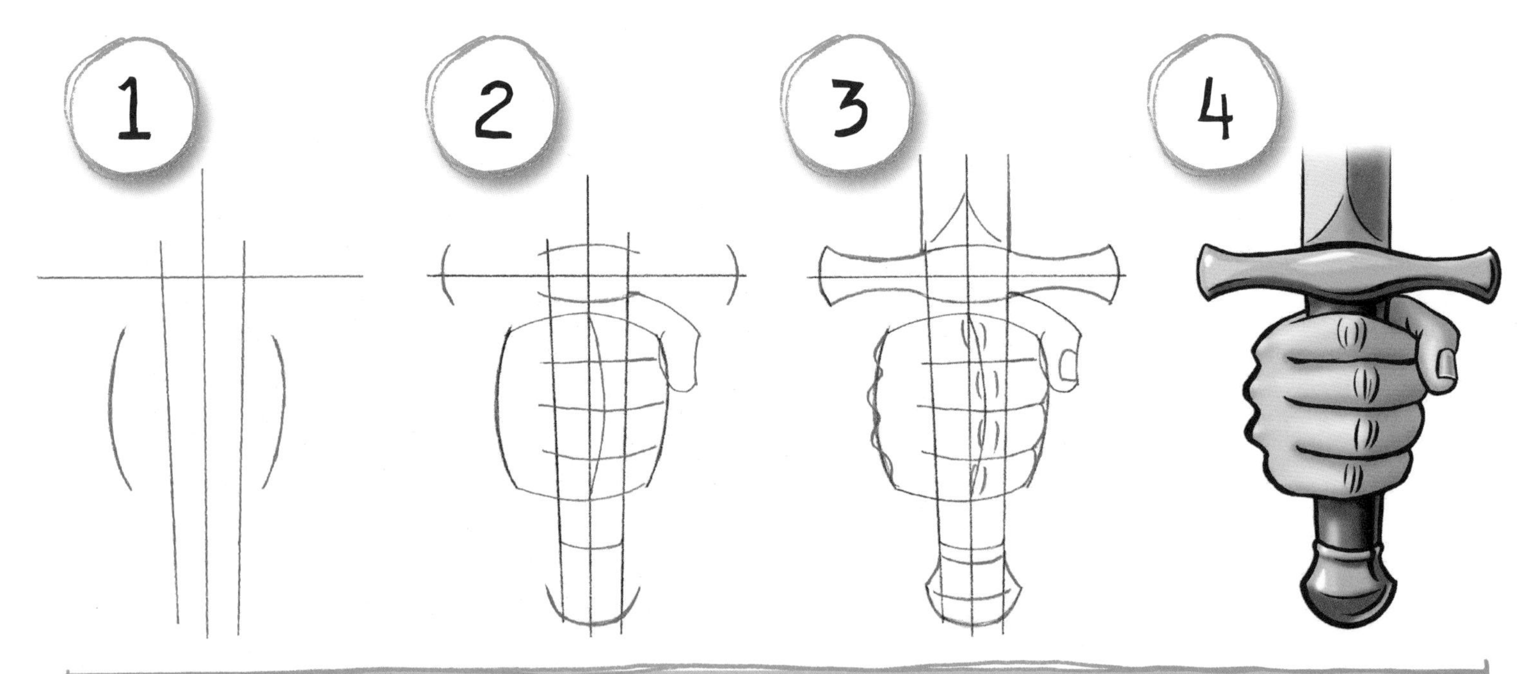

1. When a hand grips an object, it's best to start with the object first, in this case, a sword. Copy the drawing to position the sword, and mark the edges of the fist.

2. Next, draw the top and bottom of the fist using the curves as a guide. Mark the fingers and thumb, adding a curve for the knuckles. Start adding details to the sword.

3. Draw the wavy outlines that end the fist, and add detail to the knuckles. Give the thumb its fingernail. Shape the sword's handle and blade, then erase the guides.

4. To create realistic skin tones, blend yellow, pale pink, and brown. Vary the proportions for different skin colors. Add purple for the darker areas. Leave the knuckles pale for highlights.

OPEN HAND

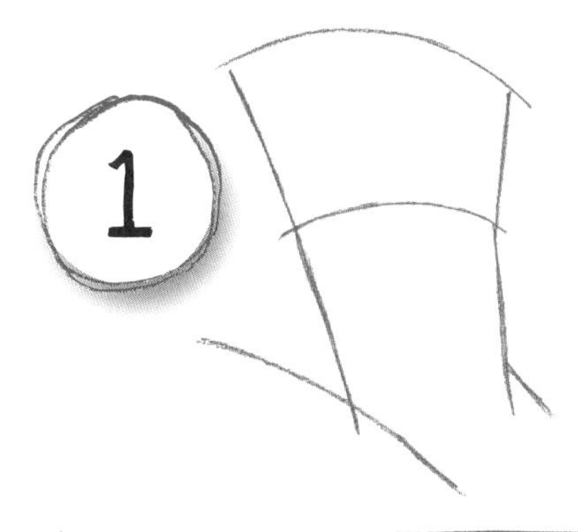

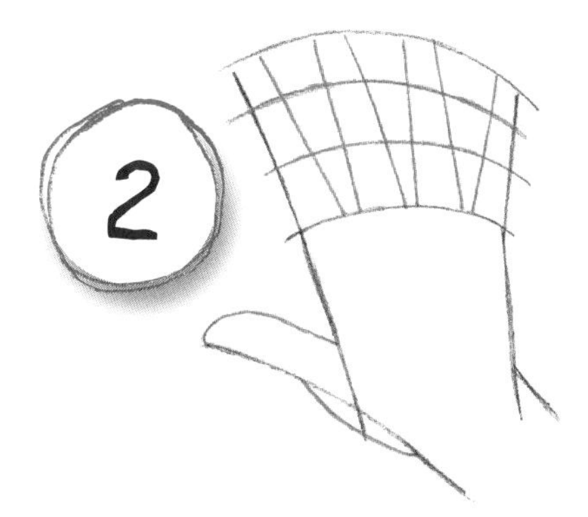

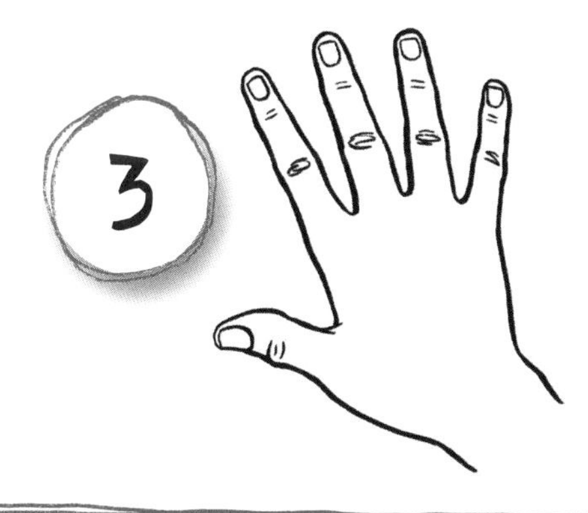

1. This open hand is almost a fan shape. Start with the bottom half, and mark lines for the thumb and wrist. Then add two guidelines with a curve on top for placing the fingers.

2. With the fingers, it's easiest to draw three wedge shapes first. Mark the curves for the knuckles, then shape the thumb and fleshy part underneath.

3. When going over the outline, remember that the fingers should bulge slightly at the knuckles. Carefully draw the fingernails, and add small crease lines for the joints.

POINTING HAND

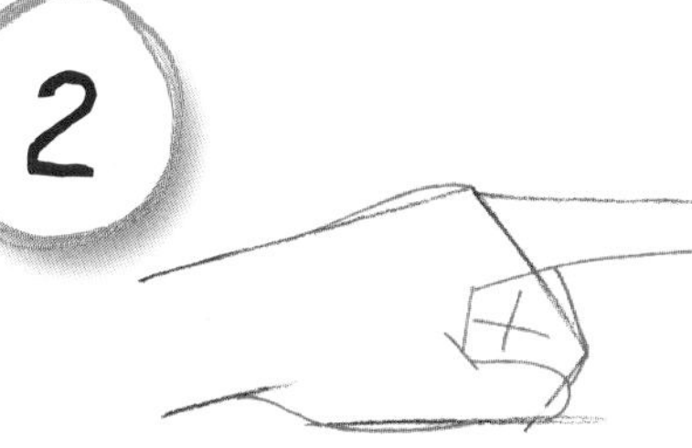

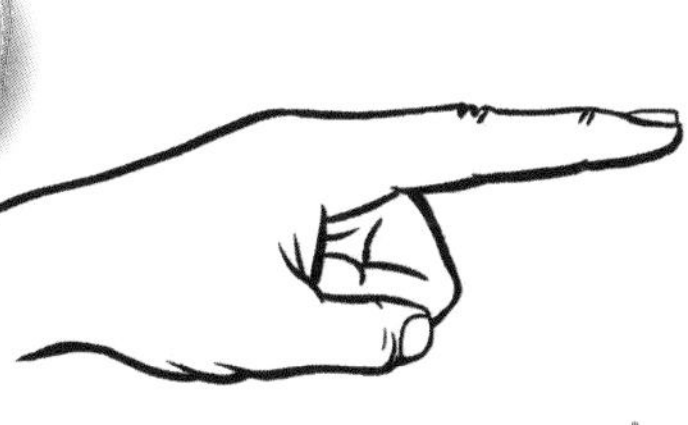

1. Shape the ball of the hand first, making sure that the bottom part where the thumb will be is flat. Add a short line to mark the wrist and a long line for the pointing finger.

2. Now add shape to the fingers. Lightly curve the pointing finger, and make the bottom of the thumb fleshy. Mark a cross above the thumb for the hidden clenched fingers.

3. Press hard with your pencil to give the pointing hand a strong outline, and make it look solid. Press lightly to create the finer creases. Don't forget to include the nails.

FEET

Feet are made up of just as many bones as hands. Although your human characters will often be wearing shoes, they will sometimes be barefoot-if they practice martial arts, for instance.

1

BARE FOOT

Here is a right foot and ankle drawn from different angles. Notice that the two bones that jut out on either side of the ankle are not directly opposite each other—one is higher up.

The two main bulges on the foot itself are the ball and heel. And just like the bones of the hand, the toe bones run in lines along the feet, radiating from the ankle.

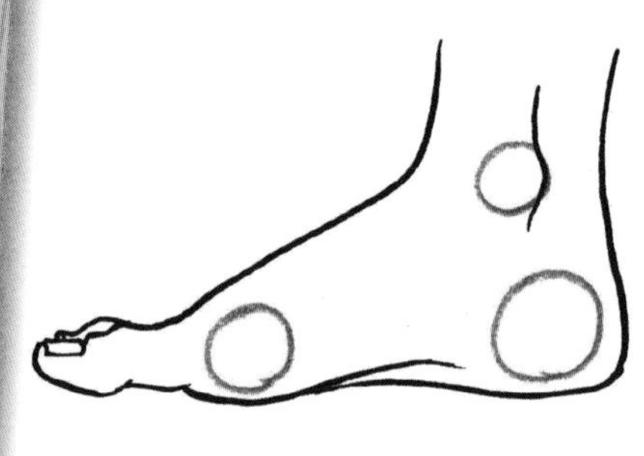

INNER FOOT

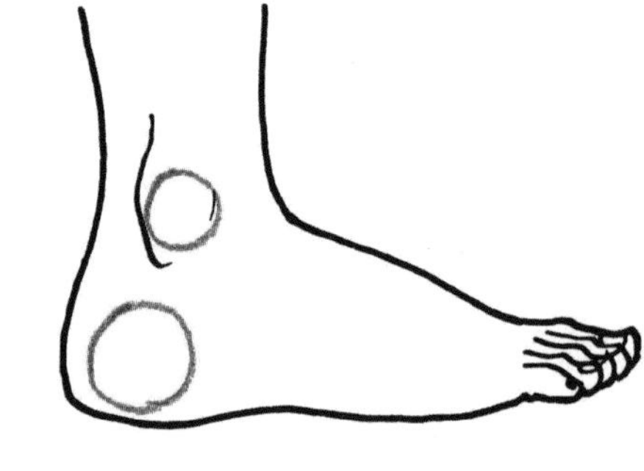

OUTER FOOT

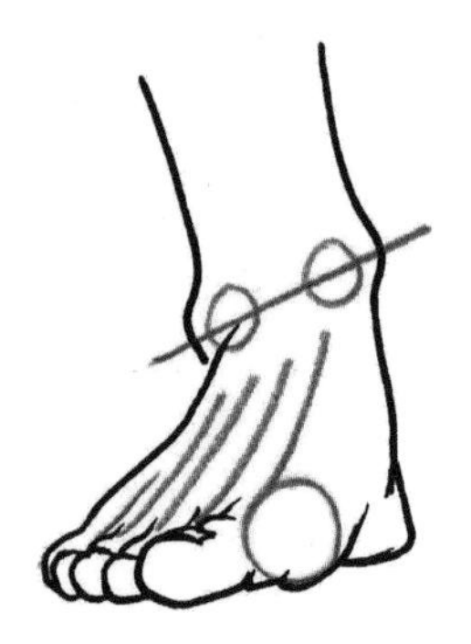

FRONT

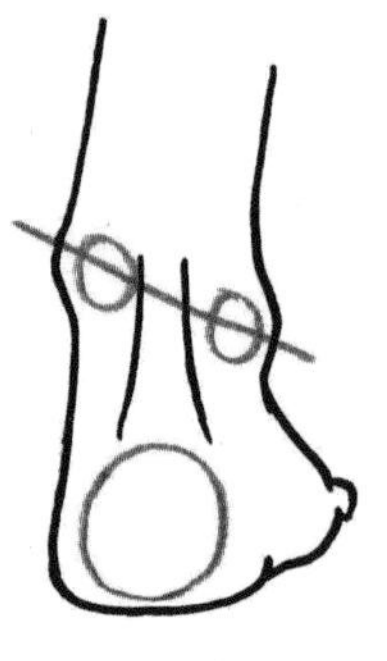

BACK

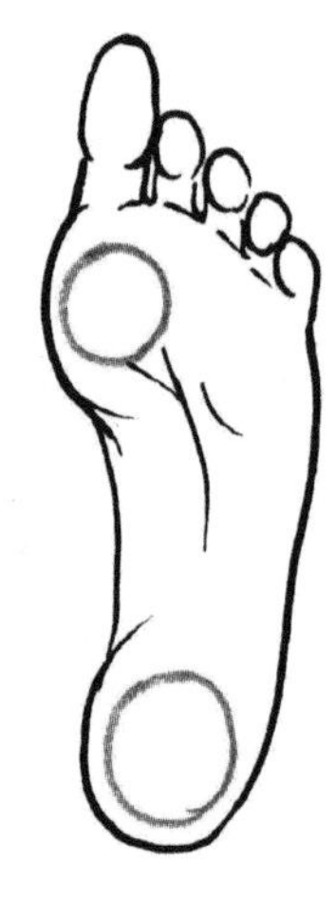

BOTTOM

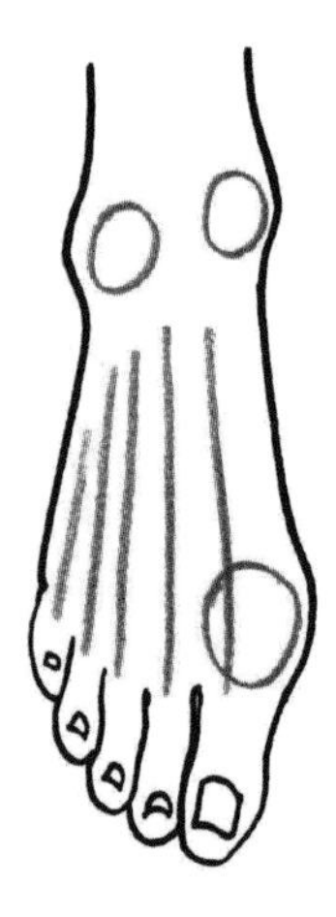

TOP

FEET INSIDE SHOES

Even when you are drawing characters with their shoes on, it will help you to imagine the shape of the foot inside the shoe.

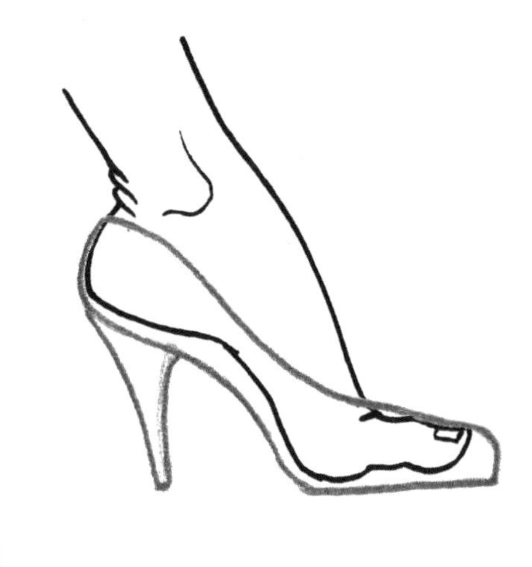

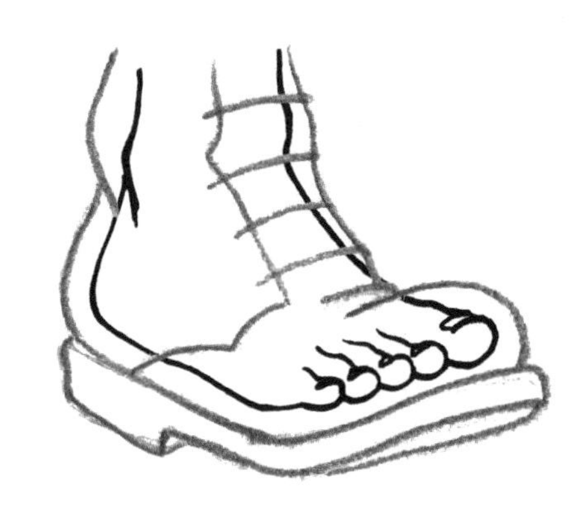

3

BASIC SHAPES

Try to think of feet as triangles to begin with. If you get this basic shape right, the other details should fall into place.

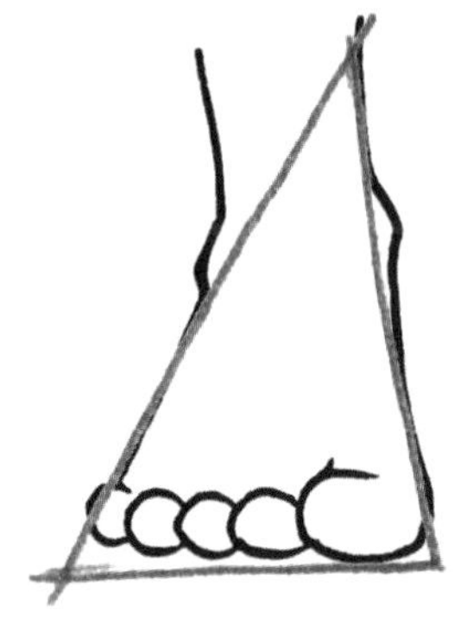

SIMPLE FEET

Even if you decide to simplify the feet, it's still important to get their basic shape right. The toes should form a pointed shape, as in the first picture. If you draw them like they are in the second picture, they will look too square.

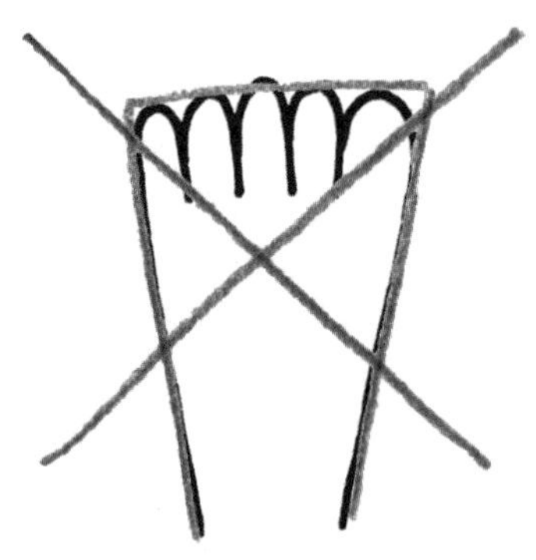

CHAPTER 5

MONSTERS

ALIEN

This alien is not a friendly extraterrestrial. A powerful, fearsome creature in a dynamic pose, this character is one to take your time with. Luckily, this monster is a fantasy rather than a reality!

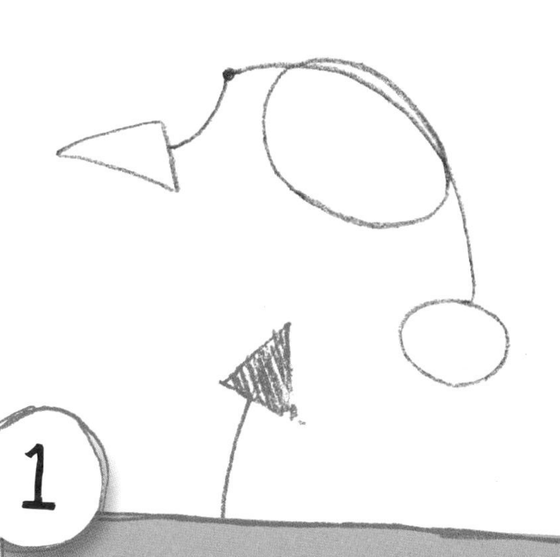

1

Although this alien's overall body shape is quite human in form, there are some vital differences in the make up of its skeleton. The outline for the head is triangular, and I've put an extra joint in the neck to make this longer and more mobile. Notice the dramatic arch of the spine too. The chest oval is much larger than the oval for the hips.

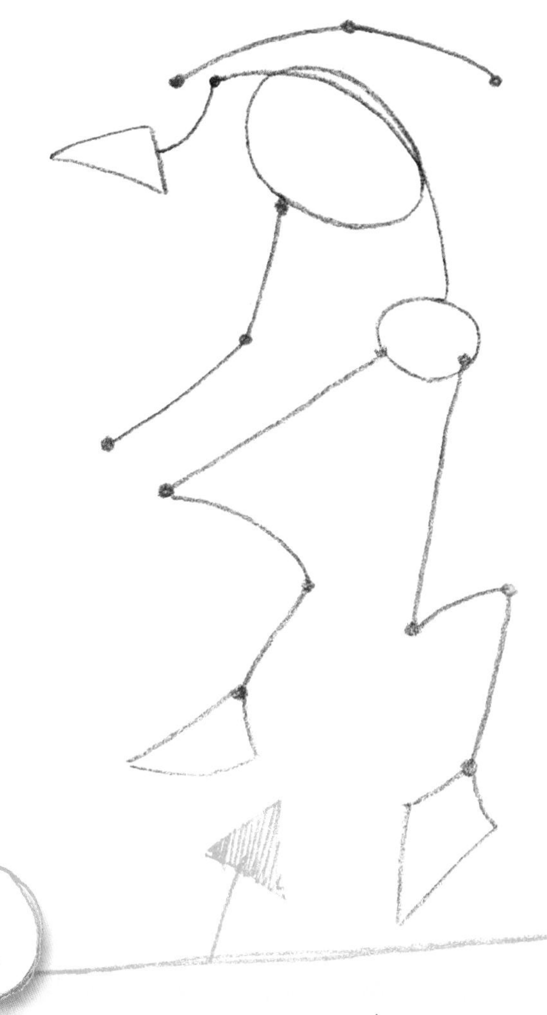

2

Place the arm bones and joints as shown. For clarity, one arm is drawn as if it isn't connected to the body. Notice how the legs differ from a human's. The section between the knee and ankle is short and the ankles sit high up, more like those of many animals.

3

Add the main parts of the body outline as shown—the body is made up of lots of separate segments.

4

Fill in the gaps of your alien's body outline—if you turn the page, you'll see a picture of the finished beast, which will help you work out what body parts all the different lines belong to. Work on the shape of the head too. The hands resemble a human's, while the feet are more like an animal's hooves.

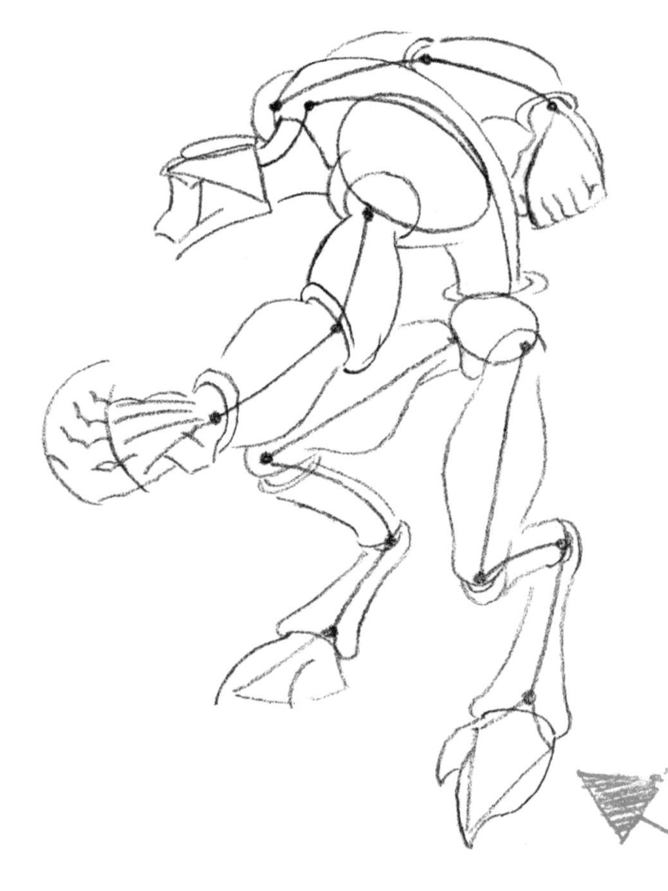

5

Build up the definition of the features gradually. Here I've drawn in the flesh of the fingers and worked on the shape around the hips and limb joints.

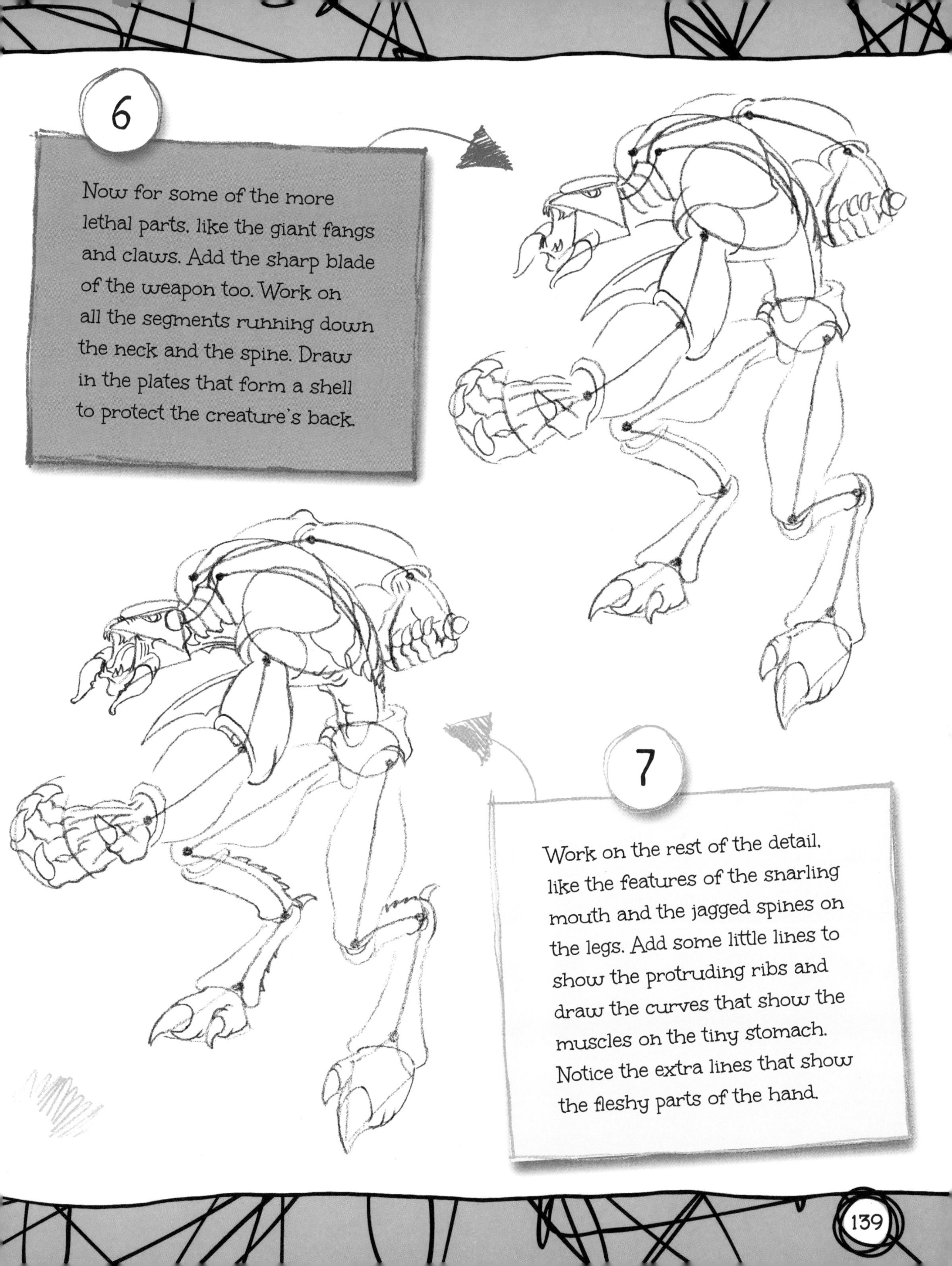

6

Now for some of the more lethal parts, like the giant fangs and claws. Add the sharp blade of the weapon too. Work on all the segments running down the neck and the spine. Draw in the plates that form a shell to protect the creature's back.

7

Work on the rest of the detail, like the features of the snarling mouth and the jagged spines on the legs. Add some little lines to show the protruding ribs and draw the curves that show the muscles on the tiny stomach. Notice the extra lines that show the fleshy parts of the hand.

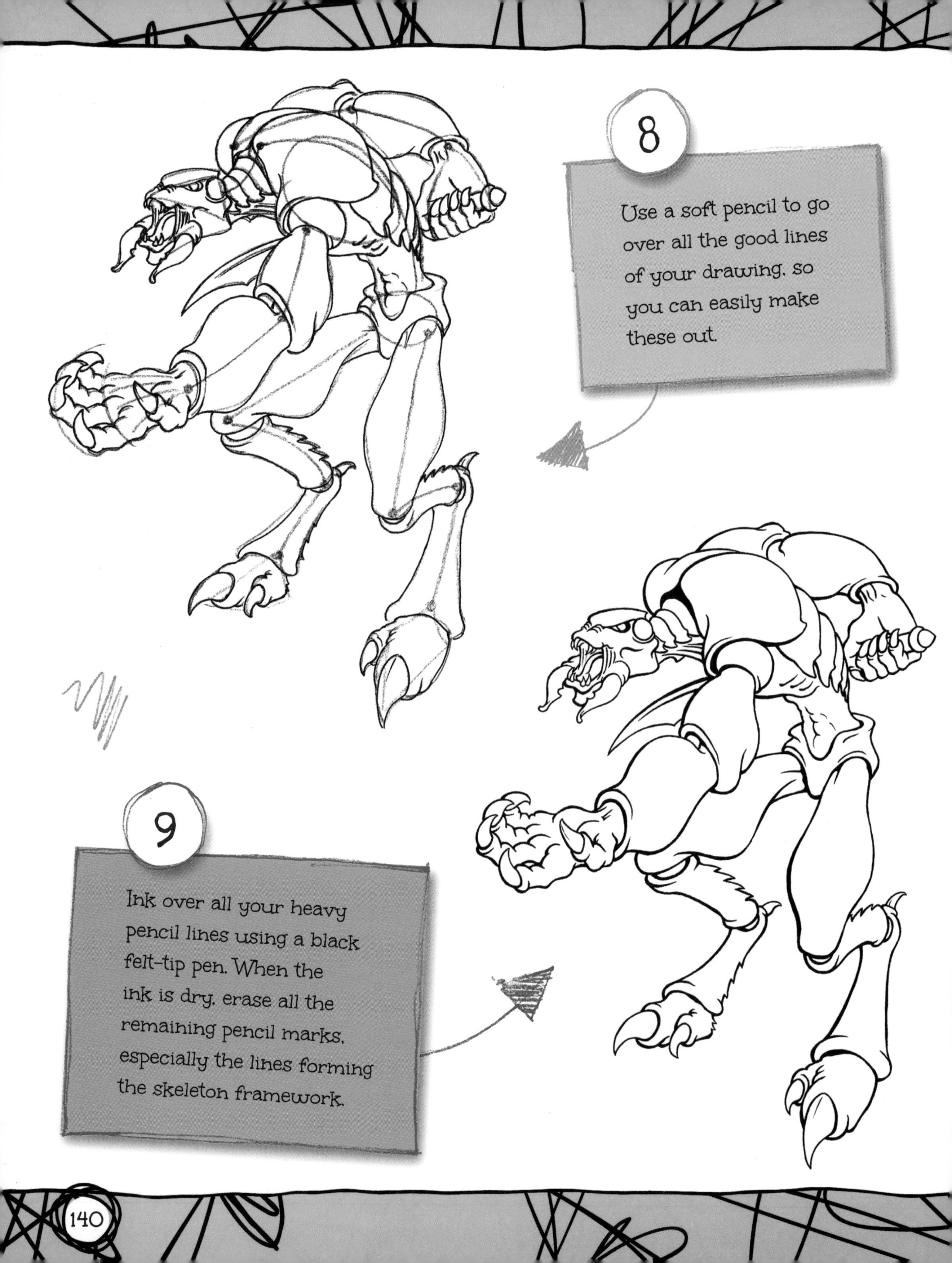
8
Use a soft pencil to go over all the good lines of your drawing, so you can easily make these out.
9
Ink over all your heavy pencil lines using a black felt-tip pen. When the ink is dry, erase all the remaining pencil marks, especially the lines forming the skeleton framework.

10

Now add color to your picture—this is what it will look like if you color it digitally. After coloring, you could have some fun thinking about what kind of creature this beast might be attacking. Once you've come up with a design for the enemy creature, put the two beasts together in one picture.

WEREWOLF

A werewolf is half-man and half-beast, so needs ferocious features and a wild expression. Dramatic, dark colors will help to make him look even more terrifying.

1

Draw an egg shape on its side with a long sweeping curve for the werewolf's back and tail. Place one small circle inside the egg and then another one just outside.

2

Now work on the hips and legs. Copy the drawing carefully, noticing the angle of the joints and the extra-long feet. Don't forget the curved line for the arm.

3

Give the werewolf its shape, making sure the feet are long and wide at the ends. Work carefully on the hand. Then draw the massive jaws and pointed ears.

4

Finally, give the werewolf its rough fur by drawing lots of jagged lines. Finish off the face, including the sharp teeth, and add the curved claws. Draw its ragged jeans.

5

To create the dramatic purple-gray fur, blend blue, red and brown. Contrast this with yellow eyes and dirty orange claws.

TOP TIPS

Check out these tips to make your werewolf look even more realistic and scary!

Work with an old scratchy paintbrush to create coarse, wiry fur. Add white highlights to make the gnarled fingers and claws stand out.

Notice how the teeth are curved as well as pointed. Paint them dirty yellow, not white, to make them look really mean!

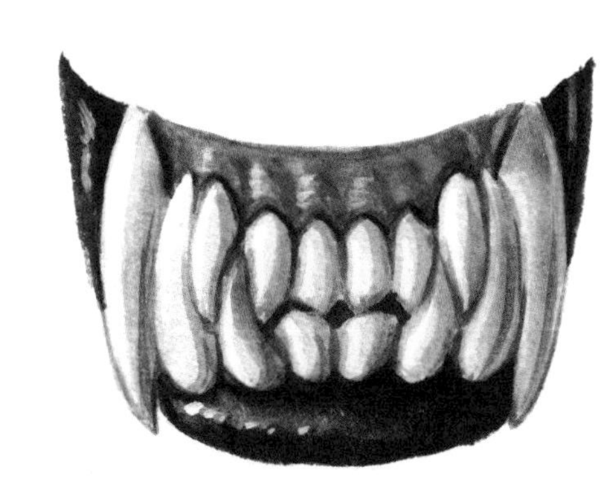

MONSTER

Have a go at creating this colorful comic book monster. Then let your imagination run riot and make up some more of your own!

1

Start with a series of curves for the body and long neck. Notice how the neck lines curve the opposite way to the body for a cheeky twist of the head. Mark on two lines for the arms.

2

Outline the arms, hands and feet. The fingers and toes are simple points, so they should be easy to draw. Then develop the head to include the horns, eyes, and giant open mouth.

3

The last step is to give your comic book creation personality. Work on the buck teeth and wriggling tongue, then outline the lips. Draw thick eyebrows and batlike ears. Don't forget to finish off the tail.

4

A cheerful character like this needs to be colorful! Create a rainbow effect by blending purple into red, orange, and yellow—or choose your own colors.

CARTOON CORNER

Create some more funny monsters by starting with simple shapes.

1

Draw a circle to shape this purple poppet's big fat belly.

2

A triangle forms the body of this green-eyed monster.

3

Start with a diamond for this monster, then add a huge mouth and flat feet.

LITTLE GREEN MAN

Aliens could come in all shapes and sizes. But with its huge eyes and humanoid shape, this is a classic type. Follow the steps to draw a picture from a different world.

1

This figure almost looks like it's upside down—but it's not! The circle for the head needs to be bigger than those for the body. Join the circles with a line.

2

Now draw the arms and legs. Make the lines straight and pay attention to the angles. Different-sized circles form the hands and the feet are diamond shapes.

3

Outline the body, keeping it thin but muscly-looking. Draw curved lines for the long, bendy fingers and add guidelines to the head to help you draw the features. Shape the chin.

4

It's important to get the face detail right—this is what makes your alien come alive. Copy the picture and carefully follow the grid. Then shape the fingers and rub out the guides.

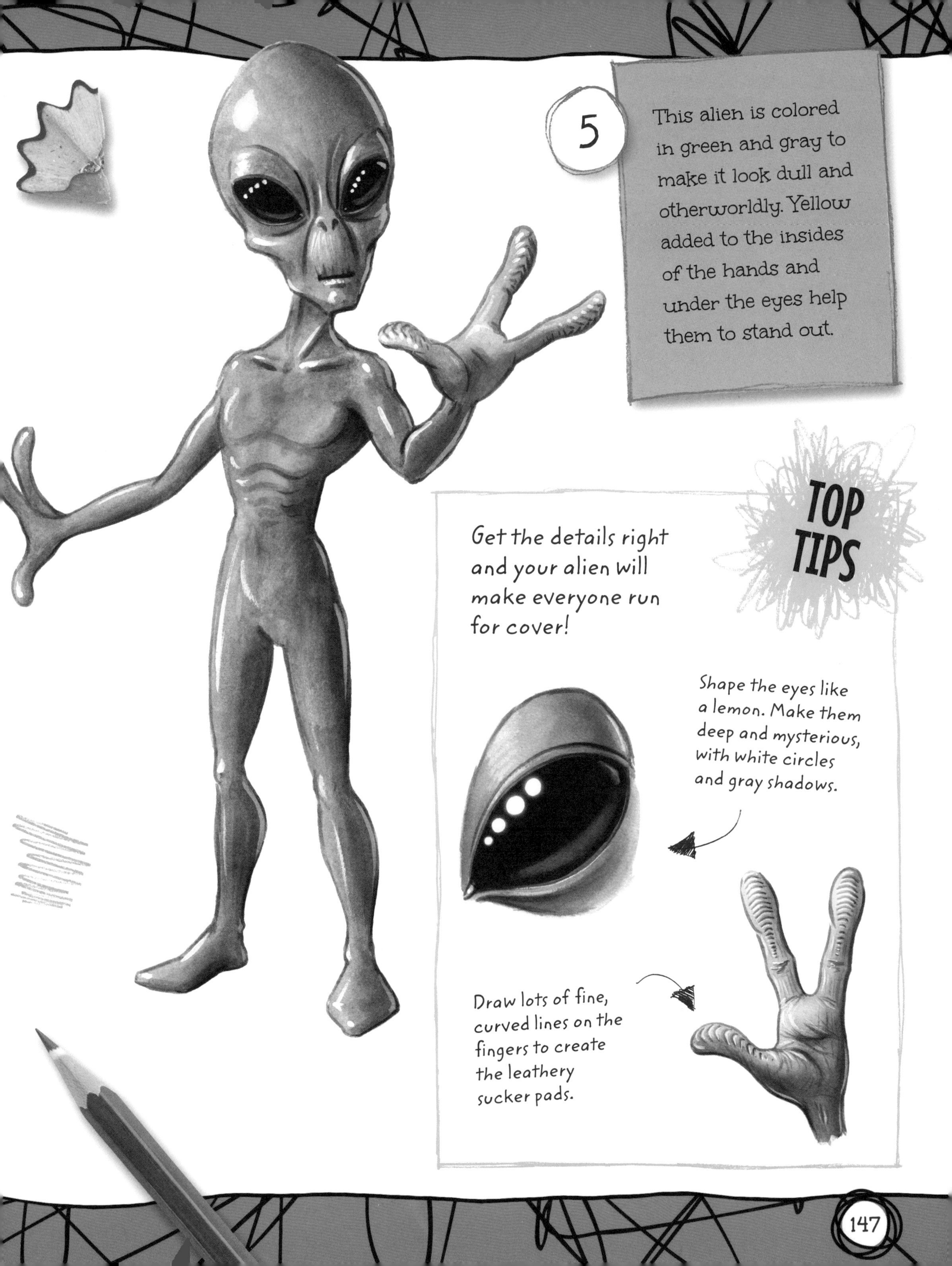

5

This alien is colored in green and gray to make it look dull and otherworldly. Yellow added to the insides of the hands and under the eyes help them to stand out.

TOP TIPS

Get the details right and your alien will make everyone run for cover!

Shape the eyes like a lemon. Make them deep and mysterious, with white circles and gray shadows.

Draw lots of fine, curved lines on the fingers to create the leathery sucker pads.

MUMMY

Yikes–there's a mummy on the loose! This is a fairly simple cartoon drawing, so you should have this bandaged horror walking off the page in no time at all.

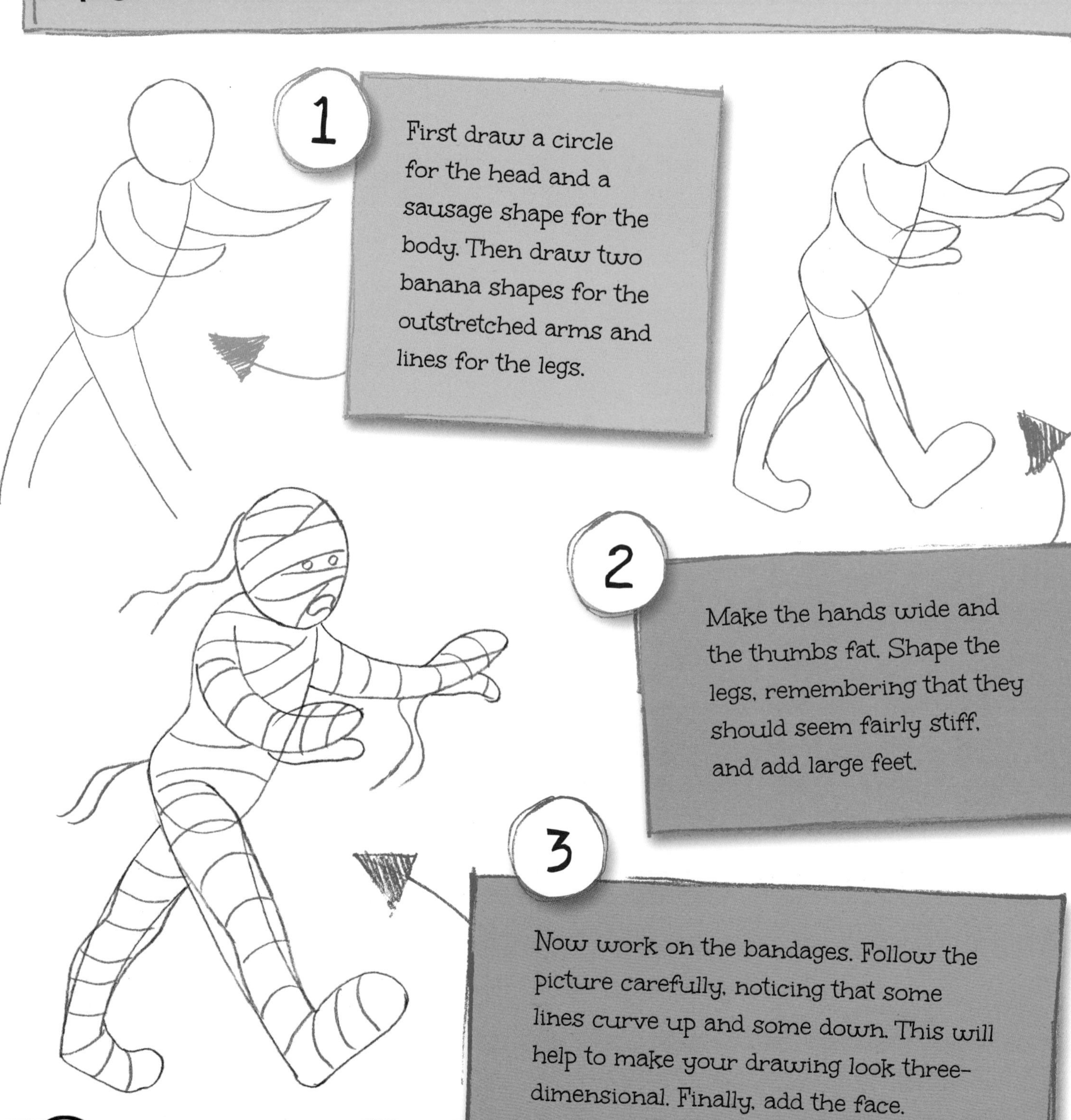

1

First draw a circle for the head and a sausage shape for the body. Then draw two banana shapes for the outstretched arms and lines for the legs.

2

Make the hands wide and the thumbs fat. Shape the legs, remembering that they should seem fairly stiff, and add large feet.

3

Now work on the bandages. Follow the picture carefully, noticing that some lines curve up and some down. This will help to make your drawing look three-dimensional. Finally, add the face.

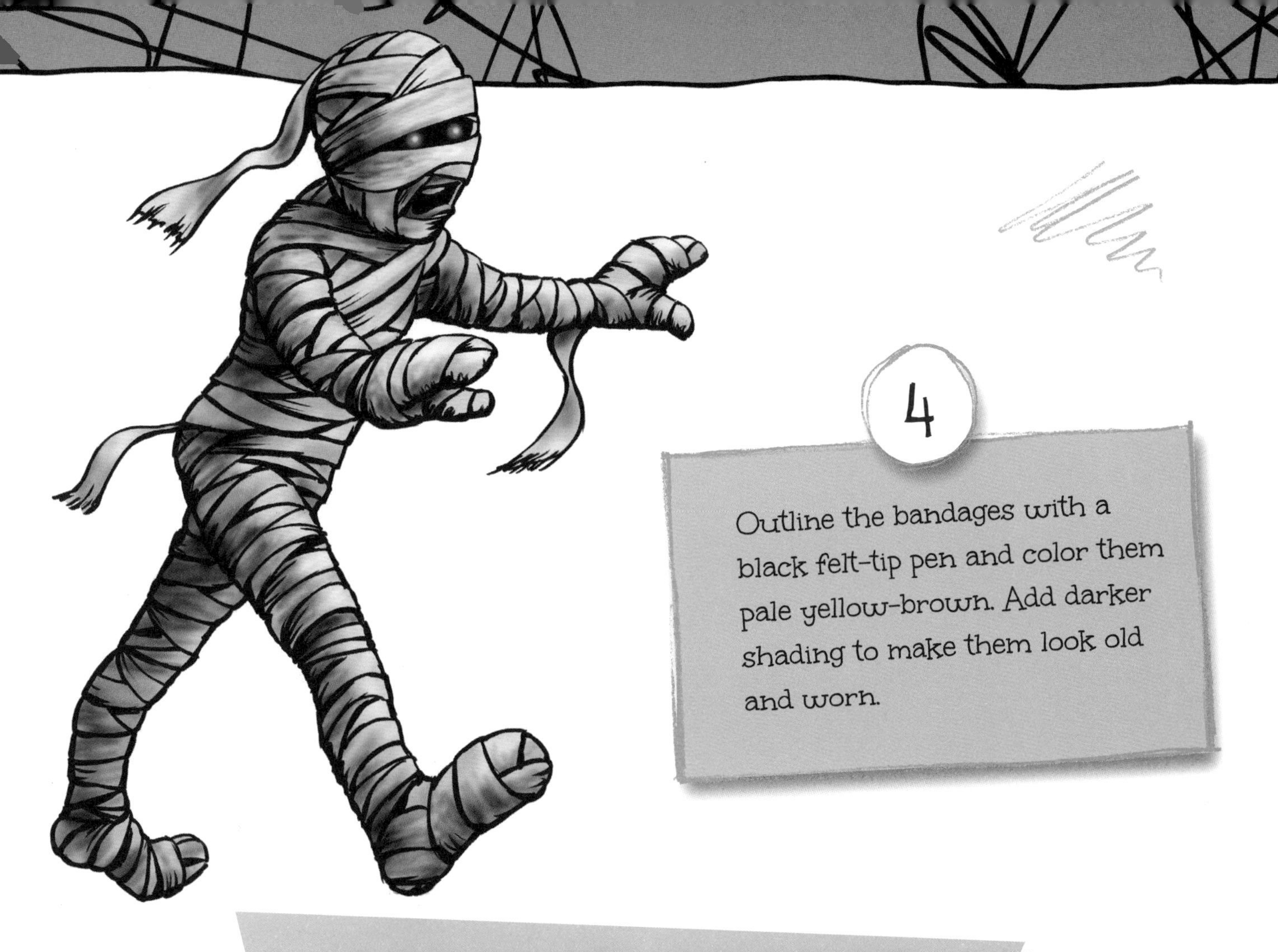

4

Outline the bandages with a black felt-tip pen and color them pale yellow-brown. Add darker shading to make them look old and worn.

CARTOON CORNER

The Egyptians also mummified their cats. Learn how to draw this one to keep your mummy company.

1

Draw a bottle shape for the body and an oval for the head. Add two ears.

2

Now shape the legs, paws and tail. Notice the cat only has one eye!

3

Finish the bandages in the same way as before. Add a loose one like a tail.

SEA SERPENT

Is it a snake? Is it a dragon? No, it's a seriously scary sea serpent! Most of the detail is in the monster's head, so take time over this part, and your picture will spring into life.

1

Start with two different-size circles. Then draw two swooping curved lines to connect the circles. You should now have a looping wormlike shape.

2

Continue the end of the front loop. Then do the same at the back—but make it thinner and taper it into a point. You have created your sea serpent's long body and tail.

3

Now draw guidelines for the head and the fins that will run along the length of the body. Add two jointed lines for the long legs and wide feet.

4

Follow the guidelines along the monster's back to draw the fins. Then finish the legs and feet. Add detail to the neck and face, including the teeth and forked tongue.

5

You can make your sea serpent any color, but blue and green work well for a watery feel. Paint more faintly toward the tail to suggest depth and distance.

TOP TIPS

A forked tongue and webbed feet are striking features. It pays to draw and color them well.

Follow the shape of the curves here carefully. Make the back of the tongue dark green, and contrast it with pink to make the forked part stand out.

Add white highlights to the feet to give them texture and make them seem scaly. Use a different shade of green for the webbing.

DRAGON

Don't get too close to this dangerous dragon! His classic features include scalloped wings and an arrow tail-but you could experiment with drawing giant horns and spines, too.

1

Draw an egg shape for the chest. Then add curved lines for the haunches and tail. Another curve with a triangle on top forms the head.

2

Now carefully outline the head and the neck. Start the legs, making sure they bend and point forward. Shape the tail, and begin the wings.

3

A dragon's wings are a litlte bit like bats' wings, and its feet are like an eagle's. Copy the picture to get them right. Work on the detail of the face, and add the arrow to the top of the tail.

4

Your dragon doesn't have to be green! This one is brown, orange, and purple. You could also give it stripes or patches instead of spots.

CARTOON CORNER

Why not try drawing a fire-breathing baby dragon, and show him standing up?

1

Start with a small circle for the head, and taper it into a muzzle. For the body, draw a pear shape. Then add the tail.

2

Work on the arms, legs, and head. To keep the baby dragon looking cute, make sure all the lines are curved or rounded.

3

Add a few spikes to the finished drawing and a puff of flames from his mouth. Keep the outline smooth and the colors simple.

ZOMBIE

When you draw this zombie, remember that it is a lifeless corpse that has risen from the dead! Make its features hideous, and give it gray, decaying flesh.

1

Draw three ovals for the head, chest, and hips. Copy the shapes and their positions accurately, then connect them with a line.

2

Next, add a long, bent line for the sloping shoulders. Draw more lines for the legs, and shape the feet. Mark the guides on the head. Your stick figure should already look zombielike.

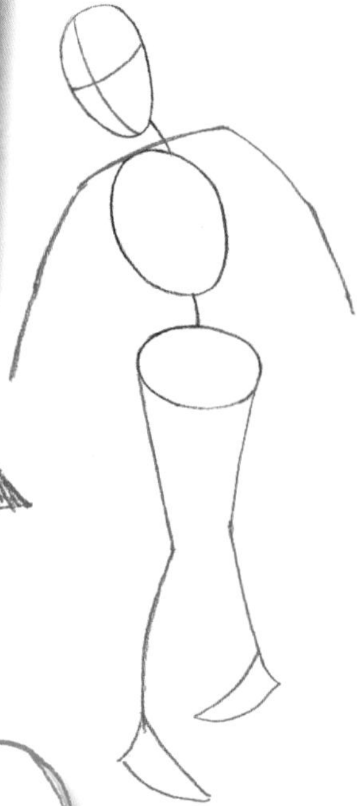

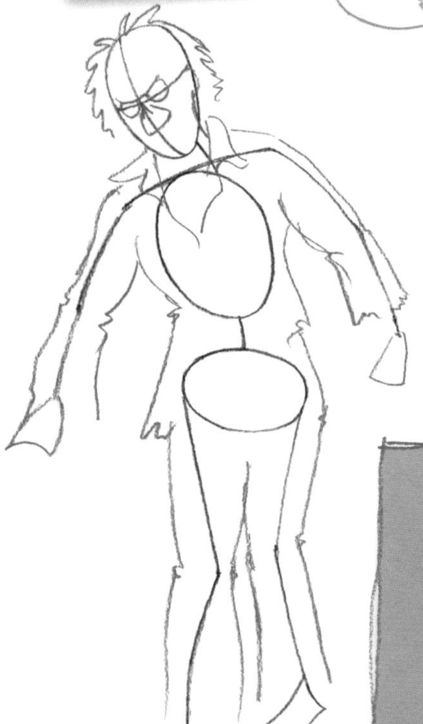

3

Bring your zombie to life by working on the straggly hair and face. When outlining the body, make the clothes look ragged.

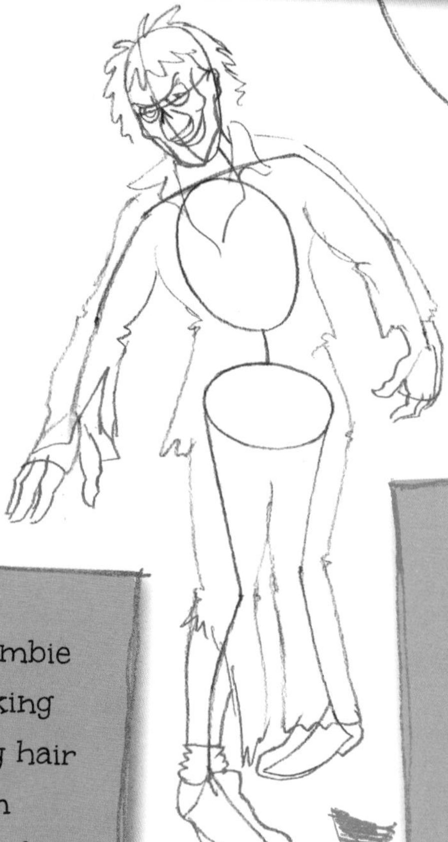

4

When drawing the hands and feet, remember that zombies are often skinny and their joints gnarled. Fill in the face, and finish the clothing. Then erase the guides.

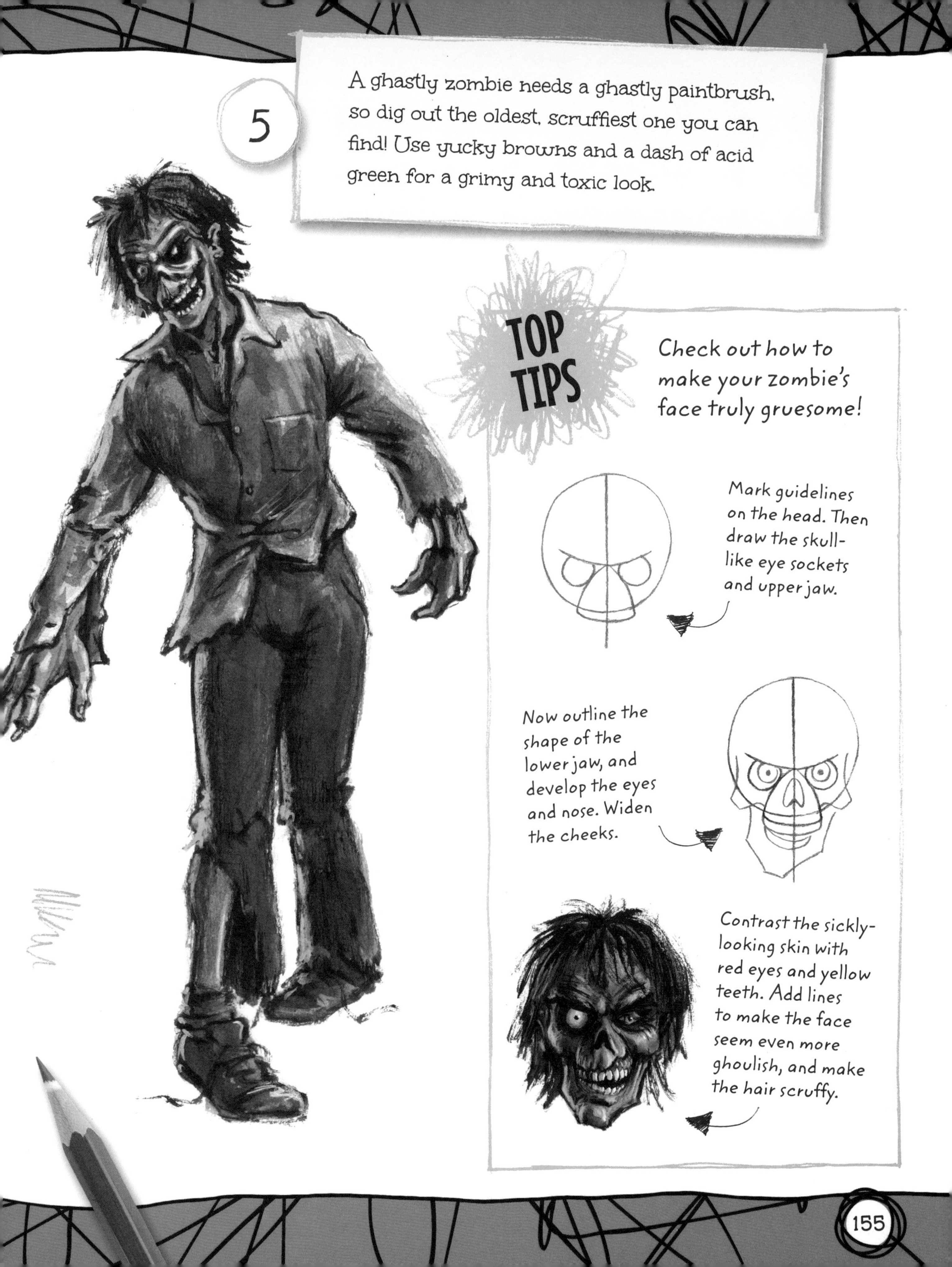

5

A ghastly zombie needs a ghastly paintbrush, so dig out the oldest, scruffiest one you can find! Use yucky browns and a dash of acid green for a grimy and toxic look.

TOP TIPS

Check out how to make your zombie's face truly gruesome!

Mark guidelines on the head. Then draw the skull-like eye sockets and upper jaw.

Now outline the shape of the lower jaw, and develop the eyes and nose. Widen the cheeks.

Contrast the sickly-looking skin with red eyes and yellow teeth. Add lines to make the face seem even more ghoulish, and make the hair scruffy.

YETI

A cuddly cartoon yeti is fairly simple to draw. I'm not sure if you'd really want to meet this legendary beast, though. Apelike yetis are rumored to be enormous!

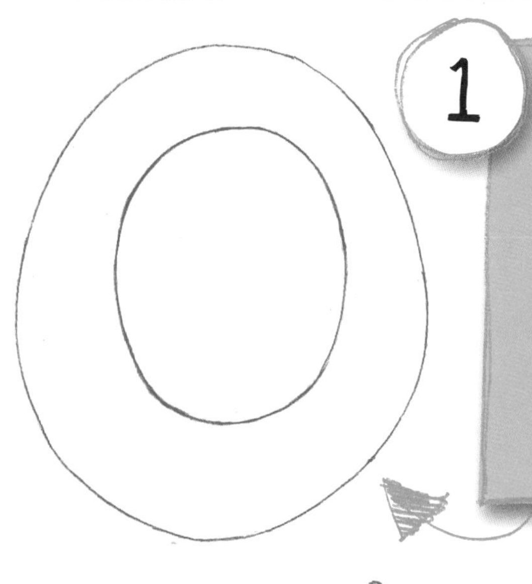

1

Start with two wonky egg shapes, one inside the other. They will form the yeti's arms and chest. Look at the picture carefully to get the shapes just right.

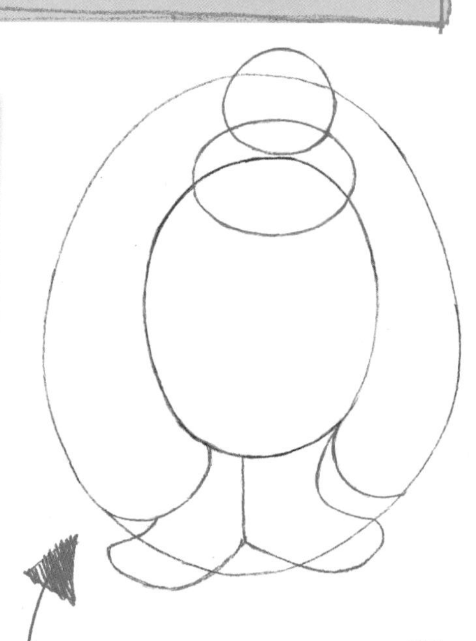

2

Next, position the head. To do this, draw a circle with an overlapping oval. Shape the bottom of the arms and the yeti's legs and feet.

3

Give the creature a heavy brow and a smiling mouth. Make his chin pointed, and don't forget the eyes. Notice that he has fewer fingers and toes than we do. This makes him even easier to draw! Erase the guides.

4

When outlining the fur, use lots of thin lines. This will make your yeti look really hairy. Remember to draw his teeth. Color him simply in pale blues contrasted with purple.

CARTOON CORNER

Follow the steps to draw this picture of a mischievous baby yeti.

1

Draw a big head, round body, and waving arms. Make the feet wide.

2

Work on the fingers and toes as you did before. Fill in the face, too.

3

Brighter colors and baby teeth make this little yeti a cuddly ball of fun!

MONSTER DOG

You can turn an everyday animal into a monster by altering the pose and tweaking the shape of the skeleton. The proportions are not realistic, but the finished effect is impressive.

1

Start with a wolflike dog in a jumping pose. This skeleton has a little more length to the spine than a real dog and a higher neck joint.

The limbs are also leaner and closer to the bone, though the outline bulges around the joints to suggest the thickness of the bone endings. The thicker, longer neck works well, as does the slimming down of the stomach area.

2

Before making a finished drawing, I figured out some more details of how I'd like the head to look. Since this is a monster dog, I stripped away all the elements that could look cute: Soft ears are reduced to leathery spikes, friendly eyes become mere slits, the teeth are sharp and pointed, and the dog has a snarling expression.

3
I think you'll agree that there's nothing friendly about this beast. Along with the changes to the proportions, I have also drawn the outline of the monster dog with a simplified, angular style. I want to convey a feral creature, ungroomed.
4
This dog is definitely a creature of the night, so I have chosen colors that will blend in with the shadows. In contrast to his body color, the bright mouth and flashing teeth and claws stand out as perilous weapons.

CHAPTER 6

FANTASY

ROBOT

Robots such as this one are known as humanoids. They have a similar body form to humans, but their features are vastly exaggerated, and you need to use angles and boxes when drawing.

1

Start with the basic masses that form the head, chest, and hips. Since this is a robot and not a human, the chest is much larger than the head and hips. Notice how the vertical guideline is in a different position on the hips because the figure is twisting.

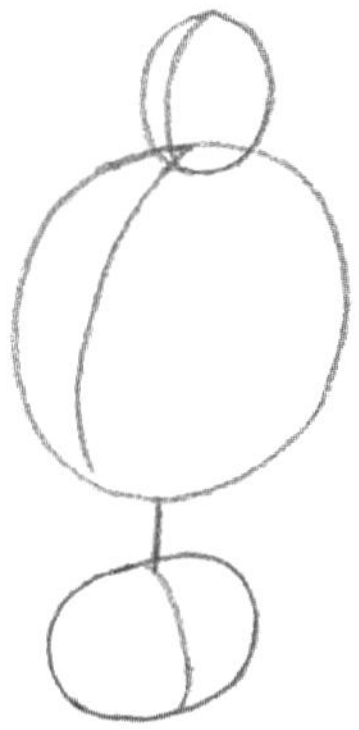

2

Although this robot doesn't really have bones and joints, drawing them will help you establish the relative lengths and positions of the robotic limbs and figure out where they bend. I've added some perspective lines to the lower body to help you draw the legs. The leg to the right of your picture is farther away, so it looks shorter.

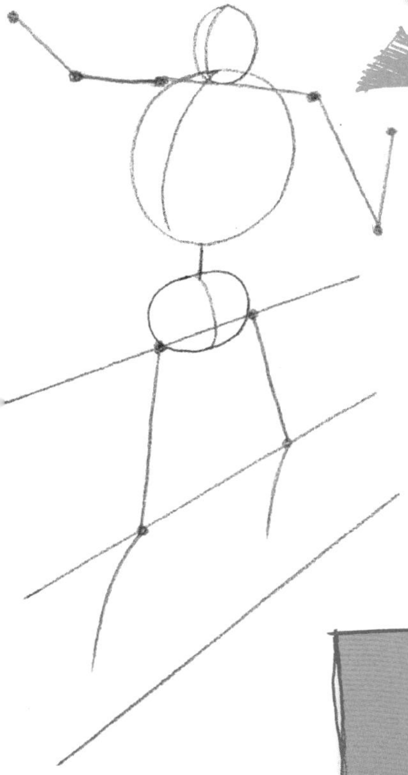

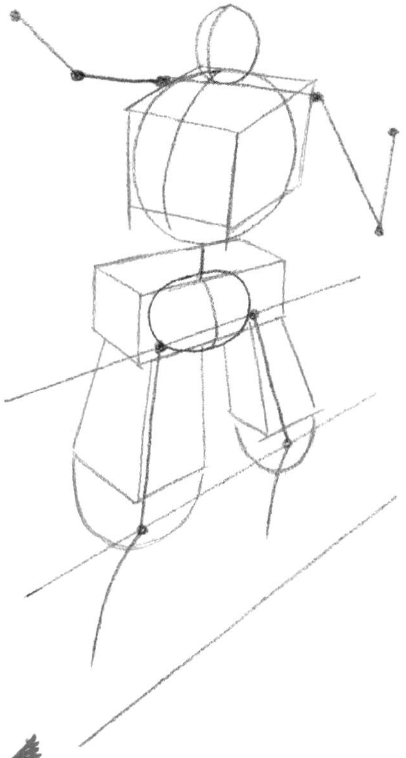

3

Turn the chest into a cube, and draw a rectangular box around the hips. Use a ruler if it helps. Copy the blocky shape of the upper legs, making the nearest leg thicker. Draw semicircles for knee joints.

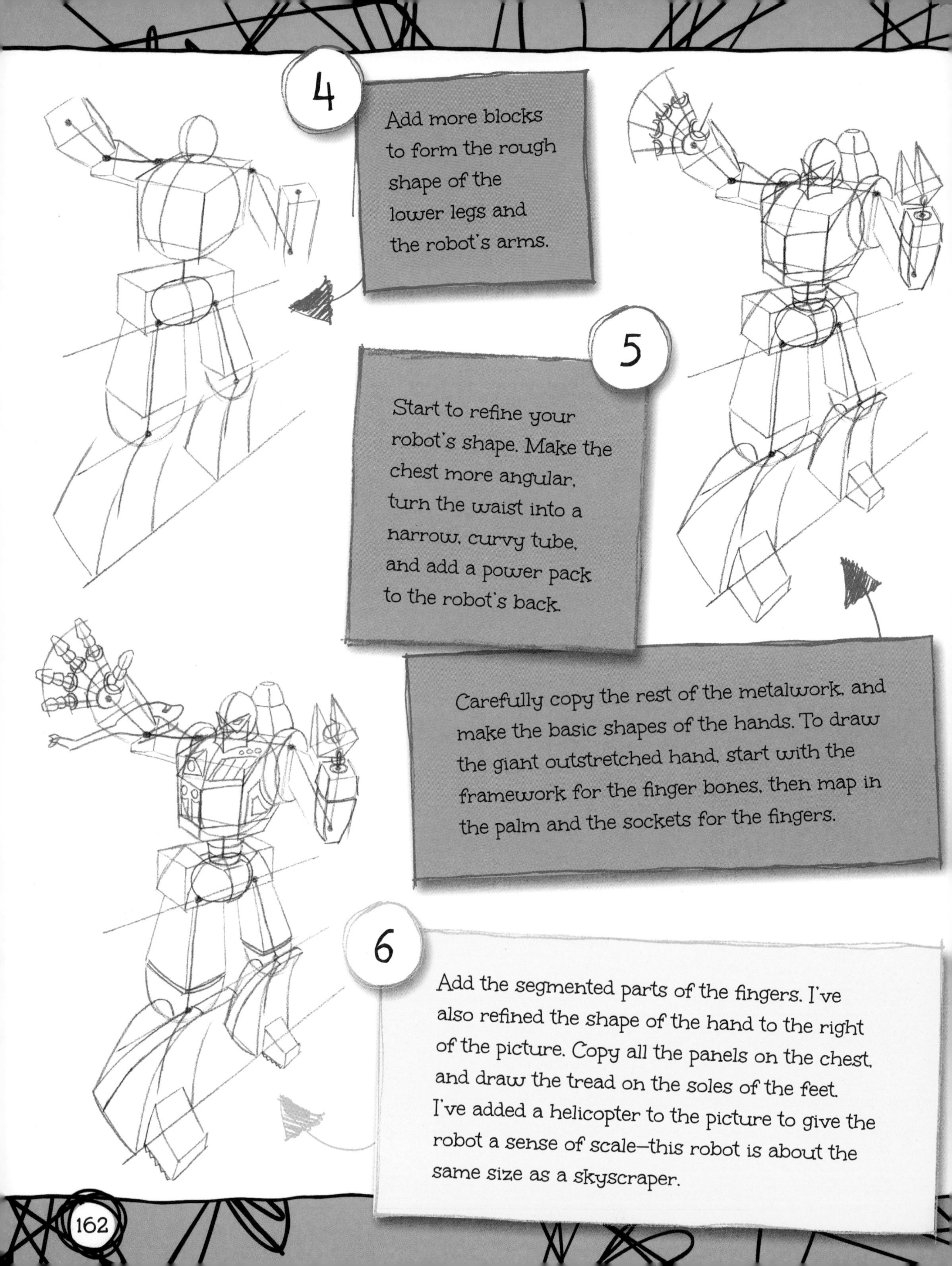

4

Add more blocks to form the rough shape of the lower legs and the robot's arms.

5

Start to refine your robot's shape. Make the chest more angular, turn the waist into a narrow, curvy tube, and add a power pack to the robot's back.

Carefully copy the rest of the metalwork, and make the basic shapes of the hands. To draw the giant outstretched hand, start with the framework for the finger bones, then map in the palm and the sockets for the fingers.

6

Add the segmented parts of the fingers. I've also refined the shape of the hand to the right of the picture. Copy all the panels on the chest, and draw the tread on the soles of the feet. I've added a helicopter to the picture to give the robot a sense of scale—this robot is about the same size as a skyscraper.

7

Go over all your good lines in heavy pencil, then in black felt-tip pen. Add some more detail to the helicopter, including the rows of curved lines that show the spinning blades.

8

When the ink is dry, erase all your pencil marks. Now you can enjoy adding color. I've added some strips of white to make the metal look like it's reflecting the light. The helicopter is bright green so it stands out against the colors of the robot's body.

FEMALE SUPERHERO

Get ready for action, and sketch this female superhero! With a superhero, the secret is to exaggerate the proportions of a human figure. Follow the steps to find out how.

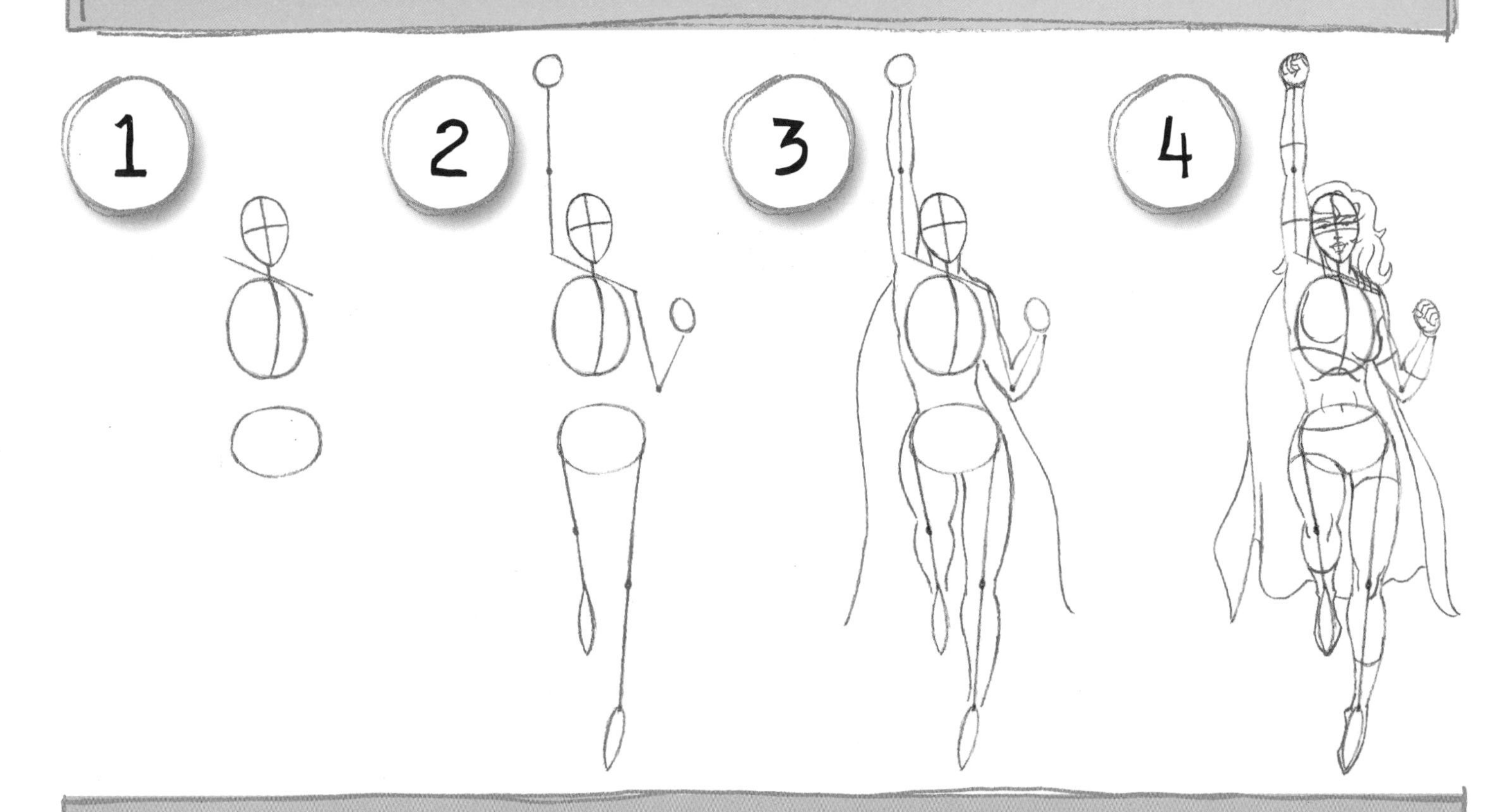

1. Start with three ovals for the head, chest, and hips. Copy the picture carefully. Mark guidelines on the face and chest. Then add a sloping line for the shoulders.

2. Next, draw stick legs and arms, paying attention to where they bend. Include dots for the joints. Notice how the front raised leg is drawn shorter than the other one. The hands and feet can be oval shapes.

3. Outline the body using slightly curved lines to suggest powerful muscles. Narrow the lines at the joints. Then start to shape the cape.

4. Finally, add the details. Work on the face and the fingers. Think of the hair as one complete shape. Develop the chest, knees, and feet. Then finish drawing the shorts and cape.

5
It's a good idea to keep to two or three contrasting colors for the color scheme to create a dramatic effect. You could show your heroine without a mask or customize her accessories.
TOP TIPS
Drawing hands is a challenge, so take your time. You'll find more tips on pages 132–133.
First, work on the basic clenched fist shape. Include lines for where the fingers and palm meet.
Now develop the fingers. Keep the shapes even. Notice how the thumb bulges at the joints.
When you go over the outlines, add more shape to each knuckle. Crease marks on the palm will help make the fist look tightly curled.

MALE SUPERHERO

In this cartoon drawing, you're going to make the details in the foreground bigger, so that it looks like your action hero is flying off the page straight toward you.

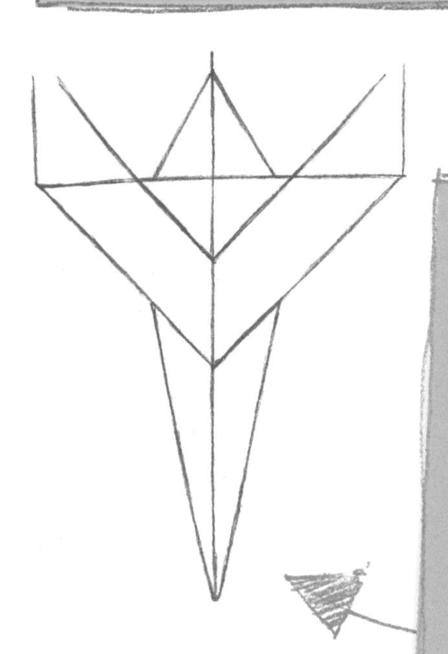

1

First, draw a cross shape, then use it to position the other guidelines. Work with a ruler to keep the lines straight, and try to make everything symmetrical.

2

Add angled lines for the chin, then position the eyes and mouth. Outline the large muscular chest and arms using lots of curved lines. Circles form the hands and domed head.

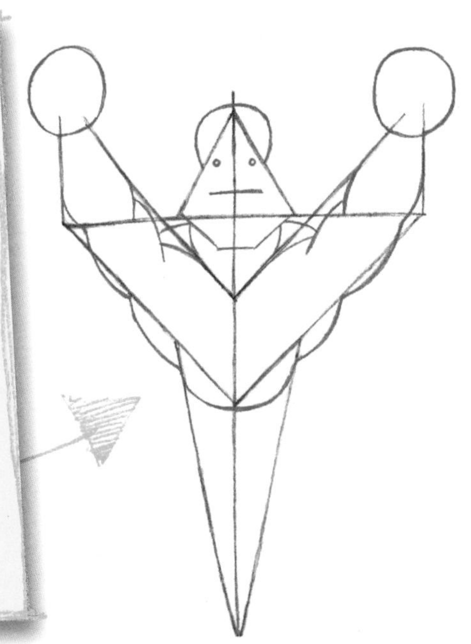

3

Shape the head, and fill in the face and hair. Then work on the muscular legs and chest. To draw the hands, look at the "Top Tips" on page 165. As a final touch, add the flowing cape. Erase your guides.

For this powerful character, use a thick black outline. Make it heavier around the head and arms and finer at the feet, so that they look like they are farther away.

CARTOON CORNER

Now try drawing these mini superheroes, or invent your own!

1

What special powers do you think this colorful superboy has?

2

Big hair, stripes, and a giant eye make this all-action girl stand out.

3

A green face and yellow eyes will make your character look wicked!

VAMPIRE

Watch out for this bloodsucking vampire-he's not the friendly kind! Give him a deathly pale face and a swishing blood-red cape to make him seem really creepy.

1

Start with two long curves to capture the vampire's overall pose, and position of his legs. Mark a line for his shoulders. Then draw the head and add the guides.

2

Shape the long legs and feet. The arms and hands can be stick lines ending in ovals at this stage. Form the cape with a straight line from the arm and a broad curve at the bottom.

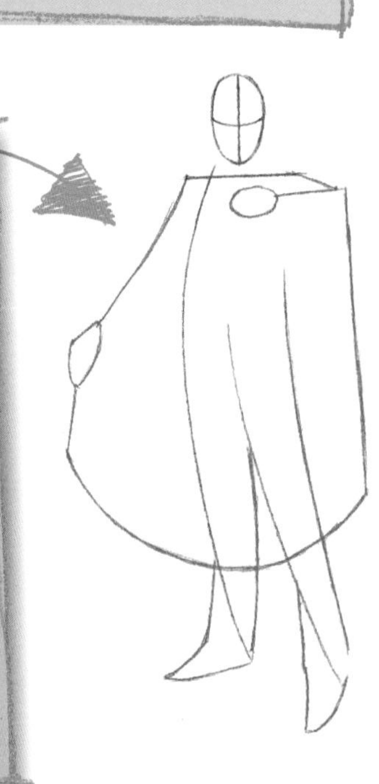

3

Include the hairline and guides for the mouth. Then draw the high collar and the vest. Don't forget the creases on the cape. Shape the loose sleeve around the arm.

4

Finally, fill in the face and hair, and shape the sunken cheeks. Include the shirt frills and vest buttons. When you have given the cape a curvy edge, erase the guide.

5

Much of the color here is solid black. The cape has two shades of red. By adding pale-blue highlights, you can create the effect of a ghostly moonlit glow!

TOP TIPS

To capture a vampire's hypnotic character, you need to spend time on the facial details.

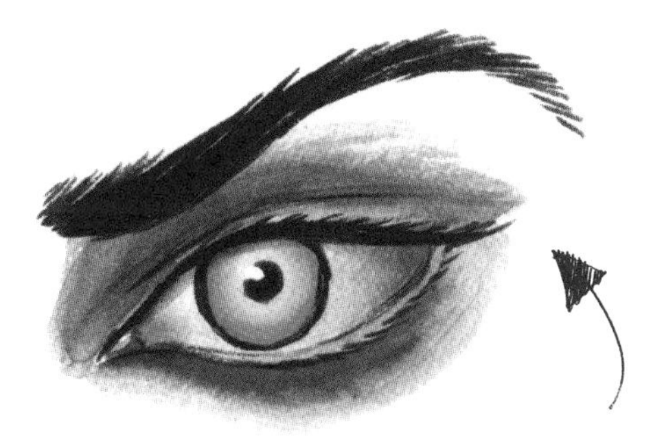

Draw catlike eyes and heavy eyebrows. Color the eyes fiery orange and yellow, then paint dark red around the rims for a spooky look.

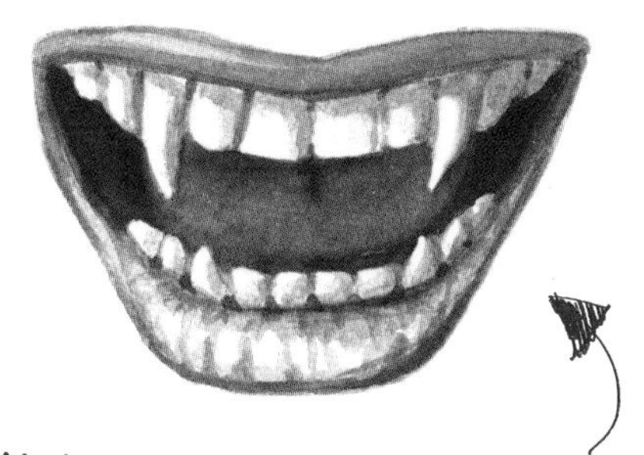

Make the lips pale so that the teeth stand out. The fangs should be pointed and slightly curved. Use yellow for the shading.

MAD SCIENTIST

Yikes! What is this crazy cartoon scientist inventing this time? What's bubbling in his lab? Once you've mastered him mixing his chemicals, try drawing the explosion that comes next!

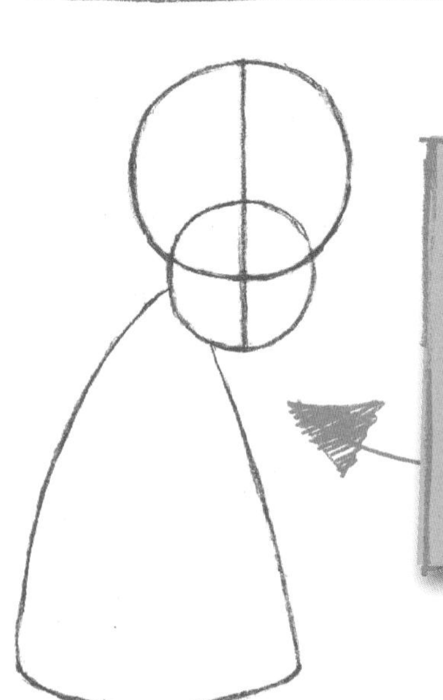

1

Draw two overlapping circles, one large and one small, for the big head. Then add a guideline down the center. A cone shape forms the body.

2

Next, copy the arms and legs. They are made up of simple lines and shapes, so they should be easy to draw. Outline the massive hair and the pointed hairline.

3

All that's left is to fill in the details. When working on the face, draw most of the features inside the smaller circle, so that the bulging forehead looks huge. Keep the clothing simple—and don't forget the equipment!

CARTOON CORNER

A crazy scientist needs some crazy equipment! Why not bring his lab to life as well?

1

A red face with puffed-out cheeks and scrunched up eyes makes this flask look like it's about to explode at any moment.

2

This test tube is on the loose. Give it waving stick arms, running legs, and a mischievous face. A few drops spilling out of the top will help, too.

4

When you start coloring, use drab browns and grays for the scientist's hair and most of his clothing. Contrast this with wacky yellow gloves, plus toxic pink and lime-green chemicals.

ORC

Orcs are fierce humanoid monsters with grotesque features. In this drawing, your goal is to capture the beast's bulky shape and his mean, but dim, expression.

1

Start with a large circle for the shoulders and overall body shape. Another circle inside forms the stomach, and three smaller circles mark the hands and the head.

2

On the bottom edge of the largest circle, draw two more circles for the knees, and add lines for the powerful legs and large feet. Start to draw the arms.

3

Work on the arms to give them a muscly look, and draw the chest armor. Mark the guidelines for the face and the sword.

4

Bring your orc to life by completing his accessories, including his cuff, knee pads, and boots. Shape his hands, and finish his face. Erase the circular guide.

5

You want an orc to look grimy, so color him in yucky greens and yellows with a hint of purple. Make his armor look dull with different shades of brown.

TOP TIPS

Follow these tips to add the finishing touches to your beast.

Make the head a dome shape and the eyes narrow. Paint your skin colors on top of each other in splotches to create a mottled effect.

Copy the shape of the sword carefully, then add a Celtic design to the handle and blade. Look in books for other Celtic designs you could use.

SEA WITCH

In folklore, sea witches had power over the waves. When drawing this wicked-looking creature, remember that she is half human and half serpent.

1

Draw three basic shapes—a small circle for the head, an oval for the chest, and a large circle for the serpent body. Then add guidelines for the shoulders and arms.

2

When shaping the arms and shoulders, spend time on the muscles. Work on the body and tail following the curve of the circle. Outline the face and add the trident.

3

Shape the body and tail further. Give the sea witch a seashell helmet and top, and flowing hair. Then add her face. Finish the hands and the trident. Erase the circular guide.

4

Before you add color, add fins to the arms and webbing to the fingers to make the creature truly fishy. Sea greens and blues work well for the body, along with a golden shell hat.

CARTOON CORNER

Draw and color a seahorse chariot for your wicked witch in three simple steps.

1

Form the seahorses using curved lines for the bodies and circles for the heads. Work on the one nearest to you first. Then shape the chariot.

2

Add the reins to the seahorses, and slot in their face details. Finish their curly tails. Scallop the edge of the chariot, and draw the cushion.

3

You can add more detail at the inking stage, such as ridges on the seahorses' bodies. Make the inside of the chariot golden yellow.

ELF PRINCESS

Make this elfin princess with pointed ears look tall and elegant rather than strong and muscular. Use lots of flowing, curved lines to achieve this graceful effect.

1

Start with a long, curved line running through the whole body to get the right pose. Then draw ovals for the head, chest, and hips. Mark the shoulders and face guides.

2

Add dots for the knees and a guideline for the front leg. The feet can be simple shapes for now. Position the arms and hands, paying attention to the angles.

3

Shape the body, starting with the chest and arm. A bell shape forms the skirt. Below, draw the legs and boots. Add pointed ears and flowing hair. Mark the facial features.

4

When you finish drawing, pay attention to the face and hands. Make the fingers long and thin. Complete the costume including the pleated skirt, then work on the face and hair. Add a flower as a final touch.

5

Color your princess in shades of green for a woodland feel. Keep the shading light and gentle. Add accessories to the figure using gold or silver jewelry.

TOP TIPS

Try drawing your princess in profile instead. Here are some tips on creating delicate elfin features.

Give her a long face and a slender, upturned nose. Make her lips small but full and her eyebrows thin and arched. Her cheeks should have a rosy glow.

VIKING

This fantasy Viking warrior is fierce and strong. You can capture this by giving him a broad body and setting his muscular legs wide apart in a fighting stance.

1

First, draw a large X shape. Using this as your guide, position a box for the body and a circle for the head. Then add guidelines for one arm ending in an oval for the hand.

Next, outline the body, making sure that the arms and legs look muscular. Mark the knee joints and the face guides. Start the shield.

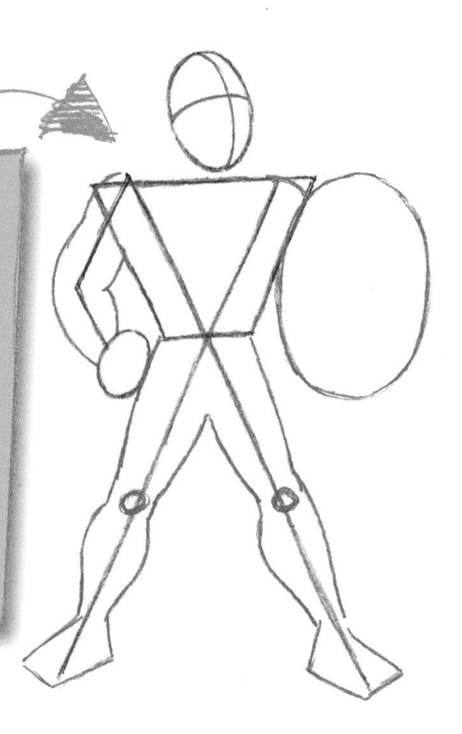

3

Now start adding the details. Copy the picture, or invent your own face, costume, and weapons. Remember to make your warrior look dangerous!

4

Think about the different textures when inking and coloring. Give the fur boots fluffy edges. Make the wooden shield hard, and make the metal clasps shiny.

CARTOON CORNER

Different warriors need different helmets. Check out these designs.

1

A full face protector makes this Spartan warrior look really scary. It also makes his eyes stand out.

2

This knight's helmet is more decorative. Make the metal shine with white highlights, and add brass clips.

3

How about drawing a Roman centurion? Check out history books for more picture references.

CENTAUR

One of the simplest ways of combining human and animal body forms is a straightforward half-and-half split. The top or bottom half of a human is attached to the opposite half of an animal. One creature that takes this form is the centaur, which has the torso of a man attached to the body of a horse.

1

Since this figure involves drawing two different species, it's best to concentrate on one creature at a time, so start by drawing the human half as shown. The chest takes the shape of an oval with a chunk cut out to show the edge of the rib cage—the oval is tilted to show that the chest is being thrust forward.

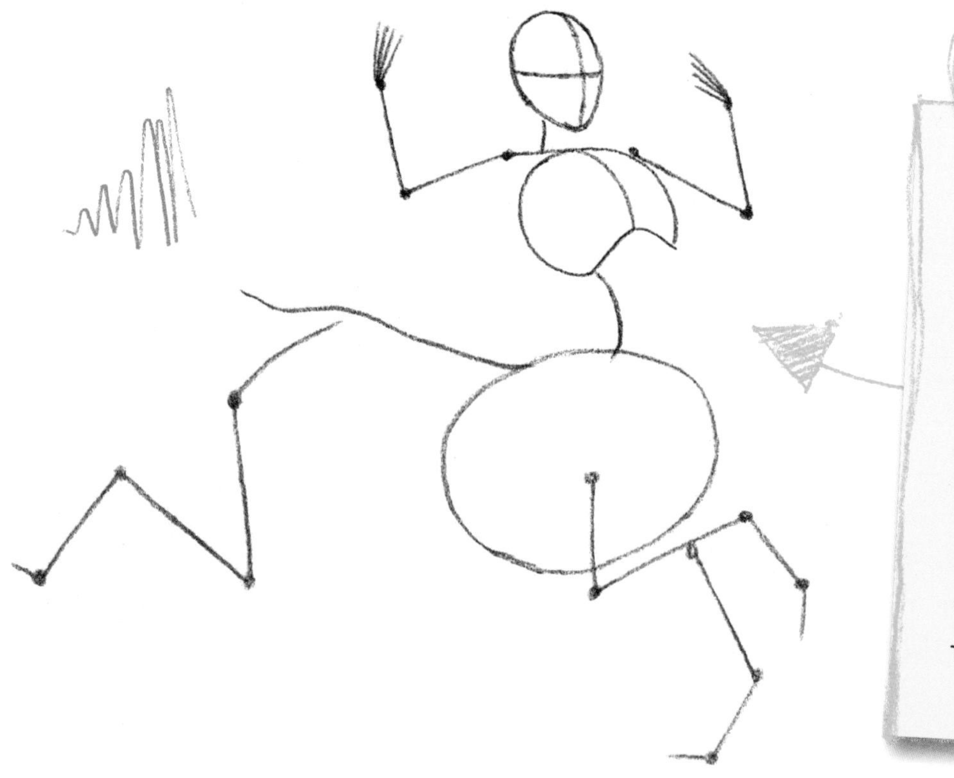

2

Now for the horse. Draw a large oval where the man's hips would normally sit to form the horse's rib cage. The man's spine is now also the horse's neck bone. Add the horse's backbone and leg bones—carefully copy their shapes to capture the centaur's active pose.

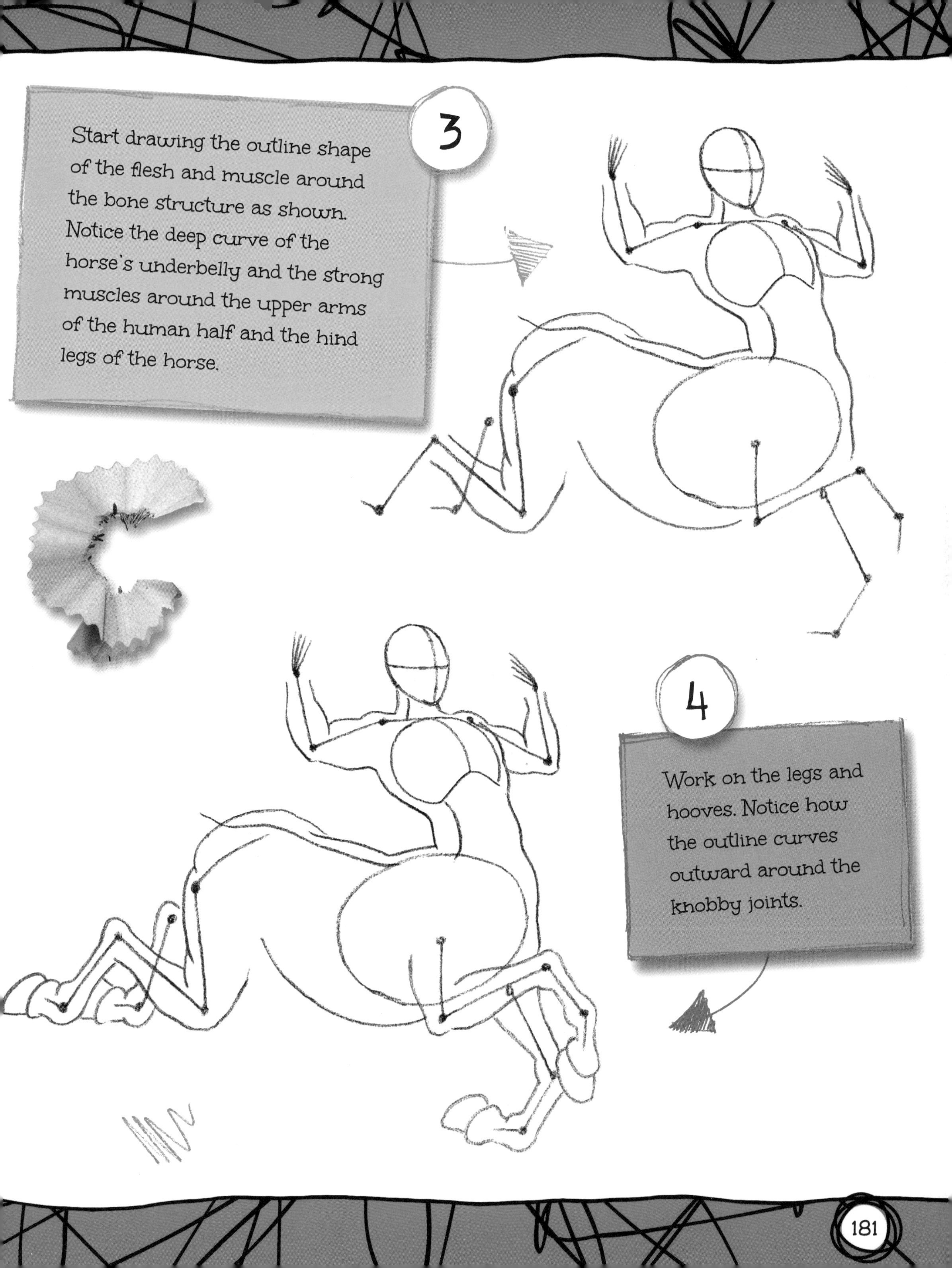

3

Start drawing the outline shape of the flesh and muscle around the bone structure as shown. Notice the deep curve of the horse's underbelly and the strong muscles around the upper arms of the human half and the hind legs of the horse.

4

Work on the legs and hooves. Notice how the outline curves outward around the knobby joints.

5

Place the facial features, and work on the shape of the hands. When you draw the sword, make sure it looks as if it has been thrust back, ready for battle. The ponytail on the head should be flying up at the back, just like the horse's tail. Use long, confident pencil strokes to create the curves of these.

6

Add some more detail to the facial features. I've made the centaur's jawline more angular and drawn lots of little lines on the upper body to define the muscle. A few more curves on the body of the horse will add more definition to the muscle and bone here, too. Notice the lines on the hair—these help to show the direction in which it is flowing.

7

Pick out the good lines of your sketch, and go over them with a soft pencil to produce your final picture. Next, go over all your final lines again using a black felt-tip pen. Shade in the eyes, leaving a tiny circle of white on each one.

8

Erase all the pencil lines that formed your centaur's skeleton framework, then add the color. I've chosen to give this centaur a zebra's body. I've made his hair black to match his tail.

JAPANESE DRAGON

This is a very sophisticated picture, so take your time with each step. Japanese dragons are usually associated with water and have serpentlike bodies, but this doesn't mean they need to be blue or green.

1

Copy the head shape as shown, then add a long, curvy tube for the body—overlap the curves of this snakelike shape as if the body is transparent. Later, you can erase the lines that make up the sections of the body you wouldn't really be able to see, since they lie underneath other sections.

2

Add the bones of the four limbs, and copy the frameworks I've drawn for the hands. They are shaped to give the impression that the beast is ready to lash out at any moment.

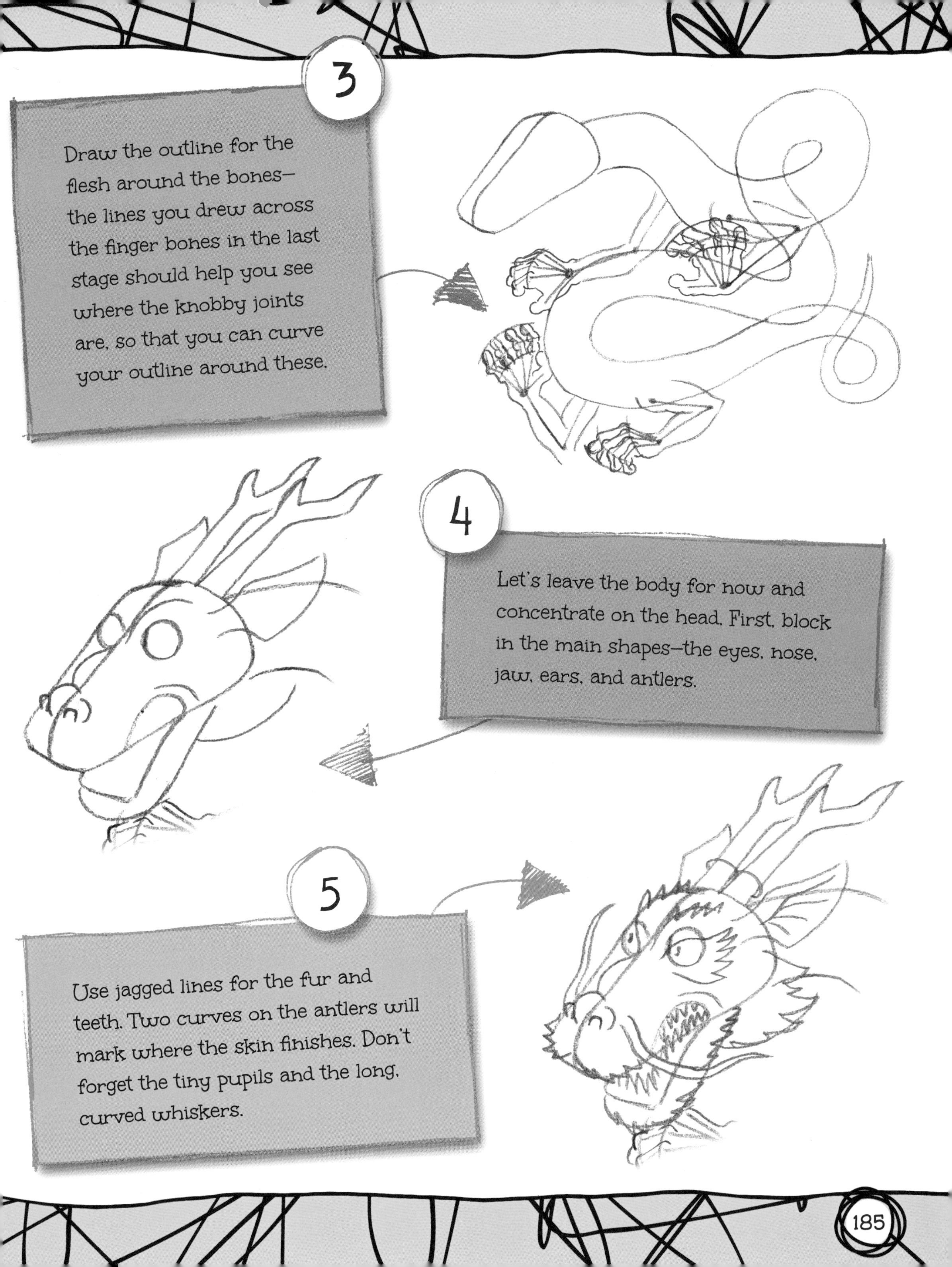

3

Draw the outline for the flesh around the bones—the lines you drew across the finger bones in the last stage should help you see where the knobby joints are, so that you can curve your outline around these.

4

Let's leave the body for now and concentrate on the head. First, block in the main shapes—the eyes, nose, jaw, ears, and antlers.

5

Use jagged lines for the fur and teeth. Two curves on the antlers will mark where the skin finishes. Don't forget the tiny pupils and the long, curved whiskers.

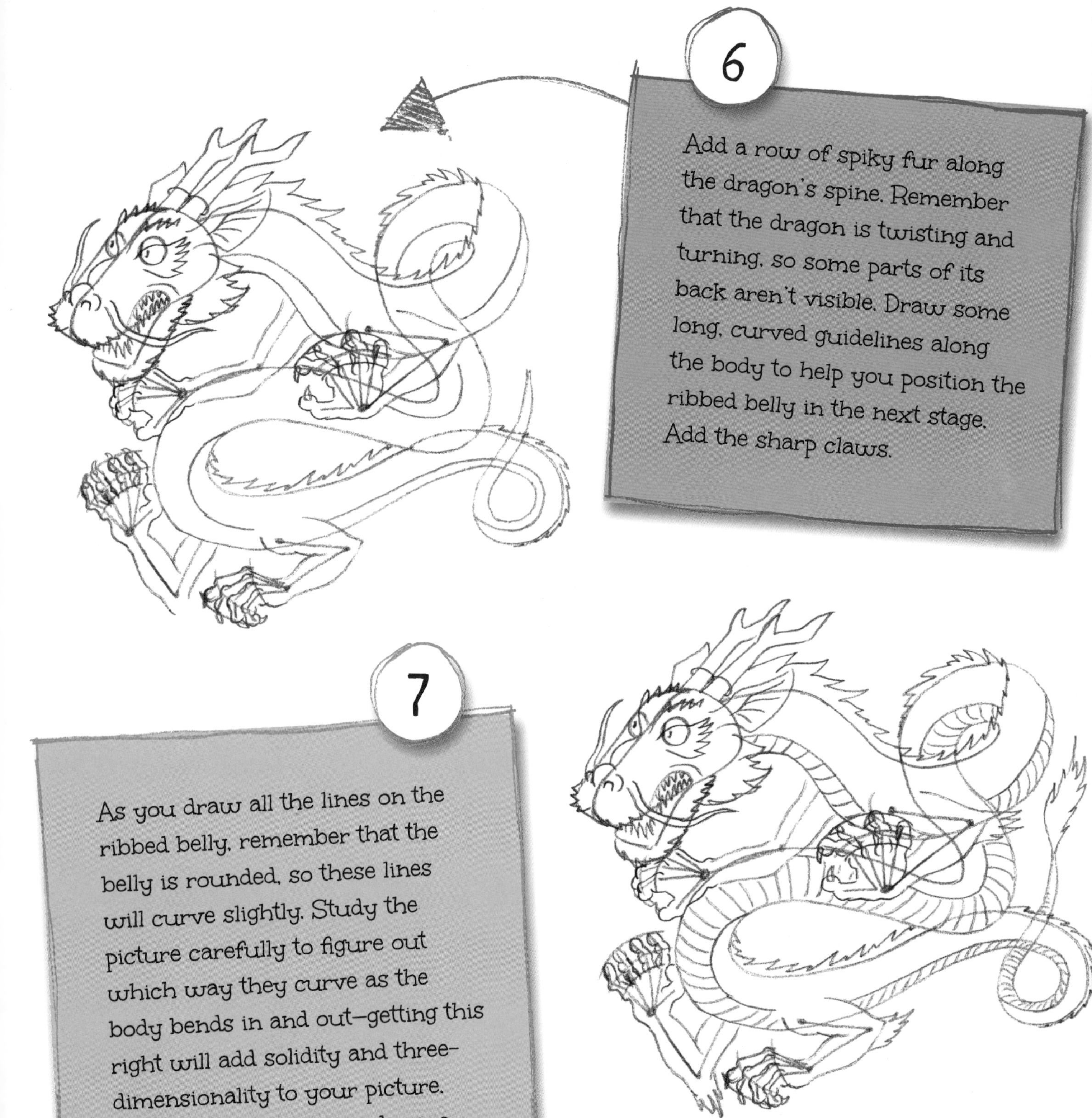

6

Add a row of spiky fur along the dragon's spine. Remember that the dragon is twisting and turning, so some parts of its back aren't visible. Draw some long, curved guidelines along the body to help you position the ribbed belly in the next stage. Add the sharp claws.

7

As you draw all the lines on the ribbed belly, remember that the belly is rounded, so these lines will curve slightly. Study the picture carefully to figure out which way they curve as the body bends in and out—getting this right will add solidity and three-dimensionality to your picture. Add the tip of the tail and some fur to the dragon's elbows.

8

Now you should be ready to pick out all the final lines of your drawing and make them heavier by going over them with a soft pencil, then with a black felt-tip pen. If you can easily see all of your good lines, then just use a pen. Study the picture carefully to see if there are any lines you missed. Add some extra black to the eyes.

9

When the ink is dry, erase all your pencil lines. Now you can decide on a color scheme. Notice the colors I've used for the fur to make it resemble flames. The inside of the mouth is black to help highlight the ferocious teeth. Don't forget to leave a circle of white on each eye.

CHAPTER 7

SPEED MACHINES

SPORTS CAR

For this turbocharged sports car, you're going to start with a simple box grid. This will help you to position the curves and get the angle of the drawing just right.

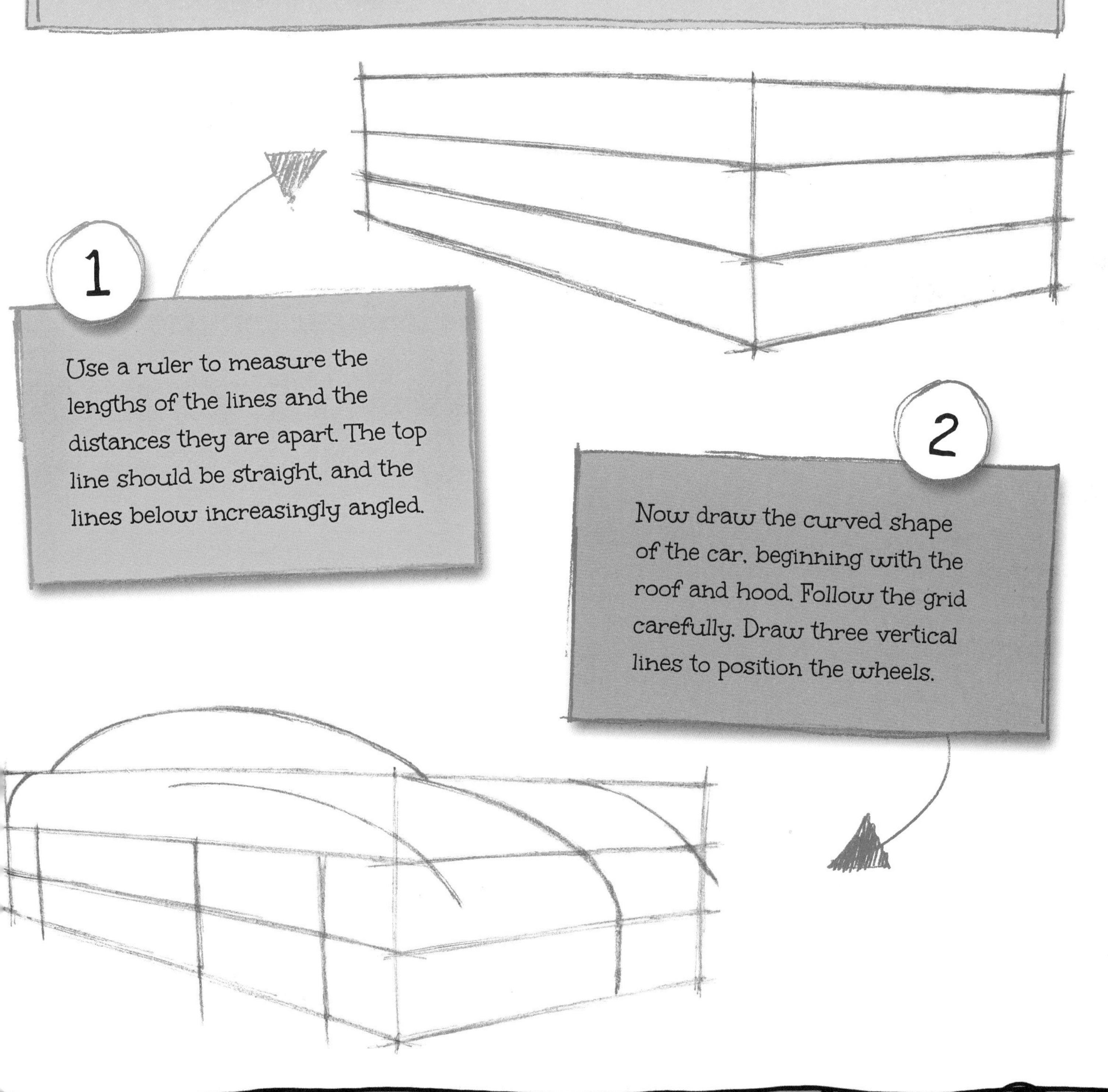

1

Use a ruler to measure the lengths of the lines and the distances they are apart. The top line should be straight, and the lines below increasingly angled.

2

Now draw the curved shape of the car, beginning with the roof and hood. Follow the grid carefully. Draw three vertical lines to position the wheels.

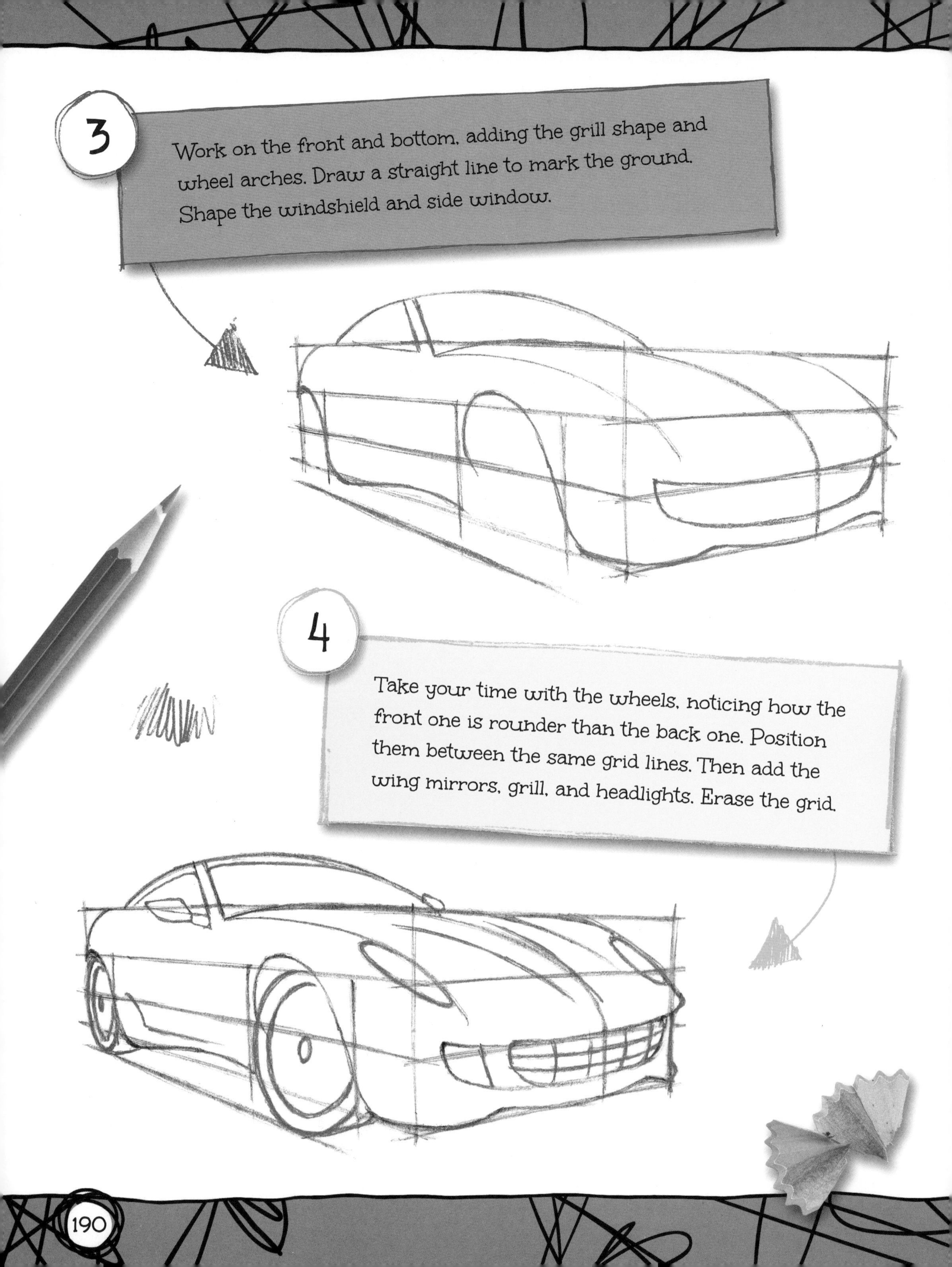

3

Work on the front and bottom, adding the grill shape and wheel arches. Draw a straight line to mark the ground. Shape the windshield and side window.

4

Take your time with the wheels, noticing how the front one is rounder than the back one. Position them between the same grid lines. Then add the wing mirrors, grill, and headlights. Erase the grid.

Bold red is the perfect color for a sports car. Keep the shading smooth, and add white highlights for a sleek, shiny finish. Shade in the road, too.

TOP TIPS

Customize your car with a few simple adjustments. As well as the hubcaps and headlights shown here, think about adding racer stripes, decals, and a personalized number plate.

Give your car class with these star-shaped alloy hubcaps. Blend gray into white to make them look shiny. For chunky tires, make the edges jagged.

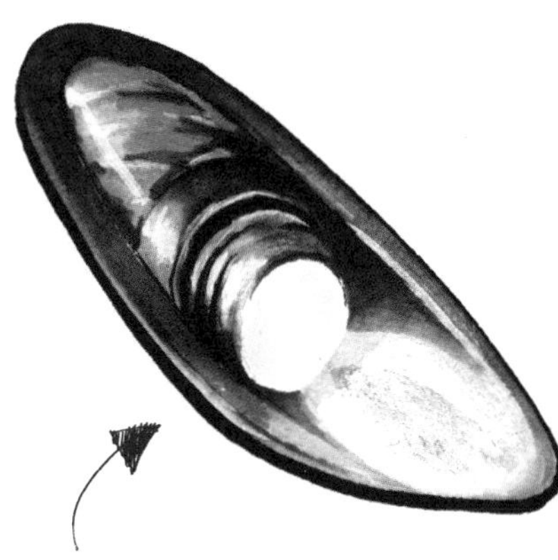

Headlights can be round, oval, or tube-shaped, like these. Color the bulb pale yellow, and add hazy beams of light with blurred edges.

F1 CAR

This mean speed machine is made up of lots of different shapes. Draw each one in the right position, and your cartoon race car will soon be zooming along!

1

Start with three horizontal straight lines. Then draw three egg shapes for the wheels. Make them tilt slightly inward. Add the top of the fourth wheel, following the guidelines.

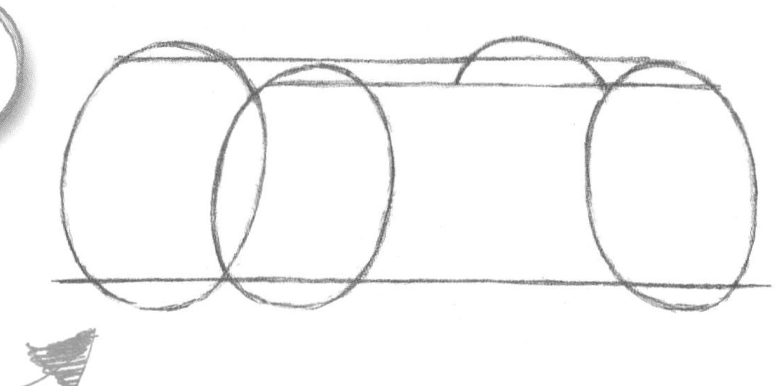

2

Draw a long curve for the hood, and shape the airfoil at the front. Add a domed helmet and the back of the seat. Be sure to work accurately. Next, draw two more guides for the rear airfoil.

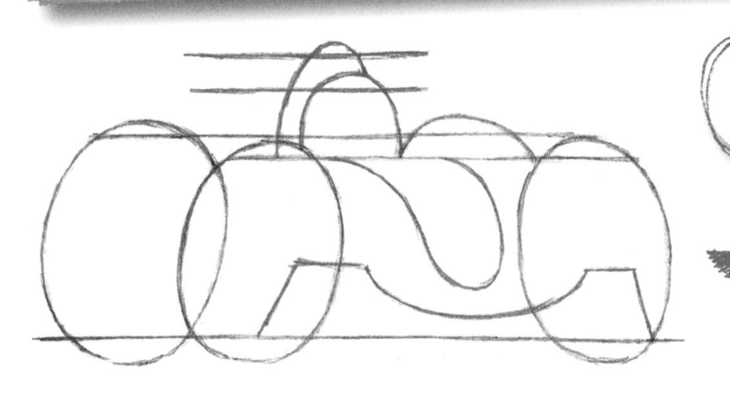

3

Copy all the shapes here to finish your drawing. Pay attention to how they fit into the guides. Keep your lines straight and wheel curves sloping for a cartoon feel. Then erase the guides.

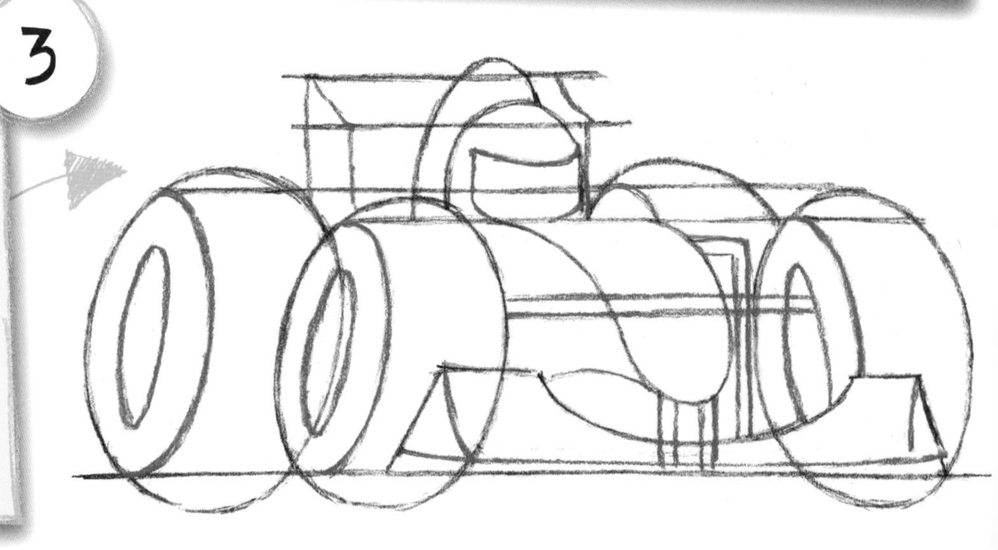

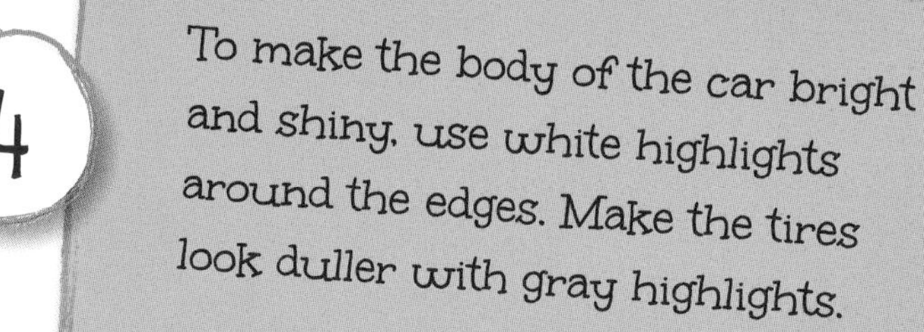

4

To make the body of the car bright and shiny, use white highlights around the edges. Make the tires look duller with gray highlights.

CARTOON CORNER

Try drawing another cartoon car, then give it a face to make it really come alive!

1

Sketch this simple small car. Follow the positioning of the lights, seats, and grill—these will become the facial features.

2

Now change the headlights and grill into eyes and a mouth! Shade in the pupils and draw teeth. Keep the seats plain.

3

For this cartoon car face, change the wing mirrors into ears and make windshield-wiper eyes! Don't forget the gnashing teeth.

JET PLANE

Get ready to launch a supersonic jet into the air! This drawing has lots of straight lines, so use a ruler and measure accurately. It will really help to get a great end result.

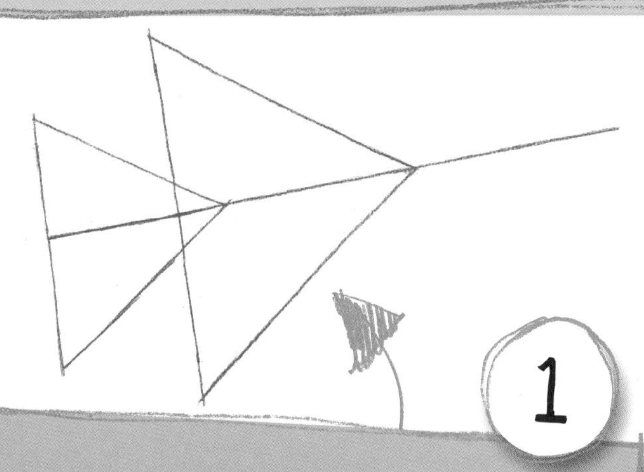

1

Start with a long, straight center line at a slight angle. Then draw two different-size triangles. Make sure they both sit on the center line so they are symmetrical.

2

Working with the center line again, draw two right-angled triangles for the twin tail fins. Next, outline the fuselage, or body, making sure you curl the nose.

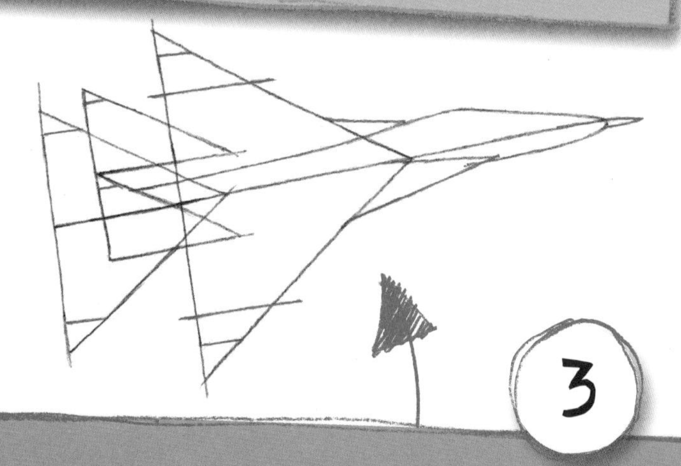

3

Draw parallel lines over the wings, tail, and fins to help you trim the edges and position the engines. Complete the wing shape, and add the pointed nose cone.

4

Erase the tops of the fins and the edges of the wings and tail, following the guides. The drawing should be much simpler now, so it will be easy to add the final touches.

5

Use a striking color scheme for your jet. Don't forget to add smoke trails for a sense of speed and drama.

TOP TIPS

Check out how to draw a realistic smoke trail. This will make your aerobatic plane look like it's speeding across the sky—and add a real sense of drama to your picture.

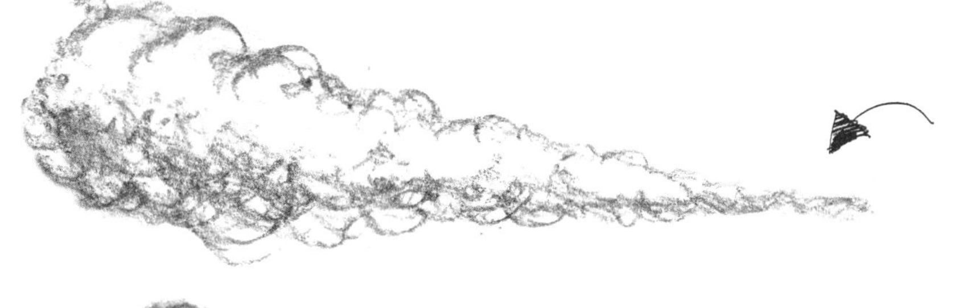

Turn a soft pencil on its side and make lots of circular movements with the lead to form a cloud shape. Leave the center white.

For a more wispy effect, use a small piece of charcoal. Smudge the trail edges with your fingertips to make them look soft.

BIPLANE

Old-fashioned biplanes are fantastic at twisting and turning in the sky. Get out your pens, and draw this cartoon version, complete with wacky pilot!

1

Draw a torpedo shape for the plane's body. Add a narrow oval for the propeller, and shape the tail. Form the cockpit with several curved lines.

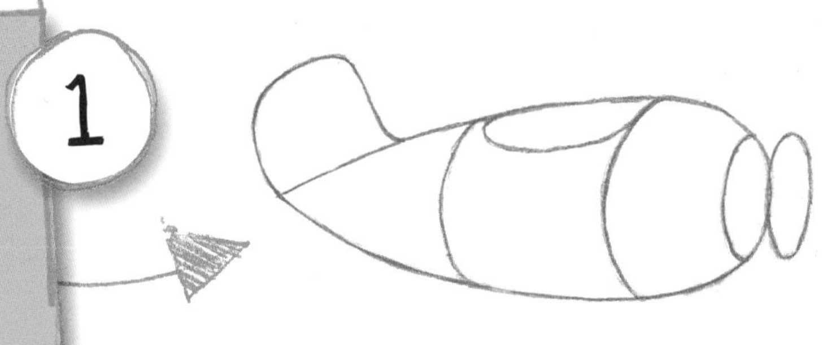

2

Copy the lower wing, then carefully draw four diagonal lines with a horizontal one across the top, and position the upper wing. Add the wheels and start the tail wing.

3

Now drawing finish the wing and wheel struts, and complete the tail wing. Work on the propeller, and fill out the wheels. Finally, draw your pilot with his old-fashioned headgear, goggles, and flowing scarf.

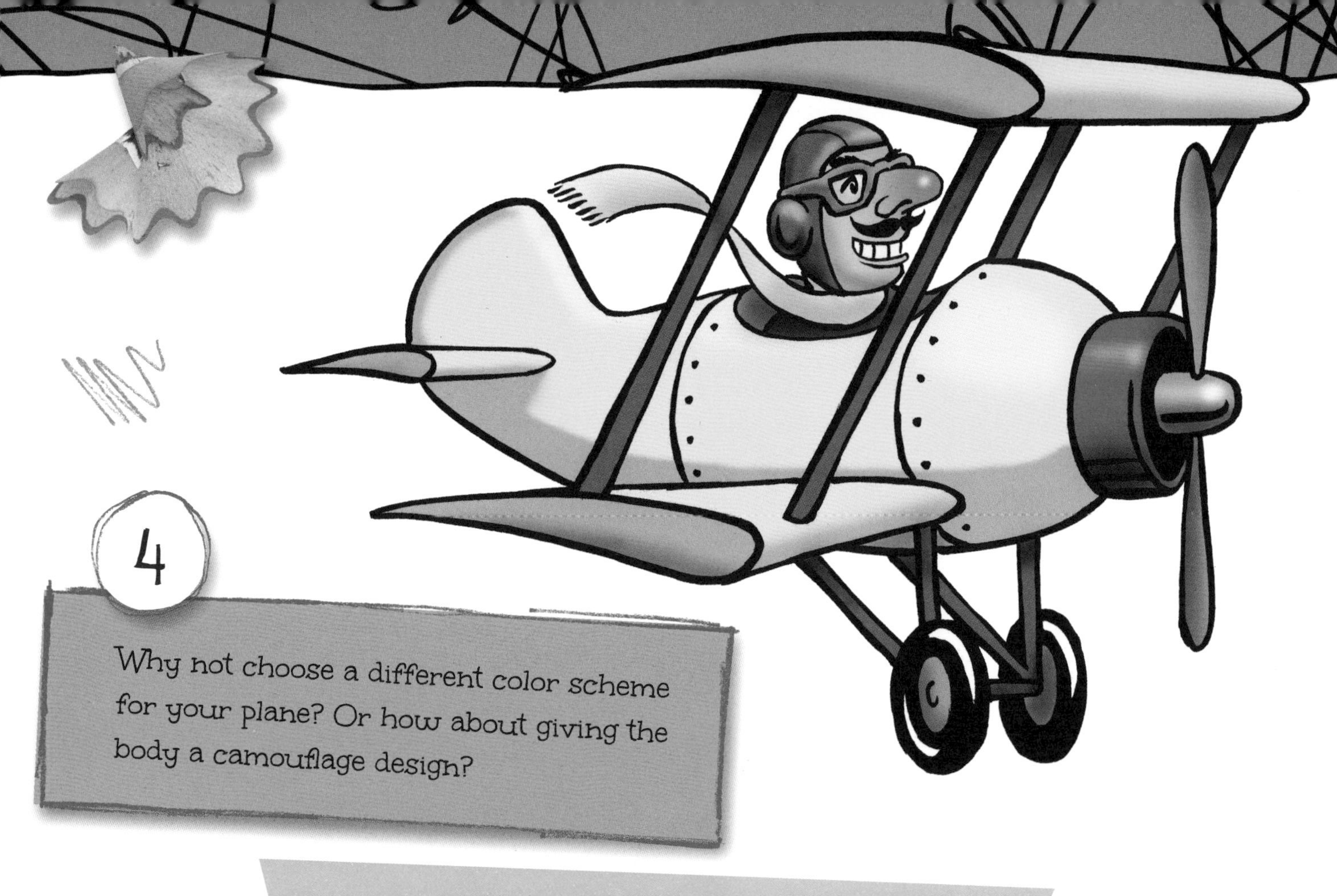

4

Why not choose a different color scheme for your plane? Or how about giving the body a camouflage design?

CARTOON CORNER

Instead of a tiny biplane, try drawing a massive jumbo jet instead!

1

This time, start with a much longer torpedo shape. Add a curve on top to make the plane take on the shape of a jumbo jet. Draw the wings and tail.

2

Soften the outline, and thicken the wing edges. Add the windows and the two engines beneath the wings.

3

Finally, work on the coloring. Jumbo jets are usually white with blocks of color here and there. Include a design for the tail.

SPEEDBOAT

Your challenge with this futuristic speedboat is to make it look streamlined. Take your time drawing the overall shape, and add curved designs in a contrasting color to achieve the effect.

1

First, draw this simple grid. It will help you to get the perspective and angle of your boat just right. Notice how the short lines across are slightly curved.

2

Draw a short curve following the center line of the grid to mark the front point of the boat. Then shape the deck using the rest of the grid. Draw the hull below.

3

Now outline the cabin including the windows. Angle the lines, dividing the windows inward, toward the roof. Add two lines at the back of the cabin to position the airfoil.

4

Fill in the rest of the airfoil, and soften the shape of the cabin. Develop the streamlined outline of the boat, then erase the grid.

5
When inking the outline, make the shape of the windows more curved. Use a slightly different color shade from the main body of the boat.
TOP TIPS
Why not draw your speedboat powering through the water? Add splashing waves and a foamy spray to complete the picture.
Try using watercolor paints in shades of blue for your waves. To create the white spray effect, dab your paintbrush rather than using long strokes.

SUPERBIKE

When drawing this cartoon superbike, concentrate hard on getting the shapes and lines right in the first step. After that, everything should fall into place!

1

Copy the two chunky wheels. Make the one on the right larger, so that it seems nearer. Draw the straight lines leading off the front wheel, and add the three curved lines.

2

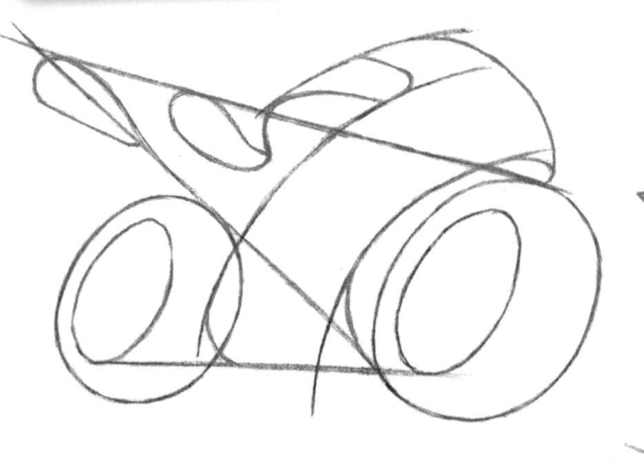

With the guides in place, develop the bodywork, including the seat and exhaust pipe. Follow the picture carefully, and watch how the bike starts to take shape.

3

All that's left now is to work on the details. Position the wheel disks and guards carefully. Then draw the handlebar and headlights. Finish the exhaust pipe.

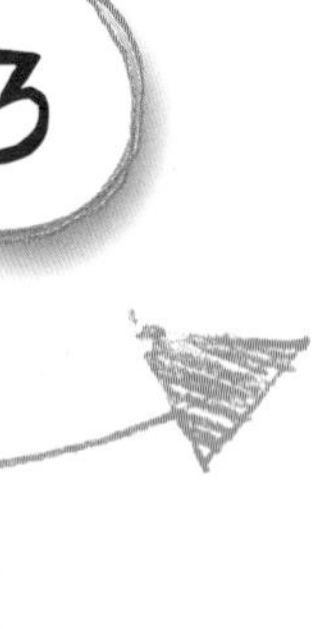

4

Before you start to color, go over your outline with a black felt-tip pen using long, unbroken strokes. This will help make the bike look really sleek.

CARTOON CORNER

Every motorcycle needs a super-slick rider! Here's how to draw one for your incredible speed machine.

1

Start with a circle for the helmet. Then draw the curve of the rider's back, shape his leg, and position his hand.

2

Finish the rider's helmet and his body. For an extra touch, raise the bike's front wheel off the ground, and change the angle at the bottom.

3

Use one block color for a streamlined rider, and add sparkly highlights to the bike's body to make it gleam.

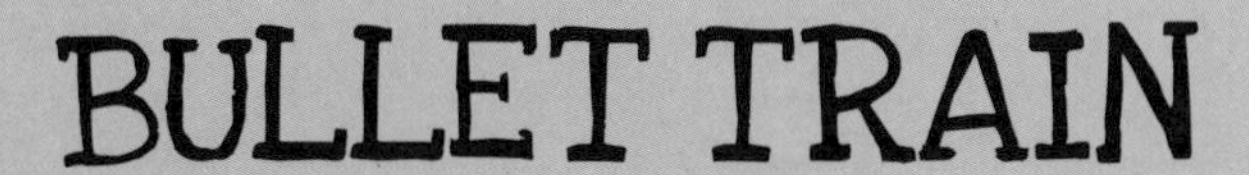

BULLET TRAIN

Draw this bullet train in perspective, so that it gets smaller the farther away it is and disappears into the distance. This will give your picture a real sense of drama and speed.

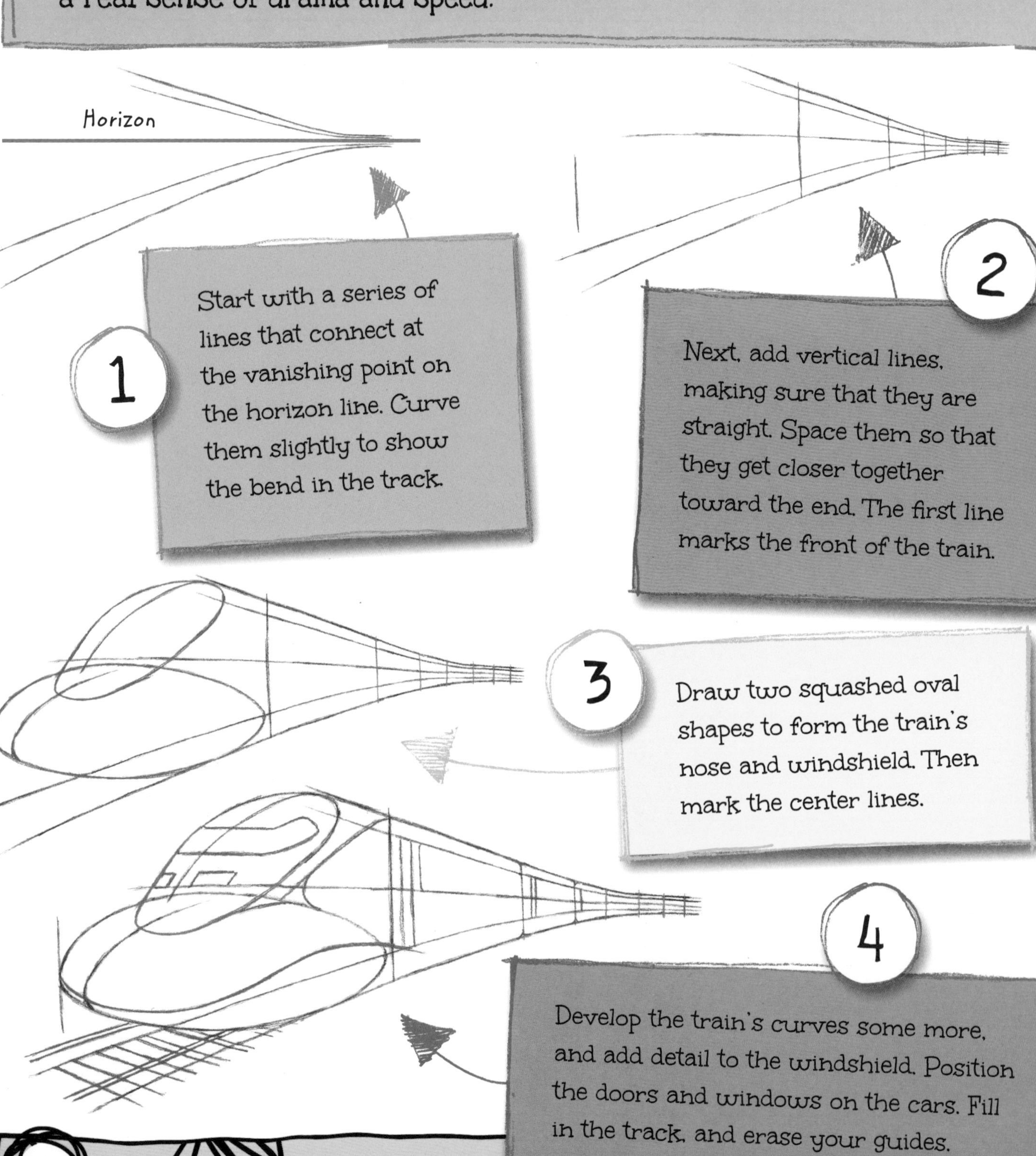

1. Start with a series of lines that connect at the vanishing point on the horizon line. Curve them slightly to show the bend in the track.

2. Next, add vertical lines, making sure that they are straight. Space them so that they get closer together toward the end. The first line marks the front of the train.

3. Draw two squashed oval shapes to form the train's nose and windshield. Then mark the center lines.

4. Develop the train's curves some more, and add detail to the windshield. Position the doors and windows on the cars. Fill in the track, and erase your guides.

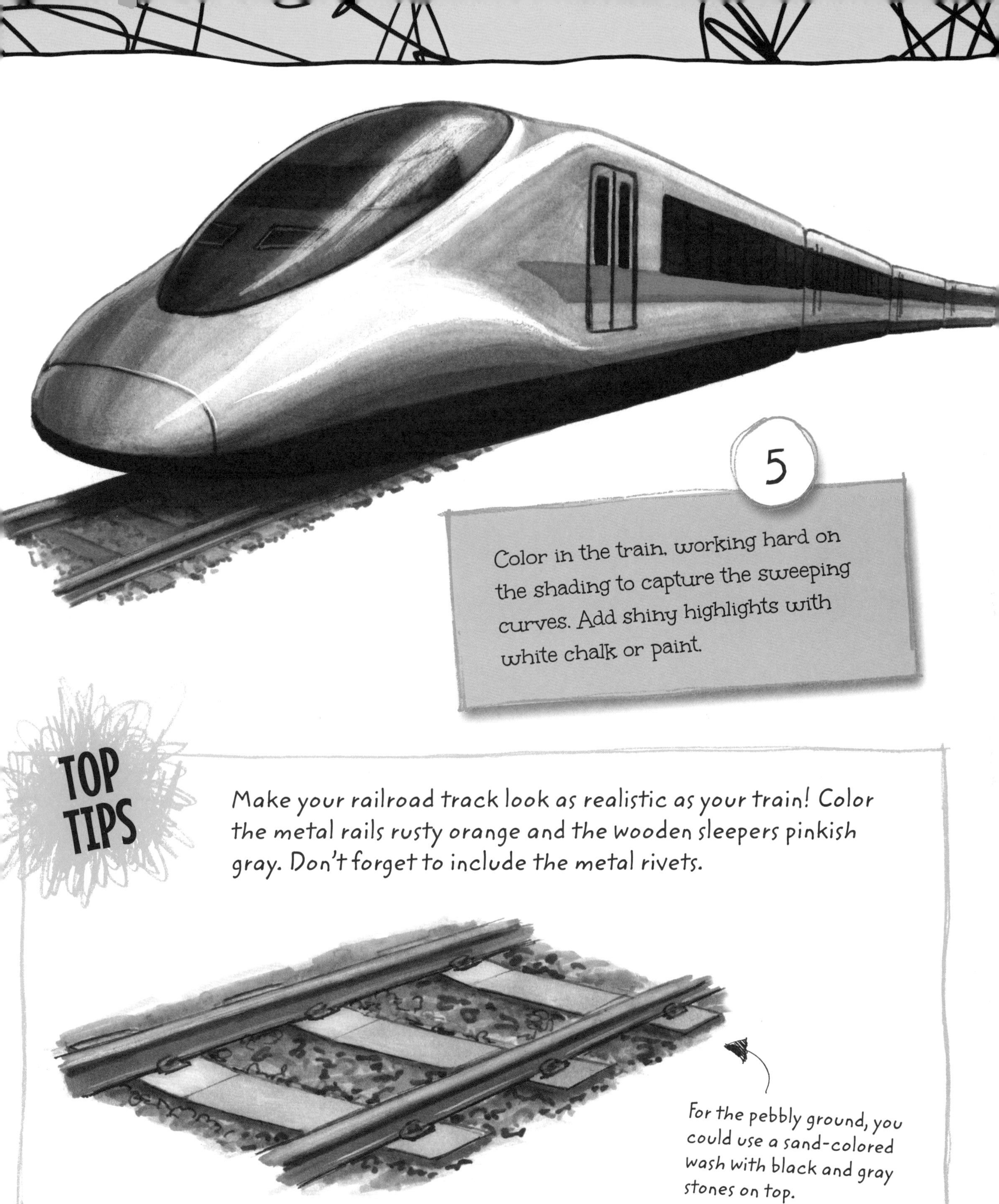

5

Color in the train, working hard on the shading to capture the sweeping curves. Add shiny highlights with white chalk or paint.

TOP TIPS

Make your railroad track look as realistic as your train! Color the metal rails rusty orange and the wooden sleepers pinkish gray. Don't forget to include the metal rivets.

For the pebbly ground, you could use a sand-colored wash with black and gray stones on top.

SPACE SHUTTLE

This space shuttle has huge rockets and a giant fuel tank to blast it into outer space. Follow the steps to launch your own cartoon version into the air!

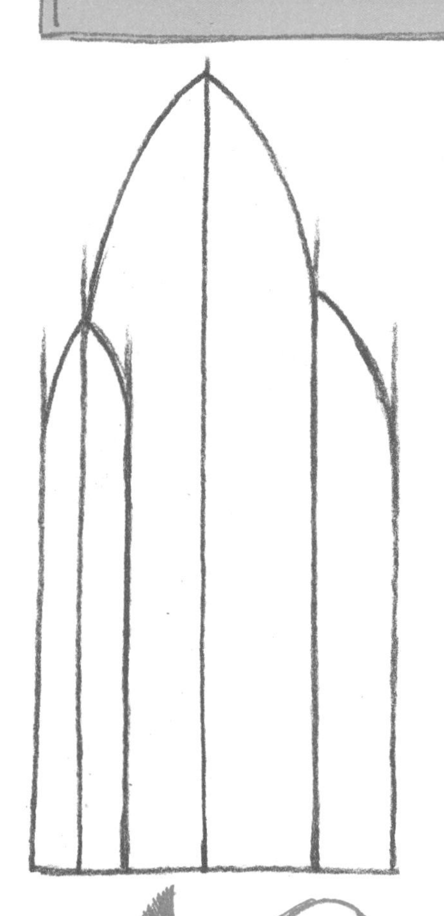

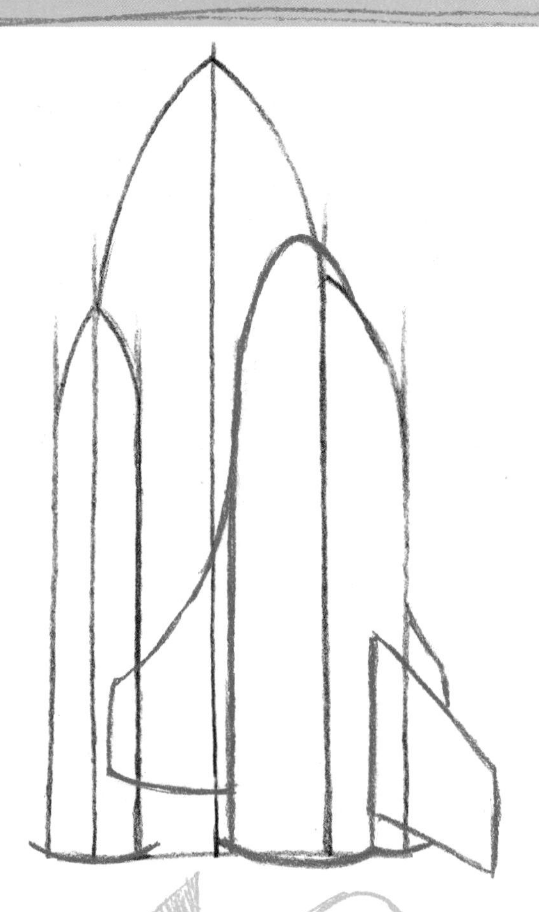

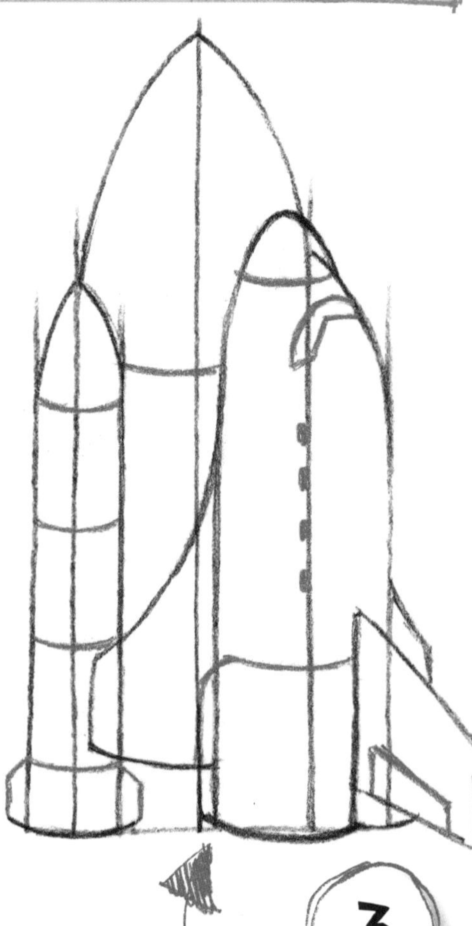

1

Draw the center line first, so that you can make the curves on the large arch shape symmetrical. Then add the outer shapes.

2

The large arch is the fuel tank, and the thin arch is a rocket. Outline the shape of the space shuttle on the right. Draw curves for the bottom of the shuttle and the rocket.

3

Now add the details. Divide the rocket and fuel tank into sections, and include the shuttle's windows, nose cone, and tail rudder. Erase the guides.

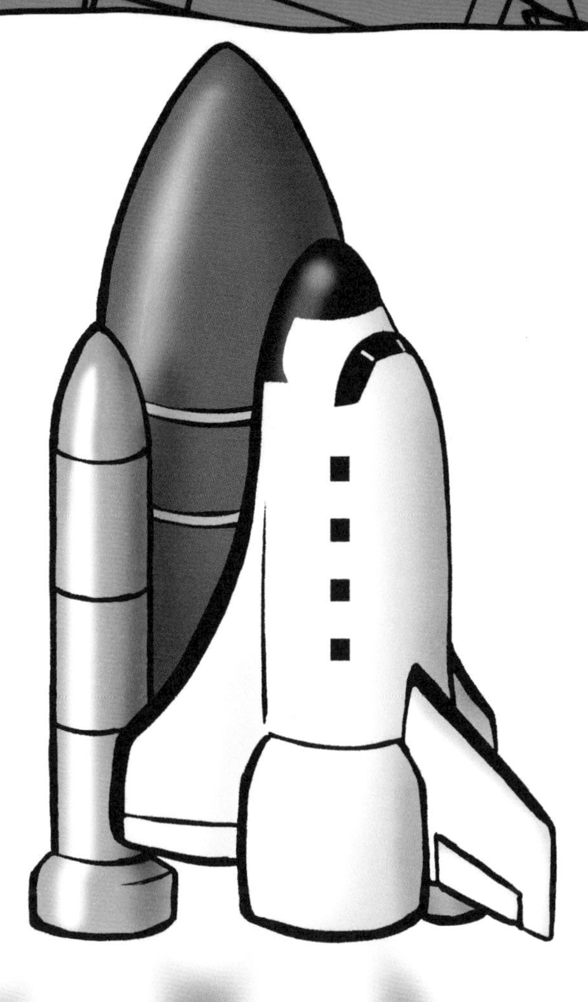

4

Take your time with the shading to make the space shuttle seem like a solid object. Even though the main color is white, introduce blue gray to darken the edges.

CARTOON CORNER

Try drawing two different types of spaceship.

1

This cone-shaped spaceship is based on two arch shapes. You can choose any color scheme, but be sure to include bright orange and yellow flames to power the spaceship along.

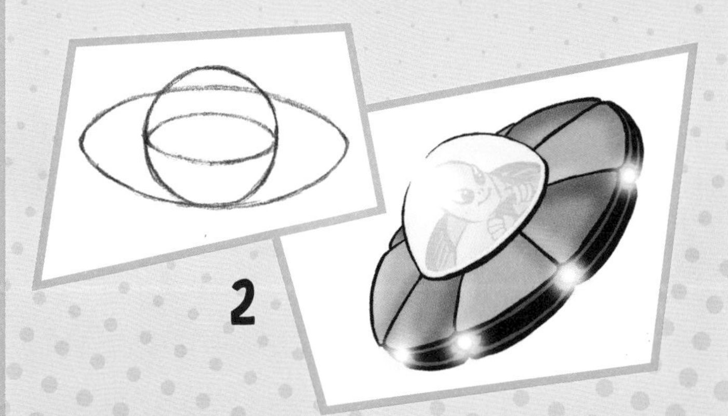

2

To draw a flying saucer, start with a ball and add an oval inside. The top half of the ball is the dome of the ship. Then draw another oval for the outer edge. Experiment with different angles.

CHAPTER 8

DINOSAURS

TYRANNOSAURUS REX

Follow the steps to draw the most terrifying dinosaur of them all-bone-crunching T. rex! Work hard at getting the shape of the body right, with all its knobbly bumps and curves.

1

Draw a big circle for the body, and work outward to shape the neck and tail. Notice how the thick tail tapers to a point. A box shape forms T. rex's head.

2

The legs and arms are pretty tricky, so start with stick drawings. Copy the picture carefully, paying attention to the line lengths and angles. Then shape the mouth.

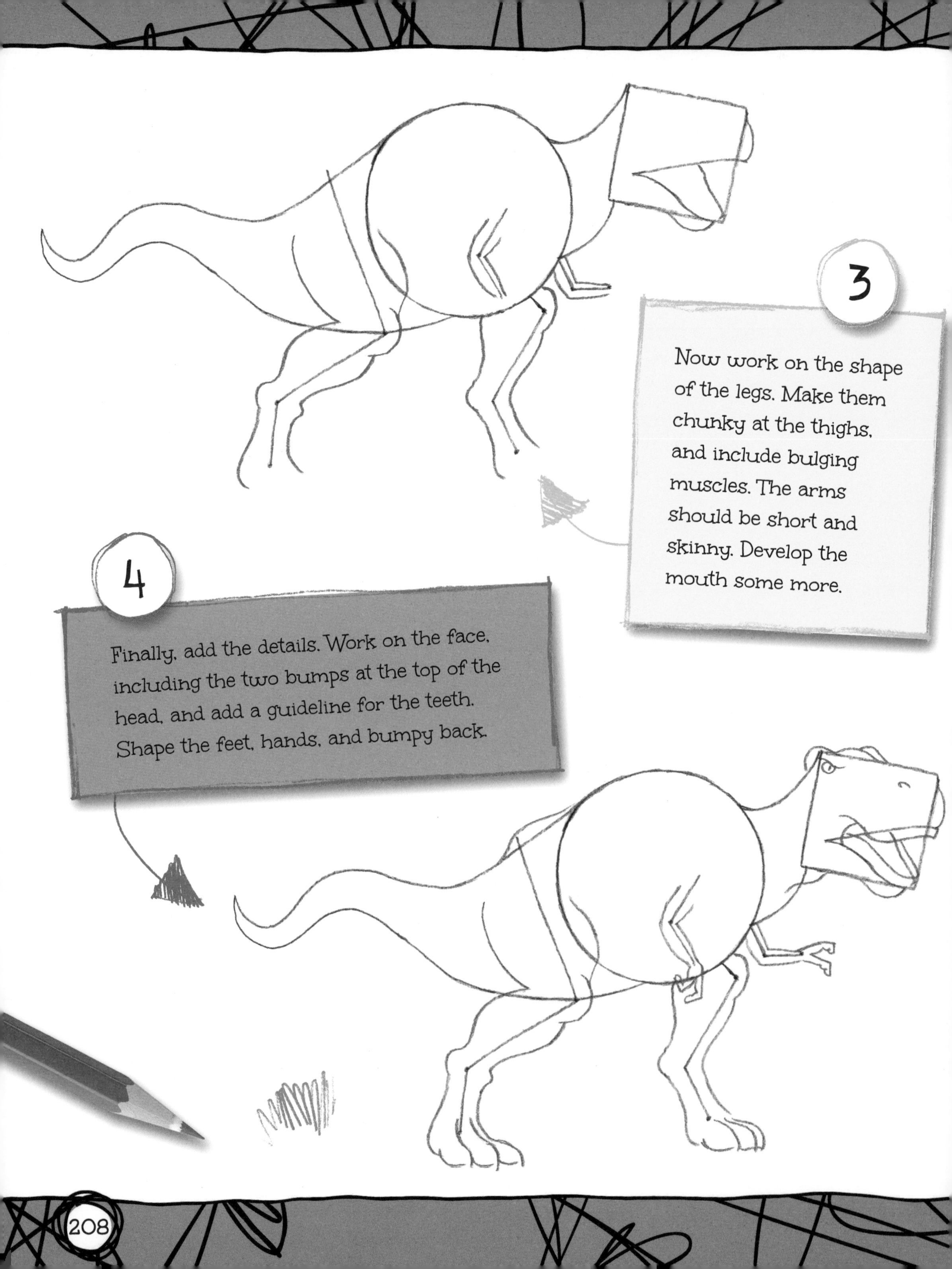
3
Now work on the shape of the legs. Make them chunky at the thighs, and include bulging muscles. The arms should be short and skinny. Develop the mouth some more.
4
Finally, add the details. Work on the face, including the two bumps at the top of the head, and add a guideline for the teeth. Shape the feet, hands, and bumpy back.

5

Use a thick pen to outline the bulky body, and color the beast. Heavy shading, especially under the eyes and around the jaw, adds a menacing effect.

TOP TIPS

Check out these tips on how to finish the sharp parts—the teeth and claws!

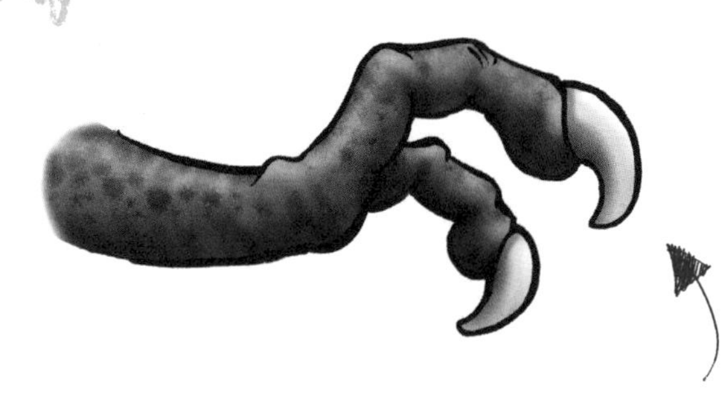

When drawing the claws, make them long and curved to show how they can grab prey. Blend orange into cream to make them look really grimy!

Your T. rex needs lots and lots of teeth to munch its dinner. Work with a fine pen to draw them accurately and to provide a contrast to the heavier body outline.

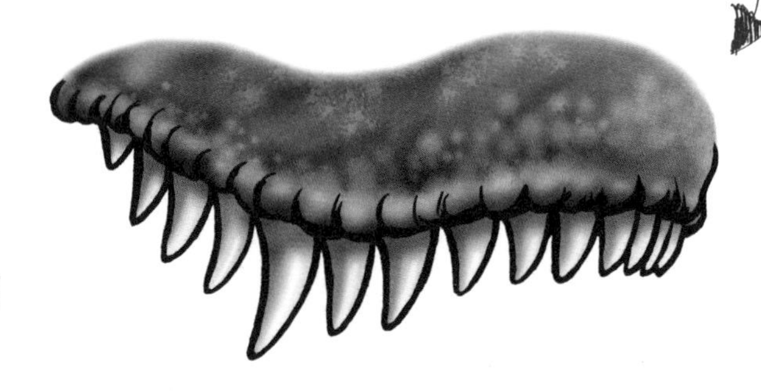

VELOCIRAPTOR

Velociraptor may not have been very large dinosaur-but it sure was vicious! Try your hand at drawing this cartoon creation, including those lethal toe claws.

1

Start with a crescent shape for the body and tail, swooping around to make the curves. Draw three swift strokes to form the pointed head.

2

Add the legs and arms, paying attention to the position of the curving lines. Add a triangle on top of the head for the crest feathers, then develop the end of the tail.

3

Velociraptors were clever creatures, so try to capture this as you finish drawing the face. Then shape the feet and sharp claws. When working on the outline, add feathery edges to the arms, head crest, and tail.

4

When coloring in, go for a dramatic effect. This picture has bold orange and brown stripes based on a tiger's coat, but you could try a different animal pattern.

CARTOON CORNER

Adapt your character to create a hatching baby Velociraptor.

1

Draw an upright oval for the egg and a pointed one on its side for the dino's head. Connect them with a curve.

2

Work on the cute face, and shape the grasping arms. Add jagged lines to show where the egg has cracked.

3

Give the baby dino its teeth, and color it as before. Choose a shade for the egg, and add fine crack lines.

IGUANODON

Iguanodon was a large plant-eater with two unusual thumb spikes. Here, you are working in a realistic style. Give the dinosaur a mottled skin to show that it is a reptile.

1

Begin with a tilted egg shape for the body. Then shape the thick swishing tail. Remember to curl it at the end. A long, curved line starts to form the neck.

2

Next, shape the arms and the legs. Draw a box for the head and add another curved line for the back of the neck.

3

Outline the hands and feet, then shape the face and neck flap. Sketch in the thumb spikes and the beak-like mouth.

4

Now, work on the details. Add in the knee joints and the curving fingers. Shape the body a little more and finish off the mouth.

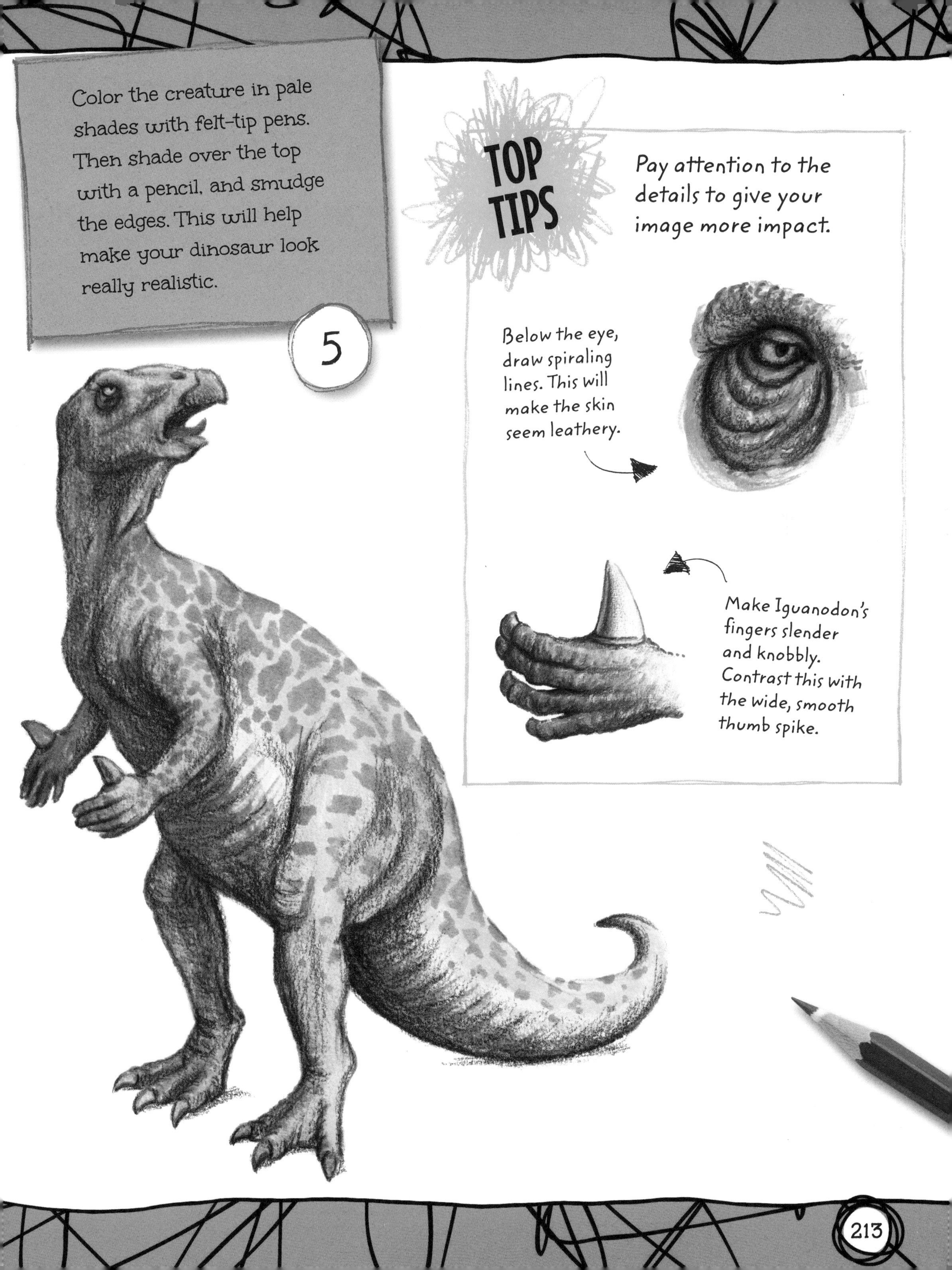
Color the creature in pale shades with felt-tip pens. Then shade over the top with a pencil, and smudge the edges. This will help make your dinosaur look really realistic.
5
TOP TIPS
Pay attention to the details to give your image more impact.
Below the eye, draw spiraling lines. This will make the skin seem leathery.
Make Iguanodon's fingers slender and knobbly. Contrast this with the wide, smooth thumb spike.

BRACHIOSAURUS

This cartoon Brachiosaurus is really easy to draw. What's more, no one really knows what color dinosaurs were–so you can choose any color scheme you want to finish the creature!

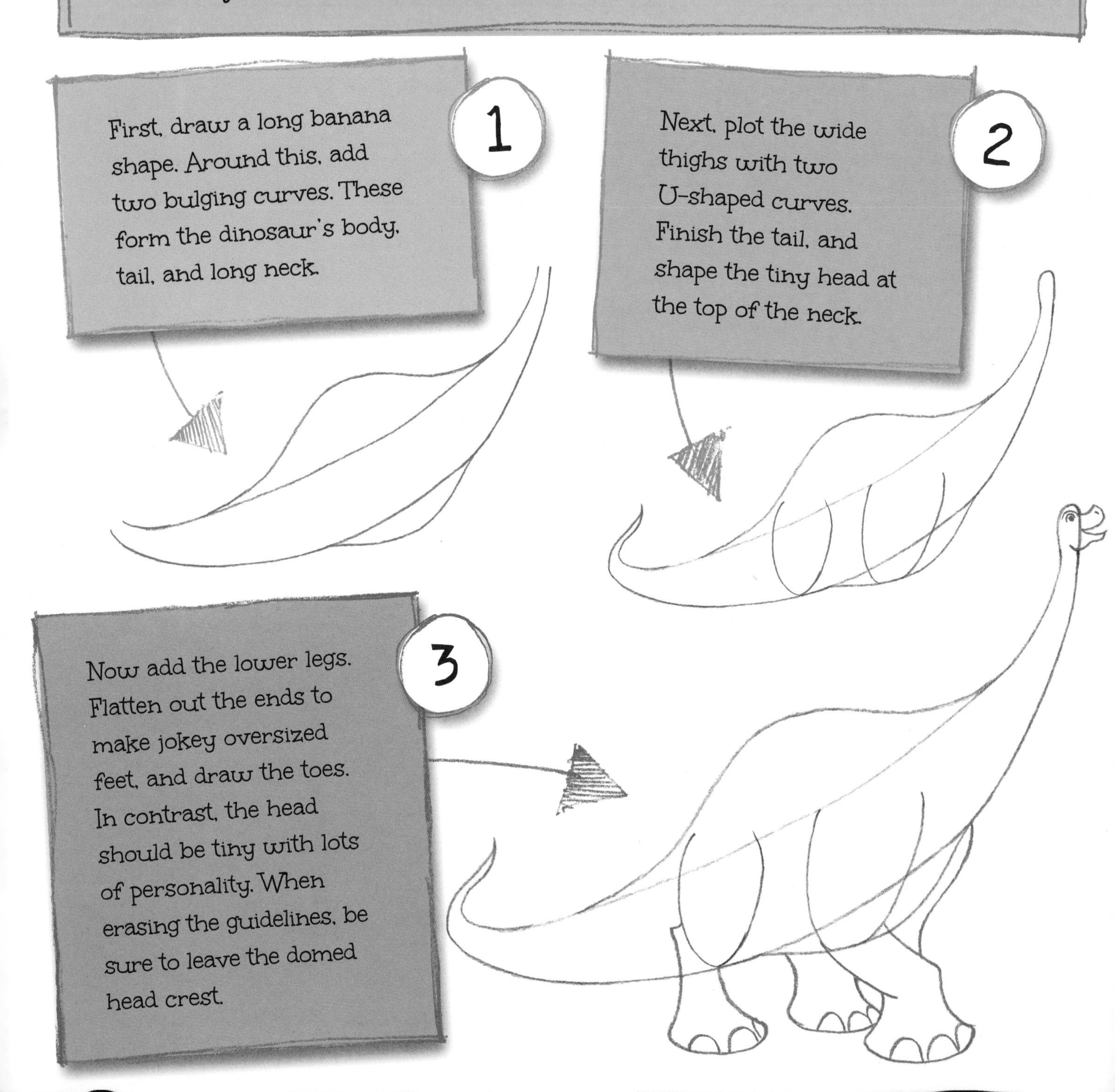

4

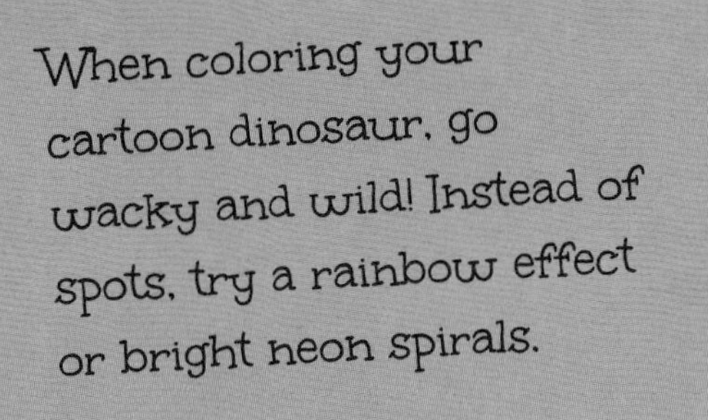

CARTOON CORNER

How about giving your dinosaur a snack to chew on or a footprint trail?

1 Brachiosaurus munched on leaves and twigs from the treetops, reaching them with its long neck. When you draw its snack, make it look like a plant from Jurassic times!

2 Brachiosaurus had wide feet. Try using a photo of an elephant's footprint for reference to show a dusty trail on the ground.

TRICERATOPS

With its pointed horns and giant neck plate, Triceratops looked fierce, but this gentle giant only munched plants. Follow the steps to draw its bulky, leathery frame.

1

Draw a crescent moon shape for the head and neck plate. Then copy the rest of the picture to form the body and tail. Make the head fairly big in relation to the body.

2

Develop the head further by outlining the nose horn and the beak-shaped mouth. Don't forget to add the eye. A series of curved lines start the chunky legs.

3

Now shape the tops of the legs with more curved lines, making sure that they look thick and muscly, and add the wide feet. Draw two long, pointed horns above the eye.

4

Work on the Triceratops' neckline and bottom of the mouth. Add a nostril and wrinkle lines to give the dinosaur its character. Finish by drawing the toes.

5

When you color, use lots of curved lines to bring out the wrinkly elephantlike skin. Work in shades of brown and white. For shading tips, go to pages 14–15.

TOP TIPS

Make your picture look even more professional with these artists' tips.

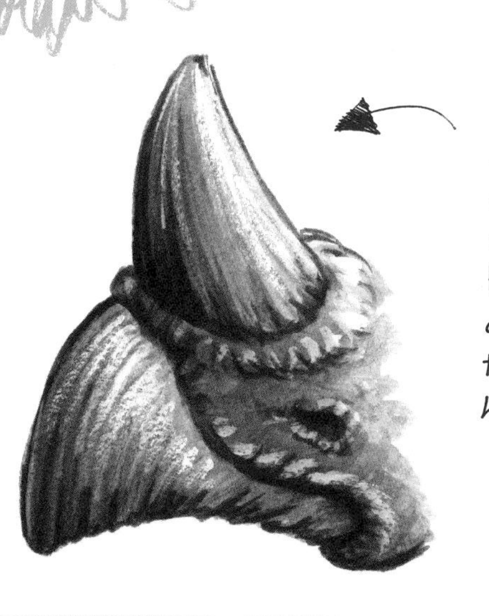

To make the horn on Triceratops' nose stand out from the rest of the body, work mainly in a yellowish-brown color. Then add dark shading at the bottom and white highlights at the top.

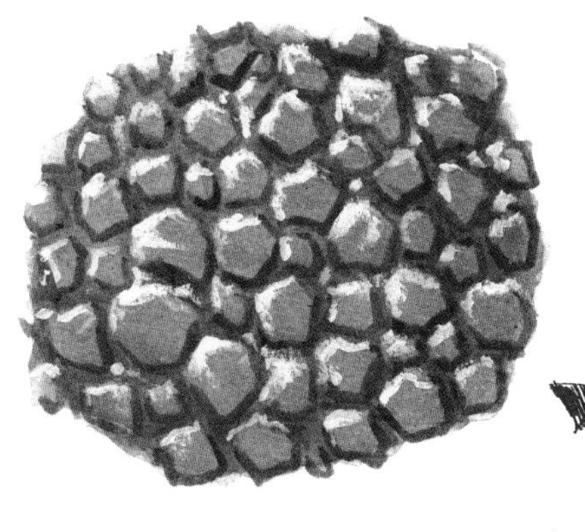

You can make Triceratops' skin look tough and scaly by drawing lots of small uneven shapes. Color the gaps a darker brown than the shapes.

ANKYLOSAURUS

Pick up your pencils and try drawing this Ankylosaurus with its swinging club tail. Ankylosaurus used its bony tail to defend itself from larger meat-eating dinosaurs.

1

Start with a giant teardrop shape for the body and tail. Then draw a swooping curve to mark the edge of the back and neck armor. A triangle forms the head armor.

2

Next, shape the head and neck, and add the face details. Give Ankylosaurus a friendly expression. Work on the legs and feet, and draw two circles for the club at the end of the tail.

3

A grid across the back will help you to position the bony armor. Draw pebble shapes on top of it, then erase the grid. Finally, add a cheek spike to the face, and finish working on the toes.

4

Giving the dinosaur a thick, dark outline will help to make it look powerful. It's also a good idea to use contrasting colors for the armor and the body.

CARTOON CORNER

Want to show your Ankylosaurus in full swing? Then follow the steps below!

1 The dinosaur is facing you, so draw a circle for the body and a triangle pointing downward for the head armor. Copy the rest of the picture.

2 As before, add the grid for the body armor and the two circles for the tail. Then work on the face shape and the two wide front legs.

3 Color your dinosaur like the main picture, or choose something different. Add swishing lines to show the movement of the tail and body.

ARCHAEOPTERYX

Archaeopteryx was a small prehistoric flying creature that lived at the time of the dinosaurs. Work hard to capture its feathered birdlike wings and scaly dinosaurlike feet and claws.

1

Draw a football shape for Archaeopteryx's body. Add a small oval for the head, and connect the two shapes together to form the neck.

2

Next, work on the wing shape. Copy the picture carefully, so that the top of the wings look symmetrical. Draw in the legs and tail, then add the eye and beak.

3

Outline the bottom of the wings and the feathered tail. Make the tail look like a paddle for now. Mark the position of the feet and wing claws.

4

The final step is to work on the details. Create the feathers with smooth curved lines. Shape the scaly feet, and add the claws. Add detail to the eye, too.

5

Erase the guidelines, then go over the feathers and the body with a fine black pen. Use lots of short delicate lines around the neck and leg area to suggest a fluffier texture here.

TOP TIPS

Feathers and scaly feet give Archaeopteryx its unique character. Here's how to draw and color them close-up.

When drawing the feet, add oval shapes with a fine black pen to create scales. Color the feet yellowish brown.

For the wings, lay down a watercolor base in green and blue first. Then on top, shade with colored pencils. This will create a feathery effect.

DIMETRODON

With its huge sail fin, sharp teeth, and crocodilelike body, Dimetrodon was a fearsome land predator that lived about 280 million years ago. Get ready to draw this beast!

1

Draw a long, flexible carrot shape with the top cut off. Imagine it lying almost flat. This will be Dimetrodon's head, body, and tail. A deep curve forms the sail fin.

2

Next, work on the wide mouth and the top of the eye. Add a scalloped edge to the sail fin. Shape the front of Dimetrodon's body, and draw the fat, bulging legs, too.

3

Bring your creature to life by shaping the eye, nostrils, and top lip—don't forget the two eyebrow ridges. Add the front leg and clawed feet. Then draw the ridges on the sail fin.

4

Once you've drawn the teeth, you can choose any color scheme or pattern for Dimetrodon. Try blending in an extra color on the sail fin to make it stand out.

CARTOON CORNER

There's more than one way to draw Dimetrodon!

1

Draw its skeleton, and you'll look like a real dinosaur expert. Make the rib cage long, and add ridges to the tail. The skull should be large and solid, but the bones in the sail fin need to be slender. Go over the outline with a fine black pen, then color the picture grayish brown.

2

Draw a baby Dimetrodon. Work with an S-shape, and include a short tail and sail fin. Add a prop, such as a bone, to give the dinosaur personality.

CHAPTER 9

SCENES

BACK YARD SCENE

You can build on the drawing skills you have learned in this book by putting your favorite pets into a scene. Here, I have chosen the cat and the dog and put them outside in a yard.

1

After playing around with various ideas on scrap paper, I settled on this composition. I decided to stand the cat on a raised surface, and to make the animals appear to be looking at each other. I reworked it, still on a small scale. Doing rough versions like this can save a lot of time later.

2

I decided that my pencil rough looked a little unbalanced, so I added a railing on the left-hand side of the picture. Then I roughly applied shade and color with watercolors to see how it would look. I restricted my palette to greens and yellowy browns, with some touches of blue here and there.

3

When I was happy with the coloring, I went on to develop the light and shade. Then I used black and white ink to strengthen the outlines and highlights. In this small rough, I have established the main areas of light and shade, which will help with the larger-scale artwork.

4

On a large sheet of good paper, sketch in the guidelines for the final artwork. The aim here is to establish a loose framework for all the different parts of the picture—the lines of the decking and fencing, and the rough shapes of the animals.

5

With the framework and positions established, you can now develop the shapes, avoiding too much detail until all the necessary guidelines are in place.

6

With a fine pencil and eraser, work in all the important details, erasing any confusing guidelines as you go. I left the fine detail that I would need for the next (inking) stage.

7

I used dark brown ink to keep the outlines from being too harsh. I watered it down to outline distant and less important features. For the dog, I used a golden-brown ink. When the ink was dry, I erased all the pencil work.

8

Using my color rough as a guide, I painted in the shadows and shading using purple brown and blue green. Then I added in the colors, leaving no white paper showing. I strengthened some of the colors as necessary, before adding highlights. I also mixed white with different greens to add texture to some of the plants.

RIVER SCENE

Now that you have mastered drawing wild animals in chapter 3, it's time to experiment by putting them into a natural scene.

1

The first stage of developing a scene is a rough pencil drawing on scrap paper. This is so that you can figure out the sizes and positions of all the elements in the scene. Don't worry if you make lots of changes and do lots of erasing before you are happy with the result.

2

Before moving on to a more detailed artwork on good paper, you can plan your colors and shading by quickly coloring in your rough drawing. The idea of a color rough is to find out what does and what doesn't work, before you start on the final artwork.

3

To complete the color rough, I have used a black felt-tip pen to define the outlines and deep shadows, as well as some white ink for highlights. I also decided to add some more foliage in the foreground and to darken some of the shading in the background and river.

4

On a fresh sheet of good paper, draw guidelines for the main shapes that make up the picture. Work across the whole surface without getting into details. Think of the plants as broad shapes.

5

Gradually build up the detail. Use the skills you have learned in previous chapters to develop the animals, then work on the surrounding elements. Draw in the details of the foreground plants, but make those in the background more sketchy. You can still make changes—I decided to alter the plants in the foreground from those in my color rough.

6

Use a sharp pencil to refine the whole drawing. Pay attention to the character of the animals. Try to keep the individual shapes of the plants clearly defined. Erase any confusing marks and guidelines.

7

It is a good idea to start inking in the elements that are closest to the front of the picture, then work backward. Use strong, confident strokes to make the plants and leaves graceful. Marks in the background should be finer and less distinct.

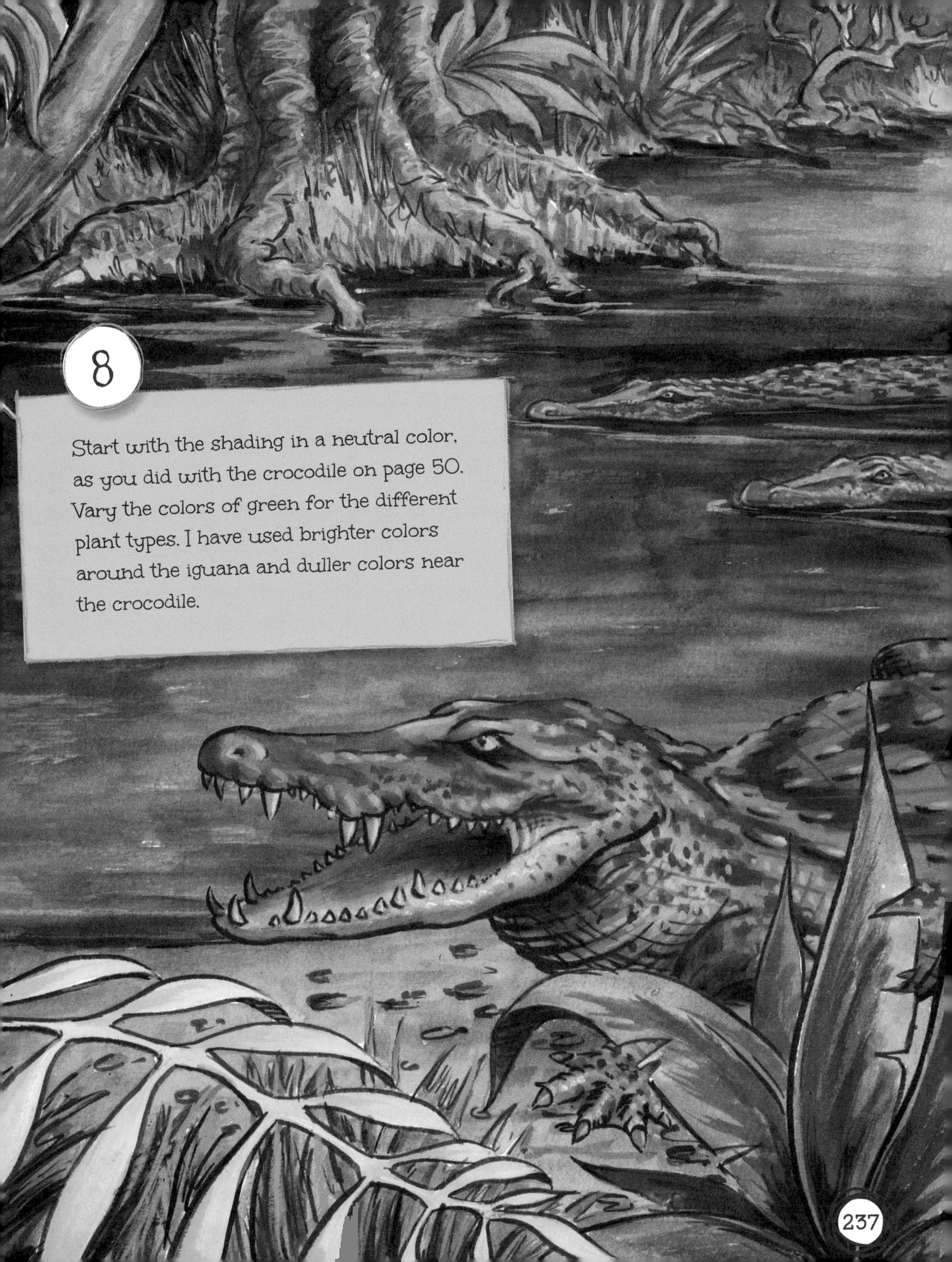

Start with the shading in a neutral color, as you did with the crocodile on page 50. Vary the colors of green for the different plant types. I have used brighter colors around the iguana and duller colors near the crocodile.

COUNTRY SCENE

Put the butterfly and honeybee from chapter 3 into a countryside scene by following these steps. I chose a bank of wildflowers as a suitable background scene for these insects. But you might want to experiment with close-ups on just a few flowers.

1

Start with a rough version of your artwork. To allow for close-up drawings of the insects, I chose a low eye level for this scene. This means that the fence is above eye level, disappearing toward the distant horizon. A cottage provides some interest in the background.

2

Next, I quickly washed on some watercolors to establish a rough color scheme. I also decided on a light source—bright sunshine coming from the right—and shaded the scene with that in mind.

3

Still working on my color rough, I used dark ink to strengthen parts of the drawing and white ink to make some features clearer. I decided that the top right part of the picture was a little empty, so I added more trees. I then added a patch of shade to the road, to provide a darker background behind the flowers.

4

Use your color rough as a guide to map out your scene on good paper. First, I established the curves that run through the picture and the main features of the drawing. The aim of this stage is to place the elements on the page, so that everything can be drawn fairly loosely.

5

Much of the detail in this scene will be added in the inking and painting stages. There's no need to draw each blade of grass. However, the cottage and the insects need good guidelines if they are to look convincing. It is also important to get the spacing right between the fence posts, to give a sense of distance.

6

Next, add detail to the insects and cottage, as well as the larger flowers. The flowers need not be precisely detailed, but they should have some individual characteristics.

7

For the inking stage, I decided to use very little black ink, keeping it for just the insects to make them stand out. To create a bright picture, I inked the foliage with green, the poppies with dark red, and the wooden details with dark brown. I used some strokes of purple watercolor for a faint horizon.

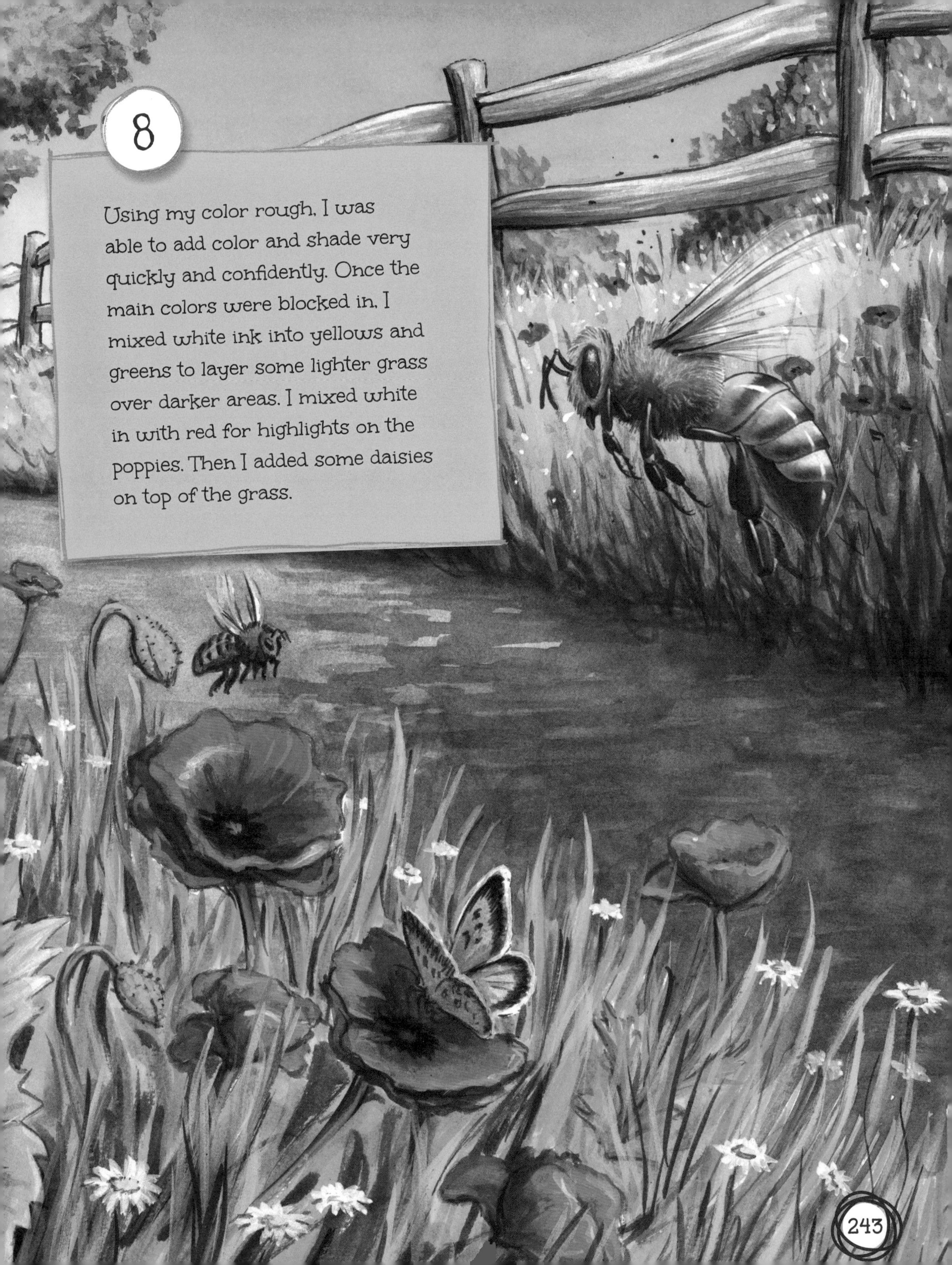

8

Using my color rough, I was able to add color and shade very quickly and confidently. Once the main colors were blocked in, I mixed white ink into yellows and greens to layer some lighter grass over darker areas. I mixed white in with red for highlights on the poppies. Then I added some daisies on top of the grass.

UNDERWATER SCENE

Dolphins are such graceful underwater creatures that I wanted to use them in a scene with a suitable background. I decided to illustrate two dolphins playing near a sunken wreck. You could add more drama by adding a shark in the distance!

1

I found lots of photos of underwater scenes and started to think about a suitable composition. Working roughly on a small sheet of paper, I arranged the boat so that it echoes the shape of the leading dolphin and makes a sweeping curve through the picture.

2

To figure out the shading and coloring, I washed some colors directly on my pencil rough. I used purply blue for the shadow areas and deep water, then yellows, oranges, and greens for the coral, plants, and the rusty wreck. For the open water, I used a paler turquoise blue.

3

Still working on my color rough, I strengthened the outlines and shadows of the dolphins, coral, and plants in the foreground with black ink and more purply blue paint. I also added some highlights with white ink. To make the scene livelier, I worked in a number of small fish, some as distant, dark shapes, and some in bright yellow in the foreground.

4

On a large sheet of good paper, I mapped out the basic shapes of the drawing in pencil. At this stage, I decided to add some extra dolphins in the background.

5

I worked up the details of the drawing over the rough guidelines, still in pencil. I didn't put in too much detail for the corals and weeds, since this can be added directly at the inking stage.

6

For the inking, I mainly used blue ink to create the effect of looking through water. I made the outlines more and more dark toward the foreground, switching to black ink for the corals, plants, and the nearest dolphin. When the ink was dry, I erased all of the pencil marks.

7

Before applying any color, I painted all the shading and shadow areas. I used pale diluted blue for the distant parts, darker blue in the middle ground, and black shadows in the foreground.

8

To color the scene, I started by filling in the solid blue of the sea, darker at the sea floor and paler toward the surface. I then roughly colored all the other parts with browns, oranges, and greens, and gray for the dolphins. When all the paper was covered, I mixed white ink into the colors to pick out textures and highlight edges. I also used a few touches of pure white ink for highlights in the foreground.

JUNGLE SCENE

Learning how to draw and paint animals is just a step along the way to making finished pictures. A bigger challenge is to set your animals against a background that brings out their natural behavior. Here are some of the steps I took to create a scene for the jaguar from page 98. You may choose to work with a different cat or on a less complicated background.

1

After trying many different compositions very roughly, I decided on this one and drew it quickly on scrap paper. The aim is to figure out how the parts of the scene fit together and be able to make alterations without messing up a detailed drawing.

2

Working on top of my rough pencil drawing, I added some shade and color in broad blocks of watercolor. This helped me to see how the composition works.

3

Using black and white inks, I developed the lights and darks of the scene. I decided to make the foreground tree largely dark, showing it in silhouette against the background. The ruined building is lighter against the darker background. I also decided to add another toucan.

4

On a larger sheet of heavier paper, start your artwork by drafting the main shapes and guidelines. The important principle here is to work broadly without any details at this stage.

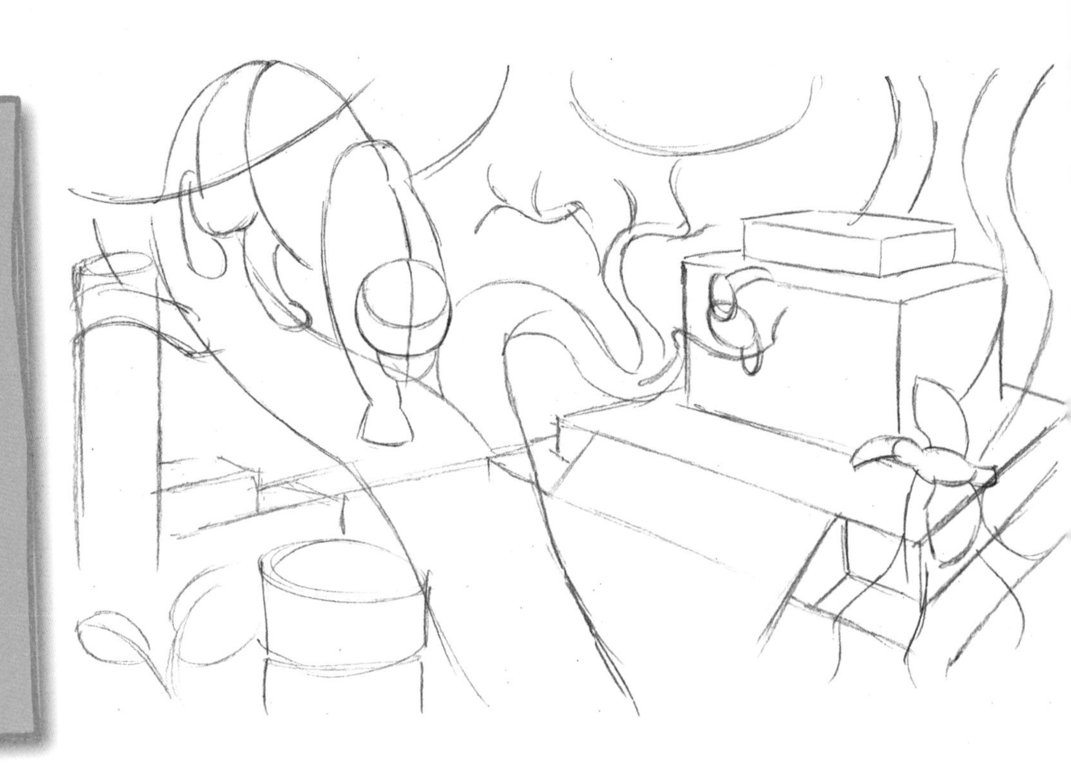

5

Gradually develop the details, bringing form to the rough masses. Although I intended the building to be a ruin, I drew it as a complete shape first, so that it would look convincing.

6

Use a softer pencil to complete the detailed drawing. Erase your guidelines as you go. I have left some of the detail sketchy, allowing some possibility for development in the ink and color stages.

7

As I inked in the various lines and textures, I decided that the main tree shape wasn't quite right, so I added another branch. When you're inking, it's important to keep in mind the light source and shading, and to add the right texture to each surface.

8
Because I had figured out most of the light and shade decisions with my colored rough (step 2), I could apply the shading and colors to my ink drawing with confidence. A few highlights helped to bring out the details of various plants.